"These moving and evocative oral histories of black, Chicana, and white working-class women . . . provide us with valuable insights into the way in which war and economic necessity interact with traditional female culture to effect change, as well as continuity, in women's work lives, and in their sense of self."
—Amy Swerdlow, Director, Graduate Program in Women's History, Sarah Lawrence College

"Sherna Gluck has changed our understanding of women workers in World War II. Her interpretation is the most penetrating one that we have on this important topic."
—Kathryn Kish Sklar, University of California, Los Angeles

"Engaging and useful . . . Demonstrating that social change is a complicated process, and that women's wartime and postwar experience was a mixture of change and continuity."
—Choice

"This book should serve as a major addition to courses in twentieth-century U.S. history, social history, and women's history."
—D'Ann Campbell, Indiana University

SHERNA BERGER GLUCK, a pioneer in women's oral history, is the director of the Oral History Program at California State University, Long Beach, and a faculty member in Women's Studies. She is one of the founders of the Feminist History Research Project and the author of *From Parlor to Prison: Five American Suffragists Talk About Their Lives.*

Rosie
THE
Riveter
Revisited

Women, The War, and Social Change

Sherna Berger Gluck

A MERIDIAN BOOK

NEW AMERICAN LIBRARY

NEW YORK AND SCARBOROUGH, ONTARIO

NAL BOOKS ARE AVAILABLE AT QUANTITY DISCOUNTS WHEN USED TO PROMOTE PRODUCTS OR SERVICES. FOR INFORMATION PLEASE WRITE TO PREMIUM MARKETING DIVISION, NEW AMERICAN LIBRARY, 1633 BROADWAY, NEW YORK, NEW YORK 10019.

Words from "National Defense Blues" by Huddy Ledbetter (Leadbelly), courtesy of Queen Ollie Robinson

This is an authorized reprint of a hardcover edition published by Twayne Publishers, A Division of G. K. Hall & Co.

Original hardcover designed by Carole Rollins

 MERIDIAN TRADEMARK REG. U.S. PAT. OFF. AND FOREIGN COUNTRIES
REGISTERED TRADEMARK—MARCA REGISTRADA
HECHO EN WESTFORD, MASS., U.S.A.

SIGNET, SIGNET CLASSIC, MENTOR, ONYX, PLUME, MERIDIAN and NAL BOOKS are published *in the United States* by NAL PENGUIN INC., 1633 Broadway, New York, New York 10019, *in Canada* by The New American Library of Canada Limited, 81 Mack Avenue, Scarborough, Ontario M1L 1M8

Library of Congress Cataloging-in-Publication Data

Gluck, Sherna Berger.
  Rosie the riveter revisited : women, the war, and social change / Sherna Berger Gluck.
  p. cm.
  Bibliography
  Includes index.
  ISBN 0-452-00911-1 (pbk.)
  1. Women aircraft industry workers—California—Los Angeles—Interviews.
2. Aircraft industry—Social aspects—California—Los Angeles—History.
3. Women—Employment—California—Los Angeles—History. 4. World War, 1939-1945—Women—California—Los Angeles.
I. Title.
[HD6073.A452U64 1988]   87-30685
331.4'0973—dc19   CIP

First Meridian Printing, May, 1988
1 2 3 4 5 6 7 8 9
PRINTED IN THE UNITED STATES OF AMERICA

Contents

Acknowledgments

This book has been many years in the making, beginning with the 1979 launching of the Rosie the Riveter Revisited oral history project funded by the Rockefeller Foundation and the National Endowment for the Humanities (RC 00019–80–1459). I am greatly indebted to the many individuals who worked on that project, and especially to my two colleagues and former students, Cindy Cleary and Jan Fischer, who each conducted a third of the interviews. The full transcripts of these forty-five oral histories—from which the material in this book was drawn—are available in several archives around the country. The moral support of my colleagues at California State University, Long Beach helped sustain me for the four years it took to complete the original oral history project.

A network of women historians around the country has provided an important arena for the discussion of my work. The sharing of ideas with others also working on the history of women during the war years has taken place in many settings, most notably over lunch at women's history and women's studies conferences.

I owe a special debt to Geri Thoma, my agent, for her faith in my work; to Anita McClellan, for her helpful editorial comments and suggestions; and to Marvin Gluck, my partner, for his critical comments and loyal support.

Last, and most important, are all the women who so graciously gave of themselves. They have been a source of inspiration, and their enthusiasm about the project helped sustain my own energy over the past six years.

Rosie
ᵀᴴᴱ Riveter
Revisited
Women, The War, and Social Change

Foreword

We sat in a circle, my women's studies students and I. As I looked around the room and we introduced ourselves, I had a sinking feeling—wondering if we older feminists had accomplished anything over the past fifteen years. Many of these young women were wearing the very items of clothing, like spike high heels, that my contemporaries had viewed as symbols of women's oppression. A stylishly made-up young woman introduced herself and expressed concern that she might not fit into the class because she participated in beauty contests and, in fact, was a "beauty queen." As she spoke about her aspirations and expectations, I pegged her as a member of the postfeminist generation, one of those young women who take for granted the gains made by women in the past two decades. As the others introduced themselves, they were sounding the same note, except for a few of the Afro-Americans and Chicanas.* Most of these students believed in "women's rights" and many had even worked for the passage of the Equal Rights Amendment, yet they choked on the label "feminist." They weren't feminists, they said, because they weren't angry.

Our realities have been so different that I wondered if we could understand one another. My contemporaries were thwarted on all fronts. Outraged and indignant, we fought with passion and zeal. We cannot understand the seeming indifference of the new generation. They, in turn, cannot fathom our anger. We are outdated relics who make them nervous. They are ingrates who make us doubt if our efforts were worth the struggle.

Sitting there, wondering how the chasm could be bridged, I lightened, remembering that I had experienced that same sinking feeling before when I interviewed a woman named Glad McLeod, a former "Rosie the Riveter," as the World War II women defense workers had been dubbed. It had been four years since I initially conceived of the Rosie the Riveter Revisited Project. Geared to that first

---

*Afro-American and *black* will be used interchangeably when I am speaking about the contemporary period. For the earlier historical period, when *Negro* was used, I will use *black*. For women of Mexican ancestry, I will generally use the term *Latina*, which is broader and less politicized than *Chicana*, unless I am referring to contemporary women who identify themselves as *Chicanas* or to women of the older generation who usually call themselves *Mexicans*. I have chosen *Latina* as the all-inclusive term because in the Southwest *Hispanic* denotes Spanish ancestry.

interview for so many years, I became depressed by what I initially perceived to be the indifference of Glad's "*pre*feminist" generation.

Three years and forty-four oral histories later, I came to a very different understanding of Glad and her generation—an understanding that gives me a fresh perspective on the young women of today. I now appreciate the subtle and incremental nature of change and understand that changes in consciousness are not *necessarily* or *immediately* reflected in dramatic alterations in the public world. They may be very quietly played out in the private world of women, yet expressed in a fashion that can both affect future generations and eventually be expressed more openly when the social climate is right.

When I first began collecting the oral histories of these women, I was looking for the dramatic. The role of women during World War II had captured feminists' imaginations in the late 1960s and early 1970s. Those strong and competent women had broken into nontraditional jobs. Why were we fighting anew, some thirty years later, for apprenticeships for women in still-called nontraditional jobs; why were we still fighting for public child care, which had been supported through public funding during the war years?

We had been taught initially that women were called out of the home to perform their patriotic duties "for the duration" and had then happily returned home to motherhood in postwar suburbia. But by 1970 we were no longer willing to accept the traditional version of women's role in history. Instead, we were asking new and challenging questions; we were looking at the facts in a different way. We discovered who Rosie the Riveter really was. She was young and old; Afro-American, Anglo, and Latina; single and married; worker, student, and full-time housewife. Contrary to popular mythology, she was more likely to be a woman who had already been working outside the home than to be a homemaker newly recruited into the work force.

The more we learned about the wartime experience of women, the angrier we became about women's lost chances. After the war, women's presence in the formerly masculine domains was again greatly diminished, if not fully extinguished. Union records did document grievances filed by some women over the violation of seniority rights, unearthing some pockets of resistance. But on the whole, not much seemed to have changed. Women's primary roles were still in the home or, if they were in the work force, in service or clerical jobs.

But was this the whole story? As part of the Feminist History Research Project, I had collected and listened to the life histories of enough women from the early part of the century to understand that women's lives were not always as neat and acquiescent as they appeared to be. I wondered what lay beneath the surface. If women were able to tell their own story, might we discover a whole hidden history of World War II?

To uncover that hidden history, an oral history project was designed. Over two hundred former southern California women aircraft workers were first interviewed by telephone, and then a group of forty-five was selected for in-depth life history interviews. (For a description of this project, including the selection process, see the Appendix.)

When the project was launched in October 1979, the *Los Angeles Times* ran a lengthy story about it. The very day the story appeared, I arrived at my office shortly before 9 A.M. The phone was already ringing off the hook. For the next several weeks, we received calls from women all over southern California who had been Rosie the Riveters—and from their children and grandchildren and nieces and nephews. One woman told me she cried when she read the newspaper article: "I thought nobody remembered us." I also received a few crackpot messages, including a threat to have my communistic research investigated.

During the next two years, as my colleagues and I collected the full life histories of the forty-five women, I felt as if I were on an intellectual and emotional roller coaster. I left my first interview disappointed and confused.

Glad McLeod was gracious and forthright. At age fifty-eight, seriously debilitated by emphysema, Glad was linked to an oxygen tank by tubing that snaked its way from her nostrils to a back bedroom. Housebound, she enjoyed the break in routine that the interviews offered. During our first session, Glad spoke candidly and in great detail about her youth, providing an intimate glimpse into the changing sexual mores of her generation. I returned the following week to record her recollections of the war years, expecting the same kind of rich details. To my astonishment, Glad hardly remembered any details about those years, as if it had been a rather unimportant period in her life. As a scholar, I understood the significance of that insight. But as a feminist, I felt let down.

I quickly discovered, however, that Glad's reaction was not the most common one. Buried in so many of the stories of the two hundred women with whom we spoke was a voice crying out to be heard: "I never realized what I could do."

Scores of women told us that their wartime work experiences

changed the way they felt about themselves. Being able "to hold their own with men," as Marguerite Hoffman, one of the interviewees, put it, gave a new sense of self, of competency, not only to women new to the world of work outside the home but also to those who had worked at traditional women's jobs. Urban women in the 1940s were accustomed to their work being devalued—be it in the home or in the marketplace. During the war, for the first time in their lives, many women performed jobs that were viewed by the public as necessary and valuable, and that were often physically challenging. Finally valued by others, they came to value themselves more.

Because I have come to know these women and to feel the intensity of their individual experiences, it is difficult for me to accept as the whole story the "facts" revealed in the labor force statistics on occupational sex segregation, marriage rates, and birthrates. Oral histories compel us to look beyond these measures of change—indeed, to challenge the very definition of change. A close look at women's lives reveals us as active players, not merely passive objects to be manipulated by men or the economy. Studying the World War II experience of women with a 1960s perspective, we tended to focus on the impermanency of the wartime changes—on the losses, not on the gains. Our vision was obscured by our own historical context and also by a definition of success that perhaps denies women's experience and the rhythm of women's lives.

As seductive as it had been earlier to view women as a group united by oppression—a fourth world, as it were—we have come to appreciate our differences. Our relationship to the world is mediated not only by gender, race, class, and ethnicity but also by our own individual life cycles. So young single women reacted to their wartime experience quite differently than older single women who, after working at dead-end jobs for many years, often seized the opportunity provided by the war job. For black women who had been relegated to the white women's kitchens, a good-paying job in an aircraft plant frequently provided the basis for real and permanent changes in the quality of their lives. These broad changes, like the more private ones experienced by individual women, are difficult to capture in the traditional historical record. It is only when individual women talk about their lives that we are able to put the whole story together: the public and the private; the dramatic and the subtle; the gains and the losses.

The oral histories of the ten southern California former aircraft workers presented here are not unique. These particular Anglo, Afro-

American, and Latina women were chosen because their experiences were typical of other women like themselves. Each has her own story and tells it in her own personal style. Though their accents are not captured on the printed page, some spoke with a thick regional dialect, others with the lilting intonation characteristic of northern Mexico. Some are born storytellers and rose to the occasion; others are more reserved and delivered their narrative or answered questions without much embellishment. Some leisurely reconstructed a sense of time and place and people; others hurtled forward, rushing from one experience or feeling to the next.

These oral histories are not mere snippets about the war years but full life stories. We see the women as rounded human beings with a past and a future. But their reconstruction of the past and their vision of the future is a product of a particular moment in time and reflects their mood at the time of the telling. Illness or loneliness or depression can produce one picture, optimism another.

But if we listen carefully, we find clues to the meaning of an event or the weight of an emotion by how a phrase is turned, how words are repeated. The words and phrases are those of the women themselves, with little alteration. The interviewers' role was to help extract these words. My role as a historian was to provide a historical and social context; to make sense out of each individual story; to find the threads that connected them; to organize the materials in a way that illuminated how these women were both molded by events and, in turn, influenced them.

The women have been grouped according to the role they played on the eve of the war: long-term worker; young new workers; and full-time homemakers. As we shall see, however, change is not always so logically organized, and individuals do not always fit into neat categories.

I hope this work will contribute to a better understanding of the process of social change and to a more complex picture of how the World War II work experience affected the lives of women in the United States. I also hope that it will contribute to thinking about the present differently. Once I reminded myself what I had learned about the process of change, I looked around at my students and realized that I would not have trouble bridging what I intially thought was a chasm between myself, the "older feminist," and my younger students, the "postfeminists." In fact, at the end of four months these terms seemed irrelevant.

Rosie THE Riveter Revisited

Women, The War, and Social Change

PART I

Introduction

CHAPTER 1

This Is the Way the World Was

The United States on the Eve of World War II

*Yesterday, December 7, 1941, a date
that will live in infamy, the United
States of America was suddenly and
deliberately attacked by naval and air
forces of the Empire of Japan. . . . I
ask Congress to declare that since the
unprovoked and dastardly attack by
Japan . . . a state of war has existed
between the United States and the
Japanese Empire*

Sixty million people gathered in front of their radios on December 8 and listened to these words by President Franklin Delano Roosevelt. The attack by the Japanese and the declaration of war against the United States by Germany and Italy a few days later were to profoundly alter the lives of all Americans. The earlier effort to maintain neutrality had already been eroded, and with the direct attack on the United States, the last vestiges of isolationism were quickly swept away. The Depression Era retreat to traditional values, with their emphasis on domestic life, could no longer sustain people nor prepare them for the task ahead. To wage a sustained war for almost four years, the entire population would have to be mobilized. Prevailing attitudes toward women, blacks, and people of other racial and ethnic groups would have to be set aside, if not changed. By war's end, the spirit and values of the country were far different than they had been on that fateful day in December 1941.

On the eve of the war, the country was still recovering from the Great Depression. Unemployment rates, though reduced, remained high and the hostility toward married women working had not abated. In fact, on December 8, 1941, the lives of most women closely resembled those of their mothers. The advances in household technology that had begun to lighten the arduousness of women's daily lives became meaningless when money was no longer available to buy goods and services or when installment payments for labor-saving devices could not be met. The depression reinforced women's role as the mainstay of family life, and their household chores often harked back to a past when women provided food and clothing for the family with their own hands. Bread had to be baked, fruit and vegetables canned, clothing sewn. Working-class women often performed these tasks without the benefits of modern household technology.

In 1941, one-third of all households were still cooking with wood or coal; and water often had to be carried from an outside source. Even though bed sheets were changed less frequently than now, laundering them was a backbreaking task for that half of the female population who scrubbed the laundry by hand or used a hand-cranked washing machine. Both farm and city women spent over fifty hours a week in household responsibilities.

It was not only the poorest women who had to take up the economic slack, nor only those women who were full-time homemakers. The working wife, the single working mother, and the adolescent girl were all forced to expand their economic roles in the home. The realities of the depression promoted a model of womanhood that emphasized women's domestic and nurturing role and contrasted sharply with the image of independence promoted during the 1920s.[1]

Over half the population still lived in rural areas or in towns of under fifty thousand where traditional values prevailed. The nuclear family reigned supreme and was idealized in the mass media. In the popular radio program "One Man's Family," the family was represented as the very foundation of society. Father Barbour reassured the audience that it was "the source from whence comes the moral strength of a nation."[2] The problems of the well-to-do, sophisticated Barbour family were far removed from the daily adversity the average person faced during the depression, but "One Man's Family" represented the *ideal* values to which everyone, regardless of class, was supposed to aspire.

Radio was an important part of life during the depression years. A form of entertainment that could be enjoyed even by the unemployed or the underemployed, it offered fare for the whole family—if it was white.

The nitty-gritty problems of life in small-town mid-America were portrayed on the daytime serials, the soap operas. There, the white working-class woman could find characters with whom she could identify. The world of the daytime serial was populated by housewives, wage earners, and small-business people as well as by professionals and members of high society. The younger women could lose themselves in the fantasy of young love on "Life Can Be Beautiful," and "The Romance of Helen Trent" held out the promise that a woman over thirty-five "could still find romance." The announcer on "Stella Dallas" daily reminded the audience that this was a story of mother love and sacrifice. The heroine was a lower-middle-class divorcée who devoted herself to others through a life of hard work. Casting doubt on the ability of the upper classes to solve their problems, this serial celebrated the common woman.[3]

The 20 million women who listened to these and other daytime serials not only found emotional release through these programs but also looked to them as an important source of advice. The daily dramas, like the stories in the confession-style magazines, were, in effect, homilies on how to get along with others, "handle" husbands, and bring up children. Above all, they showed women how to survive, "how to take it."[4] Their appeal can best be understood by a self-description from one radio serial: "The kitchen is a corner of reality in a world gone berserk."[5]

These forms of popular culture did not portray women as weak and dependent. Buried in the melodramatic stories of hardship and romance, rather, was a depiction of women as strong and largely competent. This was the time of day when a woman could define—or redefine—her world. Women were in the forefront and men, at best, were deemphasized. At worst, they were depicted as troublemakers.[6] Women could be in charge—as long as they didn't stray too far from their prescribed roles. This same double message was subtly buried in the evening programs.

Whole families would gather around the radio during the evening hours and listen to the top comedy shows. Tuesdays they would join Fibber McGee and Molly at 79 Wistful Vista, as various neighbors dropped in to visit. Although they were depicted as solidly middle class and midwestern, for a time the McGees had a hired cook and maid, Beulah—about the only role black women ever played either on the radio or in the movies. Molly was the practical one who kept

McGee closer to reality. When he became misty-eyed about the man-
dolin that fell out of the messy, jam-packed hall closet, she took him
down a peg, commenting that it was as melodious as a slate pencil.
Mary Livingstone, Jack Benny's wife, was no clinging vine, either.
She appeared every Sunday on "The Jack Benny Show," the most
popular, highest rated comedy show in broadcasting history.

Not all the women in the radio comedies were as tough and smart
as Molly or Mary Livingstone. Often, they were a bit dippy, the master of malapropisms, like George Burns's wife, Gracie Allen. Yet,
even Gracie in her scatterbrained fashion dared to suggest that a
woman might be president and jokingly ran for the office in 1940.[7]

Despite the strength of many of the women characters on radio
comedy or in daytime serials, traditional romantic images dominated
the airwaves, particularly through popular music, which consumed
about 40 percent of all broadcast time. Some 46 million people, or
slightly over half the adult population, spent Saturday evenings listen-
ing to "The Lucky Strike Hit Parade" where they heard either
"happy-in-love" ballads or "frustrated-in-love" laments.[8] The message to the youth of the country similarly emphasized romantic love,
but a developing adolescent subculture began to raise daring questions about sexual morality. For example, Dinah Shore's 1940 hit,
"Yes, My Darling Daughter," openly gives advice on sexual behavior—though the advice was still to walk the straight and narrow. Even
in Middletown (Muncie, Indiana), the epitome of small-town mid-
America studied by the Lynds in the 1920s and again in the 1930s,
sexual activity was more openly acknowledged.[9]

Social mores, indeed, were changing and so were the expectations for marriage. Sexual enjoyment and companionship in marriage
altered women's private worlds and thoughts. But if women dared to
chart a course for themselves outside the traditional family sphere,
they were either chastised or ultimately forced to surrender to their
"natural feminine instincts." In the best-sellers of the period men re-
gained their position of dominance, in contrast to the novels of the
1920s in which women often rebelled against their secondary roles.[10]
The fate of career women in the magazines of the middle class, like
Ladies' Home Journal, and of the working class, like *True Story*, was
the same. They suffered for their success.[11]

For twenty-five cents the audience of 85 million moviegoers were
treated to a double bill or even a triple bill and door prizes. They
would lose themselves in a Busby Berkeley musical extravanganza or
a historical epic like *Gone with the Wind;* or they were treated to a more
sophisticated woman's film starring Joan Crawford or Bette Davis.

These movies, like radio, delivered contradictory messages about womanhood. Although domestic bliss clearly was to be their ultimate goal, the women characters in films were not merely helpless, dependent creatures. Even a film like *Gold Diggers of 1933*, with its extreme objectification of women in the dance sequences, portrayed three strong, bright, resourceful women. In *Gone with the Wind*, Scarlett O'Hara submitted to Rhett Butler, but she, too, was a strong-willed woman who single-handedly brought her family out of the depths of economic deprivation. An important figure for white womanhood during the depression, Scarlett was the antithesis of the genteel southern woman. Margaret Mitchell, whose book was really lamenting the loss of this gentility, was surprised that audiences identified with Scarlett rather than with the helpless Melanie.[12] Black women either were absent in these films or were portrayed as the stereotypical Mammy.

In a more sophisticated fashion, the woman's films also delivered the same double message. As a strong-willed, decisive heiress or a career woman, the character ultimately surrendered her own ambitions. Basically, these films confirmed the choices made by the full-time homemakers.[13]

But the reality of most working-class women's lives was that they had few choices. In 1940, the majority of the 11.5 million employed women were working out of economic necessity. Less than an eighth of women workers were the career women depicted in films. The young, white middle-class woman or the upwardly mobile working-class woman often joined the lower ranks of white-collar workers before marriage, but after marriage she usually withdrew from the labor force. If economic necessity forced her to return to work, she would most likely become a blue-collar, domestic or service worker.

Since the early days of industrialization in the United States, it had been unusual for women to continue working outside the home after marriage. But, in order to satisfy the needs created in the 1920s by the rising standard of living, married women were increasingly attracted to the work force.[14] By 1930, one in nine married women was a wage earner. Most came from the 42 percent of families who lived at or below the subsistence level, but many of them were working for more than just bread and butter. They were helping the family achieve a higher standard of living. Even small-town working-class wives in middle America were as likely to work to assure their children an education or to buy extra clothing as they were to be forced into the job market for basic necessities.[15]

During the 1930s, however, as the effects of the Great Depression deepened, it was basic economic need that drew married women into employment outside the home.[16] By the end of the decade, almost 15.5 percent of all married women were gainfully employed. The husbands of over a third of these women made less than six hundred dollars annually, barely half the median income in 1939. The majority of these working wives of the poor were not likely to earn more than two hundred dollars, but their economic contribution often provided something as basic as a roof over their head or enough food for their children to eat.

Most wage-earning wives did not have the luxury of choosing to work or not. Nevertheless, public opinion was lined up solidly against them. The traditional hostility toward married women working was exacerbated by high male unemployment rates. In 1936, 82 percent of the population felt that wives should not work if their husbands had jobs. Furthermore, a majority believed that laws should be passed to prohibit wives from working.[17] These restrictive laws were never enacted, but the federal government did prohibit a married couple from both holding government jobs, and as late as 1939, legislatures in twenty-six states considered laws limiting married women's work. Both men and women believed that married women should give up their jobs if their husbands wanted them to.[18]

The attitudes toward working wives reflected firmly entrenched ideas about woman's proper place, not the reality of the job market. In the 1930s, men and women held different jobs. Indeed, this difference is what enabled more women to enter the work force during the depression years. The number of jobs dominated by women in the service industries expanded, whereas the number of men's jobs in heavy manufacturing contracted.

The fact that so many married women, even in the poorest segment of the population, did *not* work is a measure of the limited availability of jobs, the heavy burden carried by women in the home, and the resistance by both men and women to changing definitions of women's proper role in society. Women, above all, were supposed to be wives and mothers—even though marriage and birthrates were plummeting in response to the economic hardships of the depression.

As wives, women were responsible for carefully budgeting the pay their husbands brought home, for ministering to their physical needs, and for providing emotional support to the men whose egos were battered by the threat to their role as family breadwinner. As mothers, women had been told since the 1920s that children required full-time care and devotion, though the specific formulas regarding the nature of this care were constantly changing.[19] In the earlier part of the century, it had been assumed that working-class children would work to help support the family. But by the 1930s, a growing number of mothers went to work to assure their children's continued education. During the decade, the rate of high school enrollment sharply increased. Most working-class youths did not stay to graduation, but by 1940, three-fourths of all fourteen-to-eighteen-year-olds were attending high school.

As so frequently happens during a crisis, the family became a refuge during the depression. It was a source of comfort for the frightened and insecure. Those who were not on relief often felt that the depression was good for family life.[20] Despite the militancy of some of the unemployed, by and large people did not blame their problems on capitalism. They tended, instead, to internalize them or, through the medium of cultural forms like the popular gangster films of the 1930s, to attribute social problems to personal evil.

On the eve of the war, then, the United States was a country just beginning to recover from the devastating effects of the depression. Its social institutions were largely intact, and its people were still sustained by the essentially traditional values that had served them so well in a simpler society. But the inescapable complexity of the world was gradually changing the fabric of society.

When the United States entered the war following the bombing of Pearl Harbor, the country had to move into high gear—and fast. The war materiel already being produced for our European Allies was not sufficient for the new role we assumed. Almost overnight auto factories were converted into aircraft plants, shipyards were expanded, and new factories were built. In order to quickly fill the demands for workers in these new or expanding industries, complex jobs that formerly had been performed by highly skilled workers, like machinists, were broken down into smaller tasks that could be quickly learned.

The promise of new, well-paying jobs attracted not only the urban unemployed but also people from rural areas and small towns. The mass migration from the South, the Southwest, and the Midwest into the burgeoning industrial centers of the West and North would have an important and lasting effect on the nature of American society. In the short run, the tensions that resulted from overcrowding and from new social interaction among an increasingly diverse population often fanned the flames of race hatred. During the height of the war, race riots occurred in several northern and western cities, including the "zoot-suit riots" in Los Angeles. When the Japanese were evacuated from the Los Angeles region and placed in concentration camps, the housing they left behind was sometimes used to accommodate the new influx of black workers from Texas and Oklahoma. "Little Tokyo" became "Brownsville."

Initially, the pool of urban unemployed, supplemented by the first trickle of migrants, was sufficiently large to accommodate the expanded war economy. But as men went into military service, new sources of workers were needed and old prejudices had to be overcome, as President Roosevelt made clear in his Columbus Day speech in 1942: "In some communities employers dislike to hire women. In others they are reluctant to hire Negroes. We can no longer afford to indulge such prejudice."

And so began the entry of women into new, uncharted territories. By 1944, 16 percent of working women held jobs in war industries. In a city like Los Angeles, almost one of every eleven women workers was employed in aircraft production, where they made up over 40 percent of the work force.

This change did not happen overnight, however. In 1940 almost a fourth of all white women and nearly 38 percent of black women were wage earners but most worked in either the lower paid "feminized" clerical or service jobs or in manufacturing. (Black and Latina women were only just beginning to find manufacturing jobs.) The nondurable manufacturing industries in which women were concentrated—clothing, textiles, and shoes—paid considerably less than the male-dominated durable manufacturing industries of machinery, automobiles, and steel.

These working women didn't need much convincing to change jobs. Beginning in 1942, as news of good pay quickly passed by word of mouth, they began to enter war industries in large numbers. At first, the jobs were open only to white women. As a result of systematic organizing by black leaders, however, the doors were finally opened to Afro-Americans, including women.

A sustained battle was initiated in early 1941, when A. Philip Randolph, head of the Brotherhood of Sleeping Car Porters, threatened to organize a march on Washington of thousands of "Negroes" if the government did not take measures to stop discrimination in the defense industries and the military. In response to this threatened black revolt, President Roosevelt finally issued Executive Order 8802 banning discrimination in defense plants and government offices and services. The executive order by itself did not automatically open up jobs to black workers, however. Active community organizing was required, and the newly formed nationwide network of "Double V Committees"—victory against racism at home and victory against fascism abroad—played a vital role in this struggle.

There is little evidence of this kind of organizing among other groups. On the other hand, the Latino population did not seem to face the same kind of discrimination as the blacks. Among the Asians, there is some indication that a small number of Chinese and Filipino women did get defense jobs, but the incarceration of people of Japanese ancestry obviously removed them from the labor market. A few American Indians did find jobs in defense industries, but the migration of Indians to urban industrial centers was only just beginning during the war years.

Eventually, half of the women defense workers were drawn from the ranks of women who were already in the work force before the war. But their numbers alone were not sufficient to fill the growing need for workers, especially as more and more men were called up by the draft, so industry turned to women not holding jobs.

Students, especially those just graduating from high school, were an obvious pool of new workers. Young women who did not go to college usually entered the work force and remained there until marriage. Those who were college bound did not normally go to work, but it was hoped that the press of wartime needs could induce them to temporarily postpone further education. The problem was to convince these young single women to take production jobs in the defense industries. Left to their own devices, most young women—including those from the working class—were more likely to choose white-collar work.[21] Clerical jobs paid less than factory work, but office work was clean and respectable, an avenue for mobility—or so they thought.

The themes of patriotism and glamour were used to appeal to these young women. Their brothers and their boyfriends were off defending democracy. The least they could do was to take a war job: be the woman behind the man behind the gun. This role was glorified in songs like "Rosie the Riveter" which extolled a young worker whose boyfriend Charlie was in the marines. Magazines demonstrated how war workers could be glamorous, even fashionable. Lockheed Aircraft went so far as to hold Victory Fashion Shows during lunch hour, where shop workers modeled coordinated two-piece work outfits.

Movies portrayed the likes of Ginger Rogers dressed in slacks with a snood on her head tooling around the aircraft plant on a fork-lift. Norman Rockwell memorialized the young war worker on the cover of the *Saturday Evening Post* with his Rosie the Riveter: a muscular but pert, rosy-cheeked young woman, rivet gun slung across her lap. The double message was clear: her loafer-clad foot was firmly planted on *Mein Kampf*—symbolizing her role in stamping out fascism—but she could still remain feminine, as the powder puff and mirror peeking out of her coverall pocket reminded. The media blitz was successful. By 1944, one out of five defense workers was a recent student.

Still, the all-consuming need for more war workers could not be met, not even with the recruitment of the disabled, of high school students and businessmen for four-hour victory shifts, and of servicemen on leave. Despite the weight of traditional values, full-time homemakers had to be recruited for war work—an uphill battle. Even in early 1943, when the severity of the labor shortage became alarming, less than a third of married men gave unqualified approval to their wives taking defense jobs.[22] Furthermore, three-fourths of the homemakers themselves thought they could best contribute to the war effort by continuing to do what they were doing. The mothers of young children were especially reluctant to make any changes.[23] There was unanimity among the government agencies responsible for recruiting women war workers that the primary focus should be on women without young children at home. Recognizing, however, that mothers of young children would ultimately have to be recruited, it was recommended that schools and nurseries be provided for their children.

Like the other recruitment campaigns, those directed at home-makers played upon their patriotism.[24] The messages appealed to their domestic and nurturing roles. Self-sacrifice was required to bring their husbands and sons home safely and to preserve the way of life they cherished. The temporary nature of this required shift in roles was stressed—thereby supporting rather than challenging deep-seated cultural values.[25] In an unusual twist, the work that women performed in the home was seen as having provided them with skills that were transferable to defense work: if they could operate a sewing machine, they could easily learn to run a drill or a punch press or a rivet gun. Novel approaches were developed to get the message across. The Womanpower Commission in Buffalo, New York, set up charming little Cape Cod cottages downtown in order to welcome potential applicants with the "cheery warmth of a friendly neighbor." In Los Angeles, married Lockheed women workers served as "Victory Visitors" going from door to door in their neighborhood to recruit full-time homemakers for the factories.

The barrage of propaganda used to attract "Mrs. Stay-at-Home" to war work succeeded in breaking through the initial resistance to taking jobs. In 1944, at the height of war production, almost one in three women defense workers was a former full-time homemaker. Their addition to the work force meant that married women outnumbered single women workers for the first time in U.S. history.

Even though these former full-time homemakers made up only a third of all women defense workers, their role has assumed mythic proportions. We envision droves of women leaving their homes and flocking to the defense plants for the duration—wives fighting on the home front for their husbands at the battlefront. In reality, only one in ten new women workers had husbands in the service. (And only 8 percent of *all* women were married to servicemen.)

The former homemakers, especially the mothers, have captured our imagination. But they were not the only home-front heroines who had to do double duty, tending to home responsibilities during their "free" time. Many of the women already in the work force for years had been juggling their wage-earning and domestic roles. During the war, this double burden increased, especially for the one-third of defense workers who had children under fourteen at home.[26]

After eight or ten hours of riveting or welding or soldering, these wives and mothers had to stand in long lines in the stores and cope with rationing. By the time they reached the market at the end of their workday, the limited supplies were often depleted—unless they were fortunate enough to have a grocer who looked out for them, saving a good cut of meat or slipping a package of cigarettes into their grocery bag. The shoppers who were lucky enough to have a washing machine still had to contend with the search for laundry soap. Those who used a commercial laundry had to wait as long as two weeks or a month for the return of their clothing and linens.

The greatest problem for the mothers, of course, was how to care for their children. Who would mind them when they weren't in school? Who would take them to the doctor or stay home with them if they were sick? To assist the war workers, and particularly the mothers, special wartime programs were established by local governments and sometimes by the war industries themselves. These were not sufficient to meet the needs of the vast numbers of working women, but the special women's counselor programs and the newly established child-care centers were an important beginning (see chapter 11). Nevertheless, most mothers continued to handle their problems individually. If their husbands were present, women tried to adjust their work schedules so that the fathers could look after the children during the evening. Single mothers often had their own mothers or another relative come live with them and care for the children. Neighbors and older children all chipped in. Still, women's commitment to domestic responsibilities caused a fair amount of absenteeism and a high rate of job turnover.

The money they were earning usually compensated for the difficulties married war workers faced. Thirty-five to forty dollars a week was more than enough to satisfy the needs that had been deferred during the depression. But wartime shortages and the lack of free time meant that they would have to wait still longer. So, instead, most war workers saved their money. They were regularly reminded to invest in war bonds. The plants where they worked held frequent bond drives, often glorified by the lunchtime presence of movie stars. Promotional shorts were regularly shown in movie theaters, and booths were set up in the lobby for the sale of bonds.

The war permeated every aspect of daily life. News from overseas was regularly broadcast on the radio. One network devoted almost 40 percent of its broadcast time to news programming about the war. War themes were incorporated into the dramatic and variety shows as well. The popular comedy programs often originated from army bases and joke routines touched on life in the service. Many of the old standbys, like "Fibber McGee and Molly," incorporated war messages into the body of their programs, dealing with issues like the black market and the recruiting of nurses' aides. On other shows, the stars often gave a curtain talk at the end of the program. The daytime serials, too, went to war, and some regulars, like Stella Dallas, took a defense job.

Movie attendance was at an all-time high, with women the major audience. War themes were regularly served up, but most movies were escapist in nature, especially after 1943. The genre of women's films that had first appeared in the 1930s were still popular, and the strong characters portrayed by Bette Davis, Joan Crawford, and Barbara Stanwyck continued to survive in a male-dominated world. They were offset by the emergence of a new model, the "girl next door," as portrayed by actresses like June Allyson. Still, the work women were performing during the war was treated seriously.

Married war workers, especially those who were mothers, didn't have time for entertainment other than an occasional movie. But the young single workers had both time and money and they played hard.

Swing-shift workers often finished work, changed their clothes, and went off at midnight to dance or bowl or even go horseback riding. There was a near revolt among young Lockheed workers when their social clubs were temporarily closed by brown-outs, the dimming of lights, as a result of restrictions on the use of electricity. On the weekends, young women went to USO dances and had fun while they performed their patriotic duty of entertaining young servicemen on leave. These were largely innocent social activities, but they signaled a new era of independence for many young women.[27]

Because of their active social life, the press sometimes accused those young war workers of being frivolous, and their male peers in the armed services sometimes resented them. For the most part, though, all women war workers were highly respected, even celebrated. Newspapers and magazines regularly published stories about them, and the papers at the companies where they worked frequently cited their contributions. They were taken seriously—as long as they were needed.

By 1944, when war production was beginning to wind down, and especially in 1945, when the end of the war was in sight, the attitudes toward women workers underwent an about-face. Where earlier the working mother with her child-care problems had been the object of commiseration, she became now the object of blame for the rising rate of juvenile delinquency. Where the young factory worker had been portrayed as directly contributing to the war effort through her labor, she came to be treated primarily as a decorative object that would inspire fighting men to greater and better feats. The *Lockheed Star*, for example, had regularly run stories about their women production workers. In mid-1944 these were supplanted by cheesecake photo contests. Furthermore, there were fewer and fewer photos of women factory workers and more and more of office workers. Clearly, women production workers were being phased out—if not yet in actuality, then certainly in the public consciousness. Preparations were being made for the postwar world.

Some of the shifts in the attitudes toward women workers were subtle. Others were shrill. Astute observers understood that women had been changed by the wartime experience. Harold Ickes, FDR's secretary of the interior for instance, noted in the *Saturday Evening Post:*

> I think that this is as good a time as any . . . to warn men
> that when the war is over, the going will be a lot tougher,

because they will have to compete with women whose eyes
have been opened to their greatest economic potentialities.[28]

The equanimity with which Ickes accepted the change, even
welcomed it, was unusual. At the other extreme was the call in the
pages of the *San Francisco Chronicle* by a Barnard sociologist, Willard
Walker, for the "coming war on women." He envisioned three bat-
tles: the battle for jobs, the battle of the birthrate, and the battle of
personal ascendancy.[29]

The alarm was sounded when the results of Women's Bureau interviews with thirteen thousand women about their postwar plans
were announced.[30] The *Wall Street Journal* ran a banner headline de-
claring that 75 percent of working women wanted to continue to work
after the war. The results of this survey underscored Ickes's analysis.
It was not just those women who had worked before before the war
who planned to continue. Over half of the former homemakers announced the same intention. Furthermore, most women who planned
to continue wanted to keep the jobs they had.

How could the economy absorb both these new women in the
work force and the returning servicemen? The depression had left
deep scars and there were fears it would be repeated. Successful and
rapid conversion to a consumer economy was essential. Even before
the war ended, the public was primed. By late 1944 women's magazines were running ads promoting all-electric kitchens for the "after-
victory" homes. These advertisements played a dual role: they
suggested how wartime savings could be spent, and they served to
remind women of their proper domestic role. Preparing women for
her postwar return to domesticity, 1944 ads also increasingly drama-
tized the unhappy plight of the chldren of war workers.[31]

The majority of all married women workers planned on continuing working after the war, but this figure was considerably lower
among married defense workers.[32] A substantial proportion wanted to
take up full-time homemaking—at least for a while. They were tired
of juggling their work and domestic responsibilities. The years of
hardship, first during the depression and then during the war, had
taken their toll. A return to domesticity looked attractive. Their hard-
earned money could be used to build a secure future in a home of
their own. Many of the younger single women were awaiting the return of the GIs in order to marry and begin their domestic life.

Most women defense workers, however, did not have the opportunity to decide their postwar work plans in a leisurely fashion. Massive layoffs occurred as soon as peace was declared. At some aircraft plants, the workers were gathered into large assembly areas, where they were debriefed and their tools and badges collected. In the Los Angeles aircraft industry, the proportion of women plummeted from a high of over 40 percent of workers during the peak war production years to less than 18 percent by 1946; the figure continued to decline to a low of 11.9 percent in 1948.

The end results are hard to estimate.[33] There were clearly not enough well-paying jobs for all the women who wanted to remain in the work force. The sexual division of labor, never totally eliminated during the war, became firmly entrenched again after the war, and many women were forced back into lower-paying female-dominated occupations. On the other hand, in many cities, the proportion of women workers in durable manufacturing increased, and their proportion in menial domestic labor decreased. In Los Angeles, where the aircraft industry maintained a steady influence, the proportion of women workers by 1952 had increased to 25 percent and held there fairly steadily over the next decade.[34]

After the war, both marriage and birthrates soared. From the mid-depression low of 18.7 births per 1,000 population, the rate increased to 24.5 by 1949, or about the same as it had been in 1925. Marriage was in vogue. It is true that the divorce rate had climbed during the war, but by the late 1940s it had dropped. In any event, the institution of marriage was not threatened. Most divorced men and women were quick to remarry. Home ownership grew, spurred on by the availability of GI loans and the savings that had been accumulated during the war. By the end of the decade, the United States had become more urbanized and suburbanized; war-related benefits like the GI bill altered the social class structure; and the population, generally, enjoyed a higher standard of living.

Was the status of women changed? An increased proportion of married women were working but most defined their work as part of their family role. The Equal Rights Amendment, for which there was some brief hope of pasage in the late 1940s, fell into obscurity. The independent women earlier portrayed by Katharine Hepburn, Barbara Stanwyck, and Joan Crawford disappeared from the movie screen and were supplanted by Doris Day and Donna Reed as the wholesome girl next door and by Marilyn Monroe as the quintessential sexpot.

From all appearances, the full weight of the culture was bearing down
on women and ushering in a new idealization of domesticity.

Did the traces of pride and spirit of independence manifested by
women workers during the war simply vanish? Did women simply return to the status quo ante? The best way to learn the answers to
these questions is to listen to the voices of the women themselves—
to revisit Rosie the Riveter.

PART II

Negroes, Women, and Aliens

Women in the Work Force

American enthusiasm for production as a short cut to victory can probably be used to help tear down much of the prejudice against Negroes, women and aliens, three groups not yet fully integrated into the labor force.

Office of War Information, 1943

On December 7, 1941, 12 million women were already in the work force, comprising one-fourth of all workers. Most of these women were single, divorced, or widowed and were supporting themselves and their children. It was not yet common for married women to work outside the home, except for black women—almost half of whom did. These long-time wage earners eagerly switched from their lower paying jobs and took the better paying defense work. Eventually, they made up half of the women workers in war plants.

As long-time wage earners, Fanny Christina Hill, Marye Stumph, and Margarita Salazar (McSweyn) all faced dead-end low-paying jobs. But they were at different stages in their life cycles when they took their aircraft jobs and consequently had different expectations about their futures. The cultural differences as well as the individual differences between them colored their reactions to their wartime work experience.

CHAPTER 2

Fanny
Christina Hill

Tina Hill, 1982.

*The war made me live better, it really
did. My sister always said that Hitler
was the one that got us out of the white
folks' kitchen.*

This comment—attributed to her sister but repeated with
sufficient relish to make the real authorship suspicious—
captures the spirit of Fanny Christina ("Tina") Hill. At
sixty-seven, Tina, who looked considerably younger than
her years, told her story with dramatic flair and humor.
Tina was determined to give a lesson in black history,
and she had no hesitation making outrageous generaliza-
tions about "the Negro." These comments were outrageous not because they were inaccurate—they were usually grounded in cultural and historical reality—but rather
because Tina used such a broad stroke and so often
couched her comments in language that conjured up stereotypes.

Tina is both an actor and an observer. Her oral history not only richly details her life experiences but is
sprinkled with commentaries on them. Determined to ac-
quire the better things in life and to live the American
dream, Tina is wryly self-mocking as she describes her
ascent to the middle class.

For Tina, and for many black women, the war *was* a

turning point. The expansion of jobs in the defense industries, coupled with Roosevelt's executive order prohibiting discrimination in hiring, helped black women get out of the white women's kitchens. In Los Angeles, for instance, in 1940, over 55 percent of nonwhite women workers were in private household service. Ten years later, this figure was down 15 percent. Tina was one of those who were able to leave domestic service permanently. And the money she earned during the war years paved the way for a new life.

That new life is reflected in her home, which is filled with the material goods she has acquired. She points to these as an indicator of what the job at North American Aircraft meant to her. But her home also symbolizes the past and her own family history. The bowl that Tina's great-grandmother was given by her owner when the slaves were emancipated is proudly displayed on a shelf. Tina's quilting frame is set up in the middle of her living room. The embroidered decorations and the garden out back both reflect Tina's commitment to preserve the traditions handed down by the generations of women in her family. She feels that it is her turn to pass down these skills and this history to the next two generations—her daughter and granddaughter.

Tina told her story partially with that goal in mind. She is a good storyteller and the more excited she became—especially when she recounted showdowns with whites—the more "Texified" her speech became. A very open and outspoken person, Tina was always in command. She directed the interviews and needed little coaxing. In fact, when the third interview was completed, she lamented that she had not had the chance to talk about her granddaughter, a story that rightfully needed to be told. And so there was a fourth interview.

Tina describes herself as a go-getter and her success story is that of a fighter, set against the backdrop of the emergent civil rights movement and the wartime migration of blacks. A Texan by birth, Tina was the youngest of five children. The family was poor, but since they lived on Tina's grandmother's land they were able to maintain their own garden and raise chickens and even some livestock, the meat from which they "put up," using the local 4-H Club pressure cooker. Tina's account of her childhood in Texas recaptures both the segregated world of the South and the ways in which black and white children often mingled freely with one another—at least until they reached the age of puberty.

After her mother remarried when Tina was about six years old, the family moved to land adjacent to the Negro Vocational College. Beginning in childhood, that school played an important role in Tina's life. She attended classes there from the primary grades until she was forced to drop out when she was about eighteen. It introduced Tina to the world beyond Prairie View.

Times were hard in 1938 and Tina went to work as a domestic in Tyler, Texas. Two years later, she came to Los Angeles to make a better life for herself. Though disappointed at having to continue working as a domestic, Tina bided her time, convinced that better things were to come.

Tina went back to Texas to marry, and by the time she returned to Los Angeles after her husband went into the army, the local Negro Victory Committee had ensured that black women would be trained and hired in the defense industries. Tina went to work at North American Aircraft in 1943 at age twenty-four. Her husband returned before war's end, and she became pregnant shortly afterward. By V-J Day and the time of the massive layoffs that followed, Tina was on maternity leave. She returned to North American in 1946 and remained there until her retirement in 1980.

A very determined and willful woman, Tina was in charge of her life and took advantage of every opportunity open to her. Perhaps because she wanted to make that clear, Tina's story is very much her own. The other players in her life, especially her husband, Joseph, remained shadowy figures in her account. Although she mourned his death in 1972, Tina gave the impression that he sometimes got in her way.

More recently, especially since her retirement, Tina has begun to focus on shaping her daughter's and granddaughter's futures. Although the oral history process usually provides the person being interviewed with an opportunity to assess her life, for Tina, the life review process had a greater impact than it did for most of those interviewed. It was as if she had been sitting on her story for years, fully aware of its significance; then someone came along and validated her own sense of its importance. Tina has become something of a local celebrity in Los Angeles, in fact. As a result of publicity about the Rosie the Riveter Revisited Project, several newspaper accounts and a couple of television stories have been done locally. On each occasion, she has regularly recounted that Hitler was the one that got black women out of the white folks' kitchen. Now, however, she claims authorship.

The oral history process and the resulting attention paid to the former women defense workers have also had an impact on Tina's daughter, Beverly, who returned to college, much to Tina's delight. Beverly called me a while back to ask for sources for a paper she was writing on the training of women for defense work. During the course of our conversation, she lamented that so little women's history was being taught.

Tina and I chat by phone periodically, so I was surprised that I didn't hear from her after I wrote her about the publication of this book. Typically, she waited until she had something to tell *me*. Her news was about the Rosie the Riveter doll that had just come on the market. A friend had ordered it for her and she promised to call me once it was delivered.

I feel particularly gratified that Tina's oral history has been so meaningful to her. I tell my students that we are giving something very important back to the people we interview. Yet, at times, I worry that we may, to some degree, be exploiting those we interview. When someone like Tina is so appreciative and derives so much from the experience, it confirms my belief in the worth of what I am doing.

Tina Hill, ca. 1943

I'll never forget, my grandmother on my father's side was telling me that she was a little girl when the slaves was freed. The master's wife told her mother, which was my great-grandmother, "Nancy, now you come in the house and you get you some of the dishes and things because you're going to have to be keeping house of your own and I want you to have something that you're familiar with." She gave my great-grandmother that bowl. That thing is over a hundred years old, passed down from one family to the other. My great-grandmother gave it to her girl, which was my grandmother; my father was next and then I'm next; then Beverly and then the little baby.

She told her, "Get you some flowers, because you'll have to have flowers to go in your house also." She went out in the yard and she got some of the flowers, and two of the flowers was narcissus and jonquils. Those flowers was in the yard and I saw them for years and years. Then, about fifteen years ago, I got a bright idea: "I think I'll go back home and get some of those flowers in grandmother's yard and I'll bring 'em here and I'll plant them in our yard."

My great-grandfather was named Crawford and he went by his own name; he didn't use the master's name. He was working as a carpenter during the slavery time, and he did all the building around the plantation. He had saved enough money to buy his freedom and he had half enough to buy his wife's freedom and then he was going to buy his little girl's freedom, which was my grandmother. But then they came along and freed the slaves, so he didn't have to buy them.

He took that money and bought seventy acres of land right off of the plantation. He built them a house and they farmed that little seventy acres.

I really don't know where my grandfather came from. But the way they would do slaves when they were so bad and they couldn't handle them, they would put them up on the block and ship them down to somewhere in Louisiana where they had nothing to do but work. My grandfather was such a rebellious person, he just wouldn't stay. He just kept running away with life and he just managed to survive. That's why he left Louisiana and drifted into Texas. Then he ran into my grandmother and married her.

She must have had some kind of a background of medicine, because she called herself a "granny," which was sort of a seminurse. She would call herself doctoring on people and she always delivered babies. I remember a lot of the things my mama told me that she used to use for medicine and how it worked. My father had polio as a baby and my grandmother cured him with it. She used the same method that Sister Kenny [a pioneer in the treatment of polio] used and she didn't know anything about Sister Kenny. She took wool and then put it in the hot water and then she put it on your body. My father came out with just a limp; one leg was about half an inch shorter than the other.

My mother didn't come from this same group of people. I don't know too much about her parents because she doesn't know too much about them herself. She said they was cousins to the ones up there where my grandmother lived. The white people was almost like the Negroes: if they wasn't kin by marriage, they was kin by blood. So they were sort of the same kin in there somehow or the other. My mother was a very light-skinned woman and I know she got a lot of favors just by being that. From the black people, as well. She was almost as light as my grandbaby. And you see how dark I am? Because my father was dark.

She married my father when she was about sixteen, so from about sixteen until, oh, about thirty—I think that's how old she was when my father died. Then she was out there on her own with five children: one boy and four girls. I'm the youngest. I was born January 9, 1918.

I was born in the little house that had been my great-grandfather's. Then we moved to another little house on the same land, on my grandmother's land. My grandmother died when I was nine. I remembered the things that she did do and I decided I was going to do my best to excel in it. I was going to keep those things alive. I learned to crochet. I love that and I love to sew. I can make most anything I want to make. I can cut if I want to, or I buy the pattern. And I like to farm. I always raise a garden.

My father was supposed to have been a farmer, but he just got by by doing a little bit of nothing. Some men are like that. Mama went to work and supported us the best she could. There were times we wouldn't have anything to eat if Mama hadn't gone to work. That's why you talk about women liberation and women go out to work? The black woman has worked all of her life and she really was the first one to go out to work and know how to make ends meet, because it was forced on her.

My mother worked for this lady. And I didn't know a lot about prejudice and segregation because I would always go to town with this white woman. Everybody in this little small town knew I was Lucy's baby—which was my mother's name—and they knew that Lucy worked for Mrs. Harris. So I just tagged along and I got all the good treatment. And when her little nieces would come over to play, I was right there. I would get on the horse and ride with them. And I would ride the horse with her husband if he was going out somewhere. I don't know when I found out there was a difference in color.

So as a child, I think I had a pretty happy childhood. This lady thought so much of my mama and she treated us fairly good. She always looked after me. A lot of times I didn't go home. I slept right beside the fireplace at night to keep warm. Mama said I was just like she left me: when she'd come back the next morning, I would be right there. Sometimes I'd have the same diaper on and sometimes I wouldn't. So you often think about white people not being nice to you, but that woman changed my diapers. Nevertheless, my mama was her servant.

Tina left her childhood home in Hempstead, Texas, when she was about six years old, two years after her father's death. Her mother's new husband had bought a house on land adjacent to the Negro Vocational College in Prairie View.

We all went to this little college, but my older sister didn't make it through. She did like a lot of girls: she got pregnant and had to drop out after high school. The second girl went to college and she took home economics. Then, when she finished college, she married. Mother was going to send the last two girls to school, which was Philistine and myself, but the times was very hard. That was 1934.

We had to stay out of school a year and a half or two years. Finally we was able to go back, but times was still too hard and we didn't have clothes to wear. My mother wasn't a very good "go-out-and-getter." She didn't know how to ask people. So we dropped out of school. I was taking home economics. I wanted to do demonstrations showing people how they could cook, how they could sew, how they could build furniture, and how they could manage.

My brother started to work in this college when he was sixteen, maybe seventeen, in 1926. That's when times was sure enough hard. That was the beginning of the depression. But that kept us all through the depression, down to '38 when we finally decided to break up housekeeping and go to the city.

I decided I wanted to make more money, and I went to a little small town—Tyler, Texas. I didn't care too much for that town because I wasn't accustomed to the filth of a city. In that little college town, we had running toilets; everybody had electric lights and they had gas. People in Tyler were still using kerosene lamps and they had outdoor toilets. And the only thing I could do there for a living was domestic work and it didn't pay very much. So I definitely didn't like it.

I was working for a woman who had an apartment house with four units. One of the Connally bro'iers was there, a brother or an uncle to this John Connally that was running for president. He had a daughter, Frances, and she got married. I was talking to the maid—'cause I was a good talker and always inquisitive. I'd bounce over there and see how the wedding was coming along. All along the walls there they had the presents, and I thought this was really something and I says: "When I get married, I'm going to do this same identical thing. I'm going to get me all of this." That really did inspire me to want better things. I didn't have a wedding like she did, and it took a long time, but I got the same identical things she had: I got me a crocheted bedspread, an afghan like she had, and a tablecloth. Then I bought the silver.

But I left Tyler. I was saying, "I don't like it here because you can't make any money." I discovered I didn't have any trade. I had nothing I could do other than just that, and that wasn't what I wanted. So I decided I'd better get out of this town. I didn't like Dallas because that was too rough. Then someone told me, "Well, why don't you try California?" So then I got Los Angeles in my mind. I was twenty and I saved my money till I was twenty-one. In August 1940, I came here.

I knew I would make it. I was determined that whatever I would do, I was going to do it well. I was going to make it because I *had* to make it. There was no turning around.

Although Texas was not the land of opportunity for blacks, its rich black culture made life more bearable. As Tina recounted memories of this Texas culture, she became even more exuberant than usual. Her speech quickened and her voice rose in excitement.

Well, the white people always celebrate the Fourth of July, but the Negroes where I came from always celebrated the nineteenth of June, we called it "Juneteenth" [the day that Texas slaves learned of Emancipation]. That was the only day that we had a holiday, Christmas and Juneteenth.

That was just during the time that the corn needed plowing and chopping, and some of the cotton, you was almost through working in it. And then you had just gotten to the place where you had a little money because you'd been chopping cotton, so you was able to celebrate. That was one that we always got a dress for, Juneteenth, because we always had a picnic. A lot of times the white people would give you a calf or a hog to kill, and that's what you had for your picnic. If they didn't give it to you, you had one of your own or you went together and bought one from somebody.

The men would barbecue and we'd go down in the creeks and we'd do the thing that's illegal. We'd get in these little mudholes and seine [drop weighted nets perpendicularly] and get the fish. Who wanted a hook? And we'd also learn to dynamite them out of the water. You'd light the thing and stick that dynamite in there. We'd get the fish and bring them back and clean them and fry them.

And, oh, we had a dance or somebody could play an old guitar. You know, Negroes are musical and they could make music out of most anything. You can just take a bunch of tin tubs and old washboards and pots or anything, and turn them upside down and beat on them and bang on them and make music. So we'd always have a dance and there was always a big celebration.

Tina came west before the massive migration sparked by the expanded war industries. Although wages in Los Angeles were considerably higher than in Texas, black women were still largely relegated to domestic work. Like most domestic workers, Tina had developed a host of survival skills, not the least of which was imposing certain limitations on the work situation and relationship. These were usually unstated, but when they were exceeded, the worker simply quit her job. Tina's speech speeded up and her Texas accent became exaggerated as she recounted a run-in with her first employer in Los Angeles.

When I first came, when my aunt met me down at the station, I had less then ten dollars. I went on to her house and stayed. In less than ten days I had found a job living on the place doing domestic work. I stayed there from some time in August until Christmas. I was making thirty-five dollars a month. That was so much better than what I was making at home, which was twelve dollars a month. I saved my money and I bought everybody a Christmas present and sent it. Oh, I was the happiest thing in the world!

The family I worked for lived in Westwood. I had to cook breakfast, serve. They had a man and a wife and four kids. The smallest ones was twins and they wasn't too old. They had a nurse that took care of the twins. So I had to wash and iron, clean the house, cook. That was my job. So it was all day or practically, and I had very little time for myself. I had every Thursday off and every other Sunday. That just killed me to have to work on a Sunday, but I told myself I wasn't going to cry because I was coming out to do better and I would do better sooner or later.

They weren't very nice people. They were just plain white people that had finally got them some money. They was just—somebody. When I finally quit, he was mad. I came home one Sunday and somebody told me about a job and I went and got it. When I came back Monday morning it was payday. He should have paid me because it was the end of my pay time—which doesn't make any difference. You quit a job whenever you're ready; you don't quit payday necessarily.

And I never complained. Oooh, I never complained! You'd have thought I loved that job, the way I worked. I put everything into it

I did everything nice, just like you're supposed to. That has always been my trick: I'll never complain about anything. I'll be just as nice to you to the very last minute and then when the time comes, I will just say—boom—"I don't want to work for you anymore."

And so he was mad at me and he said something to me. And I wasn't used to fighting. I didn't tell you that, but in my household there was very little fighting going on; very little lick-passing, no fist-icuffing. And they kinda got talking too loud for me and I wasn't accustomed to that. So he said, "Well, I don't know why you'd quit." And I said, "Well, I don't like the idea—you guys had a fight here not too long ago and I saw blood on somebody's clothes." And he said, "Well, that was our business." I said, "Yeah, but I'm living in the house with you. I didn't know when you was going to run into my room!"

But I didn't like the idea of staying out there at night. That was the main problem. I thought I was supposed to come home to my own bed.

Tina worked at several jobs, including waitressing, but none suited her. She returned to live-in domestic work on the condition that she would be able to go home the night before her day off. After continuing with one employer for almost a year, Tina quit to return to Texas to marry. She had not talked about Joseph Hill earlier in the interview. Her decision to return to Texas to marry him was rather casually embedded in the broader account of her life in Los Angeles.

Believe it or not, Negroes and white people do work under different circumstances, and their value of things is quite a bit of difference. The average Negro that came out from Texas or came out from the South—the people who had been here a long time didn't have as much going for them. Just like me, I was determined to buy me a house when I came out here. I wasn't accustomed to renting. A landlord? What's that? He coming and telling you what you can't do. Ooooh, that was something I didn't know existed! So my first thought was to get me a house.

I always seemed to have been a type of person that had something going for me. Whenever I could sew, I always could do something to make you look good or make you look pretty. So I didn't have time for a lot of evil thought. Then, too, I'm not one of those religious people that believes in getting dressed every Sunday to go to church, so I spent my time doing other things.

I liked to go on outings a lot. So when I first came to California, when I'd have my day off, I'd go to the parks and to the beach and museum. Just go sightseeing; walking and look in the windows. Sometimes my aunt would go along with me or I'd find another girlfriend. But then I had a sister here pretty soon.

Los Angeles was a large city but I adjusted to it real well. It didn't take me long to find a way about it. I knew how to get around, and I knew how to stay out of danger and not take too many chances. I read the *Eagle* and I still get the *Sentinel* once in a while. [The *California Eagle* and the *Los Angeles Sentinel* were local black newspapers.] I have to get it to keep up with what the black people are doing. I used to read those papers when I was a child back home. That's what give me a big idea. I used to read a little paper called the *Kansas City Call*, and they had a *Pittsburgh Courier* that all the Negroes read.

Anyhow, then I decided I wanted to get married. Looking at the boys here in California, they weren't as nice as the men I was used to back home. They had just drifted in here from somewhere, and they thought they was the smartest things because they was able to leave home. I didn't care for them. I thought I liked this fellow I was going with back there, so I just went on back there and married him.

He said one of the reasons he married me was because he knew I was from the country and I could take care of myself. He felt like he didn't have to offer me so much—which he didn't. And he didn't want to be bossed around by his wife's family, and since I didn't have a father, he didn't have to contend with that. So that's how he stepped down—as I would like to say it—to get married. See, he was light-skinned and I don't think his family cared for me too much. My mama was real light skinned and I was so used to my mama, 'cause when I was born that's the first woman's face I looked into and her face was white. So I was accustomed to that. When that time come for me to get married and find a husband, it seemed to me as though I was just geared to a light-skinned man, which was unusual. I stepped across the line, as you would say. I was supposed to get a brown-skinned man, but that wasn't my calling. And we did stay together for thirty years, until he died.

But I knew I was only going to Texas to marry, and then I was going to persuade him to come back to Los Angeles. I stayed there for about nine months until he went into the service. Then I came to Los Angeles. I told my sister, "Well, I better get me a good job around here working in a hotel or motel or something. I want to get me a good job so when the war is over, I'll have it." And she said, "No, you just come on out and go in the war plants and work and maybe you'll make enough money where you won't have to work in the hotels or motels." Well, I was very good on taking advice from another person. And what I liked about it was the money. I felt like if I could make more money, I could do more with it.

It wasn't difficult for Tina to find an aircraft job. By 1943, when she returned to Los Angeles, the Negro Victory Committee, led by the Reverend Clayton Russell, had organized a march on the local U.S. Employment Office and had forced an expansion of training and job opportunities for blacks. The Los Angeles group used the pages of the *California Eagle* to inform and mobilize the community. Women were especially targeted, and advice was regularly offered, especially to former domestic workers, who were not accustomed to the industrial setting or to the ways in which the unions could help them.

The goal of the wartime black organizations went beyond the short-range objective of opening up jobs. The National Council of Negro Women, for example, mobilized a "Hold Your Job Campaign." They hoped to ensure that the inroads made during the war years were not lost. The council offered its services to employers and workers alike in an effort to integrate women workers into these new jobs. A series of wartime employment clinics were set up, primarily in the Washington, D.C., area. The inclusion of charm clinics and classes on behavior and attitude indicates that the black woman was being trained how to fit in and be accepted—how to be white, as it were. It is no wonder that Tina Hill and many other black women were conscious of the historic role they were playing. One of the pamphlets issues by the National Council of Negro Women contained a War Workers' Pledge: "I shall never for a moment forget that thirteen million Negroes believe in me and depend on me. . . . I am a soldier on the Home Front and I shall keep the faith."

Tina didn't want to work at Douglas Aircraft, where her sister had a job, and instead applied at North American Aviation, which was located closer to the heart of the black community. Both because of its location and because of the pressure placed on it by the United Auto Workers union and the local civil rights groups, North American had a higher proportion of black workers than any other aircraft plant.

I don't remember what day of the week it was, but I guess I must have started out pretty early that morning. When I went there, the man didn't hire me. They had a school down here on Figueroa and he told me to go to the school. I went down and it was almost four o'clock and they told me they'd hire me. You had to fill out a form. They didn't bother too much about your experience because they knew you didn't have any experience in aircraft. Then they give you some kind of little test where you put the pegs in the right hole.

There were other people in there, kinda mixed. I assume it was more women than men. Most of the men was gone, and they weren't hiring too many men unless they had a good excuse. Most of the women was in my bracket, five or six years younger or older. I was twenty-four. There was a black girl that hired in with me. I went to work the next day, sixty cents an hour.

I think I stayed at the school for about four weeks. They only taught you shooting and bucking rivets and how to drill the holes and to file. You had to use a hammer for certain things. After a couple of whiles, you worked on the real thing. But you were supervised so you didn't make a mess.

When we went into the plant, it wasn't too much different than down at the school. It was the same amount of noise; it was the same routine. One difference was there was just so many more people, and when you went in the door you had a badge to show and they looked at your lunch. I had gotten accustomed to a lot of people and I knew if it was a lot of people, it always meant something was going on. I got carried away: "As long as there's a lot of people here, I'll be making money." That was all I could ever see.

I was a good student, if I do say so myself. But I have found out through life, sometimes even if you're good, you just don't get the breaks if the color's not right. I could see where they made a difference in placing you in certain jobs. They had fifteen or twenty departments, but all the Negroes went to Department 17 because there was nothing but shooting and bucking rivets. You stood on one side of the panel and your partner stood on this side, and he would shoot the rivets with a gun and you'd buck them with the bar. That was about the size of it. I just didn't like it. I didn't think I could stay there with all this shooting and a'bucking and a'jumping and a'bumping. I stayed in it about two or three weeks and then I just decided I did *not* like that. I went and told my foreman and he didn't do anything about it, so I decided I'd leave.

While I was standing out on the railroad track, I ran into somebody else out there fussing also. I went over to the union and they told me what to do. I went back inside and they sent me to another department where you did bench work and I liked that much better. You had a little small jig that you would work on and you just drilled out holes. Sometimes you would rout them or you would scribe them and then you'd cut them with a cutters.

I must have stayed there nearly a year, and then they put me over in another department, "Plastics." It was the tail section of the B-Bomber, the Billy Mitchell Bomber. I put a little part in the gunsight. You had a little ratchet set and you would screw it in there. Then I cleaned the top of the glass off and put a piece of paper over it to seal it off to go to the next section. I worked over there until the end of the war. Well, not quite the end, because I got pregnant, and while I was off having the baby the war was over.

Tina stayed at North American for almost two years during the war. Her description of housing and daily life underscores wartime conditions and is also a reminder of the extent to which northern cities, too, were still segregated in the 1940s.

Negroes rented rooms quite a bit. It was a wonderful thing, 'cause it made it possible for you to come and stay without a problem.

My sister and I was rooming with this lady and we was paying six dollars a week, which was good money, because she was renting the house for only twenty-six dollars a month. She had another girl living on the back porch and she was charging her three dollars. So you get the idea.

We were accustomed to shacking up with each other. We had to live like that because that was the only way to survive. Negroes, as a rule, are accustomed to a lot of people around. They have lived like that from slavery time on. We figured out how to get along with each other.

In the kitchen everybody had a little place where he kept his food. You had a spot in the icebox; one shelf was yours. You bought one type of milk and the other ones bought another type of milk, so it didn't get tangled up. But you didn't buy too much to have on hand. You didn't overstock like I do today. Of course, we had rationing, but that didn't bother me. It just taught me a few things that I still do today. It taught me there's a lot of things you can get along without. I liked cornbread a lot—and we had to use Cream of Wheat, grits, to make cornbread. I found out I liked that just as well. So, strange as it may seem, I didn't suffer from the war thing.

I started working in April and before Thanksgiving, my sister and I decided we'd buy a house instead of renting this room. The people was getting a little hanky-panky with you; they was going up on the rent. So she bought the house in her name and I loaned her some money. The house only cost four thousand dollars with four hundred dollars down. It was two houses on the lot, and we stayed in the little small one-bedroom house in the back. I stayed in the living room part before my husband came home and she stayed in the bedroom. I bought the furniture to go in the house, which was the stove and refrigerator, and we had our old bedroom sets shipped from Texas. I worked the day shift and my sister worked the night shift. I worked ten hours a day for five days a week. Or did I work on a Saturday? I don't remember, but I know it was ten hours a day. I'd get up in the morning, take a bath, come to the kitchen, fix my lunch—I always liked a fresh fixed lunch—get my breakfast, and then stand outside for the ride to come by. I always managed to get someone that liked to go to work slightly early. I carried my crocheting and knitting with me.

You had a spot where you always stayed around, close to where you worked, because when the whistle blew, you wanted to be ready to get up and go to where you worked. The leadman always come by and give you a job to do or you already had one that was a hangover from the day before. So you had a general idea what you was going to do each day.

Then we'd work and come home. I was married when I started working in the war plant, so I wasn't looking for a boyfriend and that made me come home in the evening. Sometimes you'd stop on the way home and shop for groceries. Then you'd come home and clean house and get ready for bed so you can go back the next morning. Write letters or what have you. I really wasn't physically tired.

Recreation was Saturday and Sunday. But my sister worked the swing shift and that made her get up late on Saturday morning, so we didn't do nothing but piddle around the house. We'd work in the garden, and we'd just go for little rides on the streetcar. We'd go to the parks, and then we'd go to the picture show downtown and look at the newsreel: "Where it happens, you see it happen." We enjoyed going to do that on a Sunday, since we was both off together.

We had our little cliques going; our little parties. Before they decided to break into the white nightclubs, we had our own out here on Central Avenue. There were a ton of good little nightclubs that kept you entertained fairly well. I don't know when these things began to turn, because I remember when I first came to Los Angeles, we used to go down to a theater called the Orpheum and that's where all the Negro entertainers as well as whites went. We had those clip joints over on the east side. And the funniest thing about it, it would always be in our nightclubs that a white woman would come in with a Negro man, eventually. The white man would very seldom come out in the open with a black woman. Even today. But the white woman has always come out in the open, even though I'm sure she gets tromped on and told about it.

Joseph Hill had been stationed in northern California and returned home in January 1944. Tina became pregnant the following September.

Some weeks I brought home twenty-six dollars, some weeks sixteen dollars. Then it gradually went up to thirty dollars, then it went up a little bit more and a little bit more. And I learned somewhere along the line that in order to make a good move you gotta make some money. You don't make the same amount everyday. You have some days good, sometimes bad. Whatever you make you're supposed to save some. I was also getting that fifty dollars a month from my husband and that was just saved right away. I was planning on buying a home and a car. And I was going to go back to school. My husband came back, but I never was laid off, so I just never found it necessary to look for another job or to go to school for another job.

I was still living over on Compton Avenue with my sister in this small little back house when my husband got home. Then, when Beverly was born, my sister moved in the front house and we stayed in the back house. When he came back, he looked for a job in the cleaning and pressing place, which was just plentiful. All the people had left these cleaning and pressing jobs and every other job; they was going to the defense plant to work because they was paying good. But in the meantime he was getting the same thing the people out there was getting, $1.25 an hour. That's why he didn't bother to go out to North American. But what we both weren't thinking about was that they did have better benefits because they did have an insurance plan and a union to back you up. Later he did come to work there, in 1951 or 1952.

I worked up until the end of March and then I took off. Beverly was born the twenty-first of June. I'd planned to come back somewhere in the last of August. I went to verify the fact that I did come back, so that did go on my record that I didn't just quit. But they laid off a lot of people, most of them, because the war was over.

It didn't bother me much—not thinking about it jobwise. I was just glad that the war was over. I didn't feel bad because my husband had a job and he also was eligible to go to school with his GI bill. So I really didn't have too many plans—which I wish I had had. I would have tore out page one and fixed it differently; put my version of page one in there.

I went and got me a job doing day work. That means you go to a person's house and clean up for one day out of the week and then you go to the next one and clean up. I did that a couple of times and I discovered I didn't like that so hot. Then I got me a job downtown working in a little factory where you do weaving—burned clothes and stuff like that. I learned to do that real good. It didn't pay too much but it paid enough to get me going, seventy-five cents or about like that.

When North American called me back, was I a happy soul! I dropped that job and went back. That was a dollar an hour. So, from sixty cents an hour, when I first hired in there, up to one dollar. That wasn't traveling fast, but it was better than anything else because you had hours to work by and you had benefits and you come home at night with your family. So it was a good deal.

It made me live better. I really did. We always say that Lincoln took the bale off of the Negroes. I think there is a statue up there in Washington, D.C., where he's lifting something off the Negro. Well, my sister always said—that's why you can't interview her because she's so radical—"Hitler was the one that got us out of the white folks' kitchen."

Tina acknowledged what the job at North American Aircraft meant to black women like herself, but she was also adamant about the discrimination that black workers faced. Because she worked there for almost forty years, it was sometimes difficult for her to pinpoint the precise time frame. During the war years, ironically, the prevailing cultural attitudes about women's proper role might have benefited black women. If women were only *temporarily* taking these jobs, then placing black women in production jobs would not pose a permanent threat to the racial status quo. As a result, the black women were more often given production jobs, whereas the black men were more frequently placed in janitorial positions.

But they had to fight. They fought hand, tooth, and nail to get in there. And the first five or six Negroes who went in there, they were well educated, but they started them off as janitors. After they once got their foot in the door and was there for three months—you work for three months before they say you're hired—then they had to start fighting all over again to get off of that broom and get something decent. And some of them did.

But they'd always give that Negro man the worst part of everything. See, the jobs have already been tested and tried out before they ever get into the department, and they know what's good about them and what's bad about them. They always managed to give the worst one to the Negro. The only reason why the women fared better was they just couldn't quite give the woman as tough a job that they gave the men. But sometimes they did.

I can't exactly tell you what a tough job would be, but it's just like putting that caster on that little stand there. Let's face it, now you know that's light and you can lift that real easy, but there are other jobs twice as heavy as that. See, the larger the hole is, the thicker the drill, which would take you longer. So you know that's a tougher job. Okay, so they'd have the Negro doing that tough drilling. But when they got to the place where they figured out to get a drill press to drill that with—which would be easier—they gave it to a white person. So they just practiced that and still do, right down to this day. I just don't know if it will ever get straight.

There were some departments, they didn't even allow a black person to walk through there let alone work in there. Some of the white people did not want to work with the Negro. They had arguments right there. Sometimes they would get fired and walk on out the door, but it was one more white person gone. I think even to this very day in certain places they still don't want to work with the Negro. I don't know what their story is, but if they would try then they might not knock it.

But they did everything they could to keep you separated. They just did not like for a Negro and a white person to get together and talk. Now I am a person that you can talk to and you will warm up to me much better than you can a lot of people. A white person seems to know that they could talk to me at ease. And when anyone would start—just plain, common talk, everyday talk—they didn't like it.

I know I had several leadmen—it's a lot of work if you're a lead; a lot of paperwork to do. You know yourself if anybody catches on and learns good, you kinda lean towards that person and you depend on them. If you step out for a few minutes, you say, "If anybody come in here looking for me, find out what they want and if you can, help them." You start doing like that and if you find out he's doing a good job at it, you leave that work for them to do. But they didn't like that at all. Shoot, they'd get rid of that leadman real quick.

And they'd keep you from advancing. They always manage to give the Negroes the worst end of the deal. I happened to fall into that when they get ready to transfer you from one department to the next. That was the only thing that I ever ran into that I had to holler to the union about. And once I filed a complaint downtown with the Equal Opportunity.

The way they was doing this particular thing—they always have a lean spot where they're trying to lay off or go through there and see if they can curl out a bunch of people, get rid of the ones with the most seniority, I suppose. They had a good little system going. All the colored girls had more seniority in production than the whites because the average white woman did not come back after the war.

They thought like I thought: that I have a husband now and I don't have to work and this was just only for the war and blah, blah, blah. But they didn't realize they was going to need the money. The average Negro was glad to come back because it meant more money than they was making before. So we always had more seniority in production than the white woman.

All the colored women in production, they was just one step behind the other. I had three months more than one, the next one had three months more than me, and that's the way it went. So they had a way of putting us all in Blueprint. We all had twenty years by the time you got in Blueprint and stayed a little while. Here come another one. He'd bump you out and then you went out the door, because they couldn't find nothing else for you to do—so they said. They just kept doing it and I could see myself: "Well, hell, I'm going to be the next one to go out the door!"

So I found some reason to file a grievance. I tried to get several other girls: "Let's get together and go downtown and file a grievance" [a discrimination complaint with the Equal Opportunities Employment Commission]. I only got two girls to go with me. That made three of us. I think we came out on top, because we all kept our jobs and then they stopped sending them to Blueprint, bumping each other like that. So, yeah, we've had to fight to stay there.

Joseph Hill had resisted Tina's suggestions that he get a job at North American—partially because of Tina's assessment of how the black men were treated. But in the early 1950s he relented and went to work there until his death in 1972. Between their two earnings, the Hills were able to enjoy the life-style to which Tina had aspired, and they were among the one-third of urban blacks who were becoming home owners after the war. With the perfect timing of a born storyteller, Tina recounted her experience of moving into a predominantly white neighborhood.

When I bought my house in '49 or '48, I went a little further on the other side of Slauson, and I drove up and down the street a couple of times. I saw one colored woman there. I went in and asked her about the neighborhood. She said there was only one there, but there was another one across the street. So I was the third one moved in there. I said, "Well, we's breaking into the neighborhood."

I don't know how long we was there, but one evening, just about dusk, here comes this woman banging on my door. I had never seen her before. She says, "I got a house over here for sale, you can tell your friends that they can buy it if they want to." I thought to myself, "What in the hell is that woman thinking about?" She was mad because she discovered I was there. Further down, oh, about two streets down, somebody burned a cross on a lawn.

Then, one Sunday evening, I don't know what happened, but they saw a snake in the yard next door to us. Some white people were staying there and the yard was so junky, I tell you. Here come the snake. We must have been living there a good little while, because Beverly was old enough to bring the gun. Everybody was looking and they had a stick or something. I don't know how, but that child came strutting out there with the gun to shoot the snake. My husband shot the snake and from that point on, everybody respected us—'cause they knew he had a gun and could use it.

I was talking to a white person about the situation and he said, "Next time you get ready to move in a white neighborhood, I'll tell you what you do. The first thing you do when you pull up there in the truck, you jump out with your guns. You hold them up high in the air." He says, "If you don't have any, borrow some or rent 'em, but be sure that they see you got a gun. Be sure one of them is a shotgun and you go in there with it first. They going to be peeping out the window, don't you worry about it. They going to see you. But if they see those guns going in first, they won't ever bother you."

I did like he said, moved in here with some guns, and nobody come and bothered me. Nobody said one word to me.

When Tina had worked in Tyler, Texas, and saw the wedding gifts that Frances Connally had received, she had made a promise to herself. In a rather wry fashion she described how Alma Dotson, a fellow worker at North American who was also interviewed, rekindled that dream.

Alma was the one who started me off. She has very high ideas; just way up in the ceiling—beyond the sky. She came along and was talking about sterling silver. I'm going to be honest with you, I had forgotten about sterling silver because I didn't think it was for me to have. She said, "We're working out here and we should buy us some sterling silver. We can buy it piece by piece."

Oh, she told me whatever piece did I want? I picked my silverware; it was by Wallace and it's Sir Christopher. So she bought me one teaspoon and she paid seven dollars for that one teaspoon. She says, "We'll give each other a piece of silver for our Christmas present and for our birthdays." So that was fine. So she gave that one teaspoon, and with that one teaspoon I had to build up. I bought first one piece and then the other and, finally, I got around to it until I bought me service for eight. Once she gave me the idea, I just went crazy because I thought that was what you was supposed to do.

Tina didn't talk much about her husband in the interview except to say that he was not a "good suggester" and that she had to make most of the decisions in the family. Although upset by Joseph's sudden death, Tina said that she was also somewhat relieved. She doesn't think he would have approved of the course their daughter, Beverly, chose—at Tina's urging.

I never belonged to a club or anything myself. I always felt like I was too busy. But I was interested in my little girl and I always had a program set up for her. When she was in high school, she had a teacher that had quite a bit of interest in her, and when Beverly told her that she wanted to be a 4H Club leader, she called and found out all of the information. So we went to Encino for her to get into the 4H Club. They treated us kinda shabby, but from experience I know why they treats you shabby, so I just ignored them. Since I was so good and helped with the art, they couldn't say too much about it because she wasn't dragging. So we got into going there. We'd can and we put up the stuff and we could sew and just anything in art we was good at. So we went to the fairs and we won plenty of blue ribbons.

She went to college one semester, and then she just messed all up and wouldn't finish and didn't get no grades. After going through that two or three times, she just had to quit college. That's when she went out and got her a job. She started sewing in a little old shop.

Somebody came by to have her make a costume to go dancing in, and Beverly made the costume and tried it on. She got the bright idea that she could dance. After she danced a while, and she liked that pretty good, somebody said, "Join the circus." So she joined the circus. Then she was really into dancing and performing and she stayed with that awhile.

Some of the things I wanted for her happened and some didn't. I really wanted her to be a nurse or to be a performer in some fashion or the other. She did get on stage, so she didn't disappoint me about that. But I didn't push her with that. By that time I had given up.

I don't know what she wanted to be and she didn't know either. She always said, "Well, I just thought I'd get married and I'd stay home and be a housewife. I didn't know I was going to have to work for a living." Now she is a tax accountant, and she's going to school taking word processing so she can work with the computer, with that part of life.

I hoped she would get married, and I had hopes that she would have a family and the whole works. I don't know where she slipped. I don't think she wanted to come home and head for the kitchen and cook and he sit down in front of the TV. She thought that that's what she would end up with because it seemed all of her girlfriends, that's what their husbands do. I think that's why she lingered around so long and didn't get married.

I sure would like to discuss how we came about getting the baby. Beverly was an only child: no cousins, no nieces or nephews. So when I leave her, she's going to be alone. I told her she needed a child. She finally came to the same conclusion. But she was going to be a woman without a husband—to start out with at any rate. I told her I'd help her with the baby in every way: financially and whatever else I could do.

So she told several fellows about her plan: that she would like to have a baby and blah, blah, blah. When they found out she was real serious, they said, "Well, no, Beverly, I can't let you have a baby and you just walk off with the baby and leave me with nothing. My Mama would want to see it or want to come around." So that cleaned out two or three. She was getting desperate. She hadn't found anybody. So she ran into a Mexican fellow and he said he didn't care. She fooled around with him about three months and she couldn't get pregnant. So then she found another fellow. He happened to have been an Iranian. Finally she got pregnant and there she was—through. So that was a blessing.

She didn't tell him she was pregnant until she must have been four months. He said, "Well, fine, we can get married." And she said, "I don't want to marry you. You already had two wives, so there must be something wrong with you that you and those women are not together." Two other fellows offered to marry her, knowing that she was pregnant by another man. But she said, "Mama, I just don't think that would be the right thing to do." So that's why she ended up by herself.

So when we got ready to have the baby, we said we'd have it out here at UCLA. She went to one of these classes about natural childbirth, but she said she wouldn't go because you're supposed to have a partner. I says, "Well, I'll go with you." When she said, "Oh, no, I don't want no woman there with me," I told her, "Then you're going to be in that delivery room crying by yourself." So we went right on to the class then. The two of us together must have been a perfect show.

I should write an article on it, because I think somebody could profit by it. A lot of girls would like to have babies without being married and they don't know how to go about it. They don't know it's not near as hard as you think, if you have somebody on your side and that somebody could easily be Mama. No part of it has been hard for the simple reason that my friends are all in my corner; everybody is willing to help. I've found it's no problem at all. It's beautiful to me.

Vanessa is such a forward child. I don't think Beverly will have much of a problem. She seems to be a well-adjusted kid and she gets along with people much better than Beverly. She's not afraid. She can figure out things for herself.

When Tina's oral history was recorded, she was approaching retirement. She had worked at North American (now Rockwell International) for almost forty years, starting at 60 cents in 1943, and ending at $9.44 an hour. Despite her own achievements, Tina is not blinded to the continuing fight black women must wage.

Working at North American was good. I did make more money and I did meet quite a few people that I am still friends with. I learned quite a bit. Some of the things, I wouldn't want to go back over. If I had the wisdom to know the difference which one to change and which one not to, I would. I would have fought harder at North American for better things for myself.

I don't have too many regrets. But if I had it to do over again, if I had to tamper with page one, I would sure get a better education. I would never have stopped going to school. I took several little classes every so often—cosmetology, photography, herbs. For a little while, I did study nursing. I would have finished some of them. I would have went deeper into it.

We always talking about women's lib and working. Well, we all know that the Negro woman was the first woman that left home to go to work. She's been working ever since because she had to work beside her husband in slavery—against her will. So she has always worked. She knows how to get out there and work. She has really pioneered the field. Then after we've gotten out here and proved that it can be done, then the white woman decided: "Hey, I don't want to stay home and do nothing." She zeroed in on the best jobs. So we're still on the tail-end, but we still back there fighting.

CHAPTER 3

Marye Stumph

Marye Stumph, 1982.

*Well naturally, I was interested in any
kind of a job because I wanted to get my
family back together. I had my kids
farmed out and I was anxious to get a
steady job. . . . It wasn't that I was
particularly thinking about defense. That
was just what came along.*

Marye's description of taking a job in 1941 at Vultee Aircraft Company is typical of her approach to life. Never
the fighter, she accepted with equanimity every turn of
events, good or bad. The wartime job helped Marye (pro-
nounced Mary) to obtain better financial footing and enabled her to reestablish her family life. Yet she did not
speak about the job in momentous terms or with much
emotion at all.

A large, gentle woman who hails from what she described as a family of "robust" women, Marye's massive
hands were one of the first things I noticed about her.
Those hands had crafted the small, detailed ceramic
sculptures that fill her modest, wood-frame house. Her
whimsical animal pieces testified to her humor and play-
fulness.

Despite her competence, Marye is self-effacing. It is
not likely that she would have ever contacted me on her

own to be interviewed. I learned about her through her granddaughter, Lynn. Marye's close relationship to Lynn represents the continuation of a tradition of strong female bonding in her family.

Born in the small town of Geneva, Ohio, in 1909, Marye was raised by her mother and grandmother. Her account of her childhood and youth was presented with a great deal of verve, frequently punctuated with chuckles and laughter, in contrast with the much flatter presentation of most of her story.

When her mother's millinery business became a casualty of the consumers' increased dependence on ready-made goods, Marye had to move to Cleveland with her mother and get a job after high school graduation. It was a big disappointment for her to give up her plans to go to art school, and although she was wistful when she spoke about this reversal, she revealed no bitterness.

After working a year or so, Marye drifted into marriage in 1928. Shortly afterward, she and her husband moved to Akron, Ohio, and she bore two children in rapid succession. Her marriage didn't last long, and she seemed somewhat reluctant to talk about it, sliding over those four years rapidly.

When Marye separated from her husband in 1932, she went to live with her mother-in-law in a small Ohio town. Four years later she returned to her hometown, where she worked in a factory until 1940, when she moved to California. The job she eventually got at Vultee Aircraft in early 1941 was both enjoyable and economically rewarding. When she was laid off at war's end, Marye took up office work. She began a career in civil service from which she retired in 1974. Today she lives alone, with her aging blind dog in Long Beach and pursues her lifelong interest in art.

Marye's story is filled with details that are significant in understanding women's history. Her ability to survive as a single mother was largely a result of the close ties that she established with women, especially those in her family. There were always people to help Marye:

"Gram" during her youth; her mother-in-law after she separated from her husband; her landlady when she first moved back to Geneva; her cousin; Mrs. Horn, her employer when she first moved to California; and her mother, when Marye got a job in the defense plant. The natural allies and support networks available to women like Marye in the earlier decades of the century were not deliberately and self-consciously created as they might be today. They didn't have to be—they were a part of the social fabric.

Marye's life experience is also a reminder of the sexist society that stifled women and contained their ambitions. Marye really liked the mechanical work she did during the war and would have liked to continue in that job, but she accepted the cultural message that these were men's jobs that were only temporarily being filled by women. Marye did not fight to retain her job when the massive layoffs came in 1945, even though she had seniority. Instead, she returned to traditional lower paying women's work.

I can't help but feel both saddened for Marye and also annoyed by her acquiescence. It is hard to shake the nagging feeling that women colluded in the perpetuation of traditional values at war's end. But I have to remind myself how difficult it would have been to challenge the full weight of the culture in that period. What advocates there were for women, particularly for working-class women, were but voices in the wilderness. Women might garner support from each other on an individual basis, but it would be another two decades before there would be a *movement* to support their aspirations.

Despite the complacency Marye exhibited so often during her life, there are real glimpses of an independent spirit, too, like her adding an "e" to the end of the ordinary name of Mary. Looking at her sitting in the rocking chair that occupies center stage of her home today, I wondered if she wasn't really more the master of her own fate than the victim of circumstances who appeared so often in the interview.

I was born in Geneva, Ohio, in September 1909. My mother was born there, too. In fact, my grandmother's and my grandfather's families were pioneers in the Western Reserve area. I have a lineage check way back to the Revolution.

My grandmother and my mother and I lived together, and my grandmother practically brought me up because my mother was working much of the time. My mother and father were divorced when I was about three or four years old, so my father never played a big part in my life. My uncle lived with us until he married, and he was really the father figure in my life. I was very fond of him.

The house that we lived in belonged to my grandmother. She had a small pension from the federal government as my grandfather was a Civil War veteran. But my mother was the main breadwinner. She was a milliner. Her business was pretty good back before all the department stores started selling hats. She was a milliner back when they would take a hunk of buckram and some velvet and make a hat from scratch and trim it with plumes and flowers. They made real creations back in those days.

She had dropped out of school when she was about sixteen and went to work as an apprentice in the millinery business. Then she married in 1906. It was one of those marriages where they just weren't suited. My father was kind of an easy-going, happy-go-lucky type, and my mother, she was a real Aquarius. She was a go-getter and a real vital person. She was something else. My father, when he worked, was a fireman on the railroad. There were long times when he wasn't even home.

I was an only child and from what my mother said, she had a very hard birth. That's kind of unusual, because we're a family of big people and usually the robust type doesn't have too much trouble. I was a big baby—I weighed over ten pounds when I was born—and she was in really hard labor for about forty-eight hours. I guess she decided then that one was enough for her!

My grandmother was the light of my life and I guess I was her favorite grandchild. She was a person everybody loved. Everybody in the neighborhood called her "Gram." I never thought about her being old. I can remember in the summertime she'd give me some money and I'd go down to the store and buy a *Love Story* magazine and a big stick of wintergreen candy. We'd crack the candy up and then we'd take turns reading *Love Story*.

My grandmother was crippled with rheumatism, and most of the time that I can remember, she was in a wheelchair. From her wheelchair, she always did the cooking and the dishes. A good share of the time my mother was able to hire somebody to come in and do most of the housework. I never did like housework and so I never did any more than I had to.

I liked sedentary pursuits. I liked to draw and in my spare time I'd be apt to be drawing pictures. I never planned on being anything but an artist from the time I was quite small. I built my whole life around that.

Another one of my pleasures was when my mother would take me with her when she went to Cleveland to buy for her store. I'd sit and wait while she picked out things she needed in the wholesale houses. We had friends who lived in Cleveland, and we'd stay with them for a day or so. A little something special.

Then in 1918 my mother got the flu. She said she caught it on Armistice Day. That was a real big thing, when World War I was over. People were downtown really having a big time. She was very sick for months and months. Then she got a blood clot in her leg. Of course, they didn't have all the blood-thinning medicines back in those days. The way they treated it was to put hot towels on her leg. Her leg was swollen at least twice its normal size and they didn't expect her to live. She did get better, but she couldn't walk. They told her she'd never be able to walk again. Nobody should ever have told my mother that she'd never be able to do something!

She had other people working for her, and she had a cot put in the back room of her store. She ran her store from that bed in the back. She slept there at night. Later, she was able to be up in a wheelchair, and Uncle Harry would wheel her down to the store everyday and take her home. Eventually, she walked. It was her own determination. She was a very strong woman, physically as well as mentally.

Marye was in high school during the mid-twenties, an era usually characterized as wild. But the youth subculture that was to emerge gradually over the next two decades hadn't yet reached middle America.

We had a lot of fun as a group. We lived about four miles from Lake Erie, and my mother's sister would chaperone us when we'd go down and have weinie roasts on the sand. Back in those days, we didn't have so much going steady. We enjoyed things more as a group. When I look back at it now, we were pretty innocent compared to the kids nowadays. I wasn't one of these girls who was real, real popular with the boys anyway. But I didn't pine about it. Most of my social life was in our church. We weren't real religious people, but in a small town there's not all that much to do. We had a very nice minister, and he was always good with the young people and was willing for us to have parties in the church.

They taught languages in our school, and I had two years of Latin. French was the other language. I never, never took a book home; never did have the piles of homework they do nowadays. Still I graduated in the upper third of my class—which was only thirty-three people. I was eleventh.

I always intended to go to Cleveland Art School. It was all settled as far as I was concerned, and I guess my mother planned for me to go there, too. That was one reason that I took the subjects that I did in school. We didn't have an art department; they didn't even have art courses at all. I think my life might have been very different if I had been able to have a start in it.

I graduated in 1927. Just a little bit before that, my mother started having a hard time in her business. In all the department stores, you could buy ready-made hats. Her business just kind of petered out to where, in 1926, she sold it and went up to Cleveland. She got a job working in a big department store in the millinery department. Mostly it was waiting on trade and making little alterations. It was really quite a comedown for her.

When I found my mother wasn't going to be able to send me to art school, I just gave up the idea. That's been one of my faults all my life. I give up too easy. If it had been my mother, she'd have persevered and found some way to go. Later, I understood that there was at least one girl in my class that borrowed money and went to college. If I had known about that—I have to say, I was awful stupid.

So the day after graduation I went up to Cleveland. Mama and I lived for a while with these friends. We didn't take our evening meal there. We walked up to this boarding house that was several blocks away. Fact is, that was where I met my husband. After a few months, we took an apartment and brought my grandmother up there with us. So it was the three of us again. And so we went on.

I went to work for Ohio Bell Telephone. That was back when you said, "Number please." In a big city like that the telephone company wasn't just all in one place. Each telephone number was prefixed by a name and each exchange was a separate building. My exchange was "Pennsylvania." It was kind of small, prob'ly about thirty on one shift, and was within walking distance of where I lived.

It was very interesting work. You had your board with all your jacks and cords for your local numbers. If somebody'd call in and wanted a Pennsylvania number, why, I could just plug it in, but if they wanted a Randolph something, why then we had to go through the board to the Randolph exchange. We had rows of roll trunk jacks for all the other exchanges, and we'd plug in and say, "Pennsylvania so-and-so." And then they'd plug it up on their board. They trained us for two weeks. I remember we had to learn certain things. We weren't supposed to carry on a conversation with anybody and we had certain stock answers for everything. And they'd give us a little voice training—how we were supposed to say, "Number please." I enjoyed the work. In fact, they were sort of training me with an eye to being a supervisor.

In the earlier part of the century, single women worked not as an expression of their independence but as a filial duty. Marye, like many daughters, turned over most of her money to her mother, keeping only three dollars a week for herself. As was also customary, she quit her job when she married.

They started out all the telephone operators on split shift. I went to work from about 9:00 A.M. to 12:30; then I'd have to go back again about 5:30. As I was within walking distance, it turned out okay, but it took up most of my day and evening, so I didn't have too much time for dating. Paul would pick me up and walk me home. That's what we did; we walked a lot.

He was from a small Ohio town and had just gone to the city. There were plenty of different places to walk. He'd take me to the movies. And the museum was out our side of town and we used to frequently go out there on Sunday afternoon. We didn't do anything very exciting.

I hadn't really planned to marry. I always said that I was jinxed by being born under the sign of the Virgin. Sex wasn't a real big thing in my life. Anyway, Paul and I went together, and I must say, he was more interested in getting married than I was, but I figured, "Well, I can't go to art school, might as well get married." Nah, it wasn't just like that. But I figured life wasn't going to be what I planned.

We married in 1928. We didn't go out and get ourselves a separate apartment. He moved in with us. We all stayed in that apartment for a while and then we all rented a house on Whitehorne Avenue— I haven't thought of that for years! Paul and I lived there not too many months. He was working for the Mack Truck Company and they wanted to transfer him. That was just a couple of months till the time I was due—got pregnant right away. We moved to Akron and Mama went back to Geneva.

We decided we better get us a doctor. 'Course, that was fifty years ago and things were a lot different. I didn't plan to go to the hospital. People had their babies at home. So I woke up one morning and I started having my pains. We called the doctor right away and he was in surgery. He sent another doctor. I had a very easy delivery. I started having pains about six o'clock in the morning and Bill was born before noon with no trauma. That was March 30, 1929.

My daughter, Carol, was born in October 1930. Paul was still working and we didn't think about it as being too bad right then. He was a mechanic. There just practically wasn't anything with his hands that he couldn't do. He was interested in radio—that was the big thing back then—and he kept a couple boxes of parts and he could sit down and in one evening build a radio set. In fact, when I wanted to listen to the radio, I didn't have one most of the time because he'd be taking it apart and making it over.

I wasn't very smart with money, 'cause Mama had always done that. Paul kind of managed. Well, we had only so much money coming in and we had certain things we had to do with it. He paid the rent and I bought groceries, so I guess it was more or less a cooperative thing. If either one of us was dominant, it was probably him. But he didn't do things without consulting me.

I look back and I wasn't smart enough to be married. I didn't really know from nothing. I had never had an example of marriage. I never had a father at home. I wasn't unhappy or anything like that. It's hard to put it into words. The reason we broke up was my husband found somebody else. He finally told me. I didn't suspect anything. He was going out some evenings, but whatever he said, it satisfied me. Naturally it tore me all up. He didn't want to give her up and she wasn't about to let him go.

I had grown up in a family where women could take care of themselves and it never occurred to me that I couldn't do that, too, even dumb as I was. So at the end of 1932 the kids and I went to Mount Vernon to stay with his mother. She was a wonderful person. If my mother had been around in that part of the country, why, I naturally would have gone back to live with her, but she was married again and living in California. With a couple of small kids, I had to be some place where they could be taken care of.

We were right in the middle of the depression then. The only thing that I'd ever done, of course, was being a telephone operator, and telephone operators didn't leave their jobs until they died back in those days! Paul gave me a little money at first, but right soon after that he lost his job, so he didn't have anything either. One of his sisters would send a few dollars every week. Then I sort of eased into doing housework and I got twenty-five cents an hour. I worked mostly around housecleaning time. Back there you had to clean your wallpaper and wash down all the woodwork through the whole house. I had several different families that I worked for off and on, and I had this one woman I ironed for, and we'd take in washing. We got along—just barely. I did that just about the whole time I was in Mount Vernon, three or four years.

Just before Christmas in 1936, my cousin back in Geneva wanted me to come up and visit. I was getting awful tired of housework—the one thing I never did like! My cousin had a friend that was kind of a big shot in this mop factory. He got a job for me, so I decided I'd go back to Geneva.

When Marye went back to her hometown, the depression was still a bitter reality. The heavy basic industries which primarily employed men were not back in full gear; but the smaller, lighter industries where women were concentrated had not suffered as severe an economic setback. It is ironic that the strict sex-segregated workplace that kept women's and men's work distinct worked to women's advantage during the depression.

The kids and I moved back. I think I made seventeen cents an hour, but it was steady. It was a big change in my life, but I figured

I just didn't want to do housework. It looked like the depression was going on forever and just to get a chance to do something besides housework——. It was working on a sewing machine. They had these heavy-duty sewing machines, and this whole great big string of stuff come through the sewing machine and I sewed it onto a backing. It wasn't something you'd want to do all your life, but it was a step up from housework.

I worked there for, oh, maybe six months. Then my Uncle Roy, he was the treasurer at the Fork and Hoe, the biggest factory in town. They made the steel shafts for golf clubs and the steel fishing rods. He got me a job in the bait department tying fishing flies. That was a much better job. It was on piecework, but once I could work as fast as the other girls, why, I could average about fifty cents an hour, which was doing pretty good. I had quite a time working up to tying two hundred! At first, I'd wake up in the morning and my hands would so be stiff, and I'd have to soak them in hot water until I could bend my fingers.

Carol was in the first grade and Bill was in the second. The place where we lived, it was upstairs over a bakery, and we had a big bedroom and kitchen privileges. When the kids came home from school, Mrs. Morris would kind of watch out for them. It just seems like all my life I've fallen in with nice people that have helped me and did things for me.

After a year or so we moved to an apartment practically across the street from where my cousin and her family lived. It was the entire second floor of a house. We had five large rooms but no central heat and no hot water. We put a large coal stove in the living room, and I found a nice little four-burner flat-top coal stove which heated the kitchen. We mostly used it to heat water for baths. We had a gas hot plate for cooking. The owner rented the apartment to me for eleven dollars a month, and as the paper and paint were in pretty bad shape, he paid for the materials and my cousin and I painted and papered the whole place—even papered the ceilings.

We were only a few blocks from the school, and the teachers my children had in the second and third grades were the same ones who had taught my mother, my uncle, and myself. There were other children in the neighborhood besides my cousin's children and mine and they all played together. So with Irene watching out for them, there were no great problems.

My life seemed to kind of go in cycles of four years at that time. Yeah, I went back to Geneva in December of '36, and December of 1940, why, I finally got to California. I'd been saving my money until

I got my fare saved up. I sent the kids out during the summer and they came out on the train by themselves. Then I went out on the bus in December.

My mother and stepfather were living out in the country over near Hemet. Some friends had let them have what was really just like a shack and he was the dogcatcher. They had the dog pound right on the place. I landed out there and I knew right away that I didn't want to stay there.

Mrs. Horn, a lady I had worked for back in Mount Vernon, was down here in Long Beach. She said they'd come up and get me and bring me down for a visit. As soon as I saw Long Beach, I knew that was where I wanted to stay. The kids stayed back there in Hemet for a while and I stayed down in Long Beach with the Horns.

I started looking for a job right away, but there wasn't anything. So I found this Grau Business School, where I could have classes in the morning and then we worked in the afternoon addressing envelopes. That paid our tuition. Oh, too, I had gone to the Unemployment Office, hoping they could find a job for me, and they applied for unemployment for me back in the state of Ohio, so I got eight dollars a week. I was going to school, and I kept going down to the employment office. They found me a little work over at the YMCA cafeteria carrying trays. That was twenty-five cents an hour and that wasn't steady. And, of course, they'd take that off of my unemployment check.

Come early spring, the Horns were going back to Ohio and I still didn't have a regular job. I got kind of desperate about what I'd do with the kids and how I'd get along after they left. Mr. Horn said he'd take Bill back with him and keep him there for the summer, but I didn't know what I was going to do with Carol. Finally, I got directed over to the Children's Home Society. They had a beautiful place out there in Hollywood. They kept Carol and it didn't cost me anything and they were awfully good to her. It wasn't like an orphan home. I mean, they had such a wonderful woman in charge, and a lot of the movie stars were interested in this place and they'd take some of the kids out to their homes and treat them. That took care of Carol at least for a few months and I found a room for two dollars a week— just a little tiny room and kitchen privileges.

Marye was in the right place at the right time and was able to get a decent job in the aircraft industry even before the United States entered the war. Her low-key description of getting the job seemed to mask the real desperation that Marye had felt as she faced continued unemployment and the separation from her children.

The owner of the business school told us that we could go down to Third and Olive where they were training people for the defense plant. It was part of the Long Beach City College system. Well, naturally, I was interested in most any job because I wanted to get my family back together. It wasn't that I was particularly thinking about defense. That was just what came along. So I went down there right away. They were teaching us to work with simple wiring and pliers, things for electrical subassembly—which I never used when I did get out there.

I don't think I was there even six weeks when the foreman of the subassembly section at Vultee came down there and picked out some people to interview. It was July when I went to work. I started at 62.5 cents an hour. I thought I'd hit the mother lode!

That was the first time I'd ever worn slacks. I felt kind of funny because I didn't really have the figure for slacks. I was pretty buxom. Of course, we got quite used to it, and later I wore them all the time, even on my day off. We didn't have to wear safety shoes; most everybody wore leather oxfords. If you worked with any of the machinery, you were supposed to wear a hair net, and if you were working around welding, you wore goggles.

I had worked in factories and it wasn't too strange to me. I kind of stood around, and they decided where they wanted people to work. The planes that Vultee put out, they weren't these big bombers; they were like two-seater planes. All the names started with "V" like in Vultee. They had a training plane called the Vanguard and, later on, a dive bomber called the Vengeance.

Anyway, I went into subassembly. They had these "skins": sheets of aluminum about four feet by eight feet. These were riveted on to the sides of the plane. But they had to be cleaned. They had two tanks, one a rinse tank with clear water and one with a real strong acid. We wore big heavy rubber gloves that came way up our arms. We dipped these skins in this acid and we had to take a cloth and swab it around. Then we'd rinse them in the clear tank and stand them up on the floor and dry them with an air hose. Then they were taken over to the spot-weld machines.

After a few days I was kind of in charge of the tanks, and when they'd have a few girls in other departments who'd run out of work and be at loose ends, they'd send them over there to work with me. That job seemed to be a place where they put new people, and then they'd gradually go off to other jobs as they showed an aptitude for certain things.

After a while, the supervisor wanted me to go on the spot-welding machine. It was a big, tall machine and you just sat there and ran the pieces together and the hot iron would just come down and hit it. It just welded in a little spot, like a needle. It wasn't anything that anybody couldn't do, but the men got all up in arms. They didn't want any women on there and they all protested. So I didn't get on the spot-welding machine.

I liked anything mechanical like that and I would have liked spot welding, but it didn't break my heart because I didn't. Later, I heard that there was a vacancy over in the machine shop. That sounded interesting to me, so I just asked if I could have a chance over there. Everybody that went into the machine shop started out with burring, scraping the rough edges off of parts.

Then they started me out on a Harding lathe, which was a little, small lathe. I guess maybe the whole thing was about five foot. They didn't do too many operations on those; it was more like cutting rods to a certain length, which was very simple. I worked for a few months on that and on the drill press, and then I got a chance to go on one of the big lathes, the number three—the number fives were the big ones. I really liked that.

By that time, the war had started and a lot of the men started leaving and there were a lot of women. In fact, practically all those men on spot welding had to go into the service and they put women on the machines. Right in my own department, they never did put women on the really big, number five lathes. The men seemed to be professional machinists; they had a lot of experience and were able to do their own set-ups. Class A machinists were still men. The women got to be Class B machinists, which was as much as we expected to be. We weren't making a career of it like men. We were doing what was there to do.

Marye's description of the discrimination the women faced helps to emphasize the extent to which the status quo was enforced: women might work on the lathes, but not on the number fives; they might be machinists, but could never aspire to Class A. Despite the limits placed on women, the defense jobs paid well. Before long, Marye was earning seventy-five cents an hour, triple what she had been able to eke out from the odd jobs she had been doing before going to Vultee.

As soon as I got enough for a month's rent, I rented a little house in Long Beach. It was probably just about the first of September I got everything together, because my son came back out in time to start school. With the children's ages, I needed somebody around when I was at work. My mother had been living up in the country, and she came down to visit me and decided to stay. So the four of us lived together. I paid twenty dollars a month and it was four rooms. One room was pretty small, but we made it Bill's bedroom and Mama had a bedroom and Carol and I slept on the davenport in the living room. It was very comfortable and it had a little kitchen. It worked out real well for us. I felt safe about working and leaving the kids with her and she managed things at home. I wasn't able to save anything, not right then. It was just sort of live from payday to payday.

We kind of felt the need of making a little more money than we'd get just from wages, so we got a larger place and boarded a couple of young children. We went through the city of Long Beach and got a foster home license. This woman was working in a defense plant and she needed somebody to take care of her children. One child was just a baby, less than a year old; another little boy was about three. They stayed and slept there and she'd come to visit them. Mama managed real well and it made us a little extra money.

In fact, I suppose that's how we made enough money to put a little down payment on a house in El Monte. I think it was only two hundred dollars we had to have down on it. I sold it after eight months and came away with eight hundred dollars, and that made my down payment later for the house here in Long Beach. By that time it was about the end of 1943.

Everybody was involved with their own lives. We didn't do anything very exciting. We used to go to the movies quite a bit. That was our main thing, and I used to read a lot. I didn't date very much. Men just didn't figure too prominently in my life. In fact, I really felt like I was too busy just making a living and existing, and it didn't seem necessary to me. In the course of my life, I have not very often come across a man that interested me all that much. And if I ever did, it was somebody who was already married.

But I didn't actually think too much about the future. Oh, occasionally I did worry about what I'd do when the war ended. I could have enjoyed an assembler job. I could have just gone on and made a career out of that. But I didn't think that there was anything like that available for women. It was just an emergency that they hired women in, and I didn't figure that there was enough chance finding anything to bother trying to keep in that line.

It just ended overnight. My daughter had been visiting her aunt for the summer down in New Mexico, and I had taken a week's vacation and gone down to bring her back. The war ended while I was down there. By the time I got back, I had a telegram saying that the job was over. A ten-word telegram.

Naturally, then I started worrying about another job. I was looking around madly for something to do, because I didn't have that much money to last very long. I think my first job was civil service. They were hiring girls for temporary jobs at the center on Terminal Island where they separated the sailors from the navy. It must have been September or October when I finally found this.

Marye worked at a series of temporary jobs and applied for a civil service position. During the two years she waited for her name to be reached on the Civil Service Register, she fell back on her experience with the telephone company and worked as a switchboard operator. In 1947, she began as a records clerk at the Long Beach Naval Hospital. By 1954 she had worked her way up and had become the secretary for the chief of the engineering division. By the time she began her career in federal civil service, her children were both in their late teens. Her son, Bill, had joined the Merchant Marine before the war was over. Both he and his sister, Carol, married young.

My daughter, Carol, and I have always been very close. I was close with Bill, too, but's it's just the difference between boys and girls. I never had any brother and my father was never any figure in my life, so I just felt that I wasn't fitted to cope with the problems of a boy. He was a good boy, but he was kind of adventurous. That was quite a worry to me. It was much easier for me to understand and get along with my daughter.

Bill went into the Merchant Marines before he was seventeen, and after a while, he went into the Army Transport Corps. He was a junior officer and that just seemed to be what he wanted to do, so he spent several years in there. I didn't see him very often. He came back on leave once in a while, but sometimes I wouldn't hear anything of him for several months at a time.

His first marriage happened when he was about seventeen, and they had a baby daughter, Katy. He didn't get home very often and was never able to be much of a husband or father, and later they divorced. During the Korean War, he joined the navy and spent a four-year hitch, and then after that he was kind of ready to settle down. He met a girl and they got married. She was a nice girl, but they just weren't suited for each other and that didn't last very long. Later, he was killed in a work accident. July 3, 1973. That's one date I remember.

Carol and Bill were very close. They were only nineteen months apart and there was a strong family resemblance. They both looked more like their father's family. Carol was a good girl. She started going with this boy who was older than she was when she was still in high school, and she wanted to drop school and get married. I managed to talk her out of that, so they didn't get married until after she got out of school and worked for a little bit. I would have liked her to go on to college, but she just wasn't really interested in that. She was figuring she was going to get married and wasn't interested in preparing for anything special.

So she married, but they weren't really suited. They were both strong personalities and, eventually, they clashed. I'm beginning to think most people aren't really suited. You have to work an awful lot at it.

Carol wasn't fitted for anything particular. She kind of got into office work and from one job to another; she learned something different each job. She's gone on now where she's a very good accountant and bookkeeper. In fact, she and her present husband are working in Topeka, Kansas. She runs the office and does the administrative work and he is in charge of the shop.

My granddaughter, Lynn, we've always been real close from the time she was a little girl. I used to enjoy having her come and spend the weekend with my mother and me. I took her to Sunday school

and church and I used to take her to a movie, do things with her. I had a girlfriend back in the fifties and we used to go to the light operas. Well, she got cancer in 1960 and died, so I started taking Lynn with me. Oh, she really enjoyed that. We'd go out to dinner and go to Chinatown. We had a real close relationship. Now she looks out for me. She does a lot of things that her mother would do if she were here. If I have any problems, I tell her and she straightens them out for me. In fact, I lean on her too much sometimes.

Lynn has sort of been my favorite of all my grandchildren. I wasn't that close with my son's boys. There was still that idea that I don't know much to do about boys. They lived just a couple of houses up here from me and they would stop in and see me, but I didn't put myself out to be a good grandmother to them, so I'm not close with them now. In fact, I haven't seen either one of them for quite a while and I blame myself for that.

Once Marye's kids were grown, she finally began to pursue that elusive dream of an art education. Although she began taking classes as early as 1950, it wasn't until her retirement ten years ago that she really had the time to devote to her art.

I did go to a pottery class up at Poly High, and then after I got a car I was able to branch out a little bit. When I was working, it was a little bit of a drag, although I did always mess around with something at home. When the mosaic craze came on, I got into mosaics. In fact, Mama got interested in that and she did mosaics with me. I just did that at home. I've gone through the whole bit: pottery and mosaics and decoupage and papier-mâché. But pottery, I stayed with that and get more out of that than anything. Back in the sixties I tried working on the wheel, but I never could do anything very big. I'm more interested now in sculpture. I made that rooster over there and there's my little nativity set.

I've enjoyed it more since I retired and go to an art class. I've been trying to paint, but I'm not any good at it. My eyes are getting worse all the time, so I'm not good at mixing colors. But I do quite a bit of drawing. I think that really I should just stick with drawing, 'cause it's the thing that I do the best.

I think sometimes how my life could have been different just if I had gone to a school that had an art course. Of course, I'm just not the competitive type. I'm not interested in getting out there and see what man's job I can take on. If I'd been a more aggressive type I'm sure I'd have gotten further in the world than I have. I adapt too easily to whatever happens to me. If I could live my life over and know what I know now, I would have been more aggressive about trying to get an art education when I was young.

A woman should be able to do what she wants to do. But I can't say that I've ever been the object of too much prejudice. It hasn't ever hampered me that I was a woman except that I'm sure, even when I worked for the government—and the federal government bends over backwards trying to give women equal opportunity—there are a lot of jobs that women could do that they just naturally choose men to do, the higher paying jobs. But in my time, I just figured there was men's jobs and women's jobs, and it didn't bother me too much that I wasn't doing a man's job. I was satisfied with the work I was doing.

Some of the things the women do today kind of turn me off. But like Lynn says, "Some of them have to get out in front there and push." I realize that. If women are just too passive about it, they'll never achieve anything. Somebody has to be militant, but I'm not the militant type myself.

CHAPTER 4

Margarita Salazar McSweyn

Margarita Salazar McSweyn, 1986.

*There wasn't that much money working
as an operator and I could see that I
wasn't going to make it. The money was
in defense. You made more hours, and
the more hours you made, the more
money you made. And it was exciting
and being involved in that era. You
figured you were doing something for your
country—and at the same time making
money.*

Margarita ("Margie") Salazar was twenty-five when she
went to work at the Lockheed subassembly plant in Los
Angeles in 1942. Billboards in Spanish plastered the land-
scape of the east Los Angeles barrio; the Spanish-lan-
guage paper, *La Opinion*, carried stories about women defense workers; and the customers in the beauty shop
where Margie worked were full of stories about the good
money to be made.

Margie took the defense job for a host of reasons, not
the least of which was ambition and, perhaps, jealousy.
She wanted to be involved, the way her brothers were.
Two of them were in the service. For Margie, going to
work at Lockheed was one way she, too, could participate in war effort; and so was joining the Civilian De-

fense Corps, with its uniforms patterned after that of the WAVES. Margie spoke excitedly about the war years, and especially her role in the Civilian Defense Corps. When I arrived for our first meeting, she had already assembled photographs and memorabilia. She proudly showed me one in which, carrying a standard, she is leading a march of Civilian Defense Corps volunteers.

A pert, youthful woman at age sixty-five, Margie's very presence and surroundings reflected her domesticity—a description she had used even before she married. Dressed comfortably in casual clothes she herself had sewn, she was delighted to show off her sewing, crocheting, and baking, as well as the wooden cradle handcrafted by her husband, Alex.

Very much a family woman, Margie's oral history became a family affair. I first learned of her from her godniece, an acquaintance at California State University, who was excited about my project and eager to have her aunt included. Even before my first visit, Margie had already begun to consult with her sister, Rosie, to try to reconstruct their family history. As we progressed through the account of her life, Margie regularly checked details with Rosie and also with her close friend, Molly. Margie's husband, Alex, kept out of our way during the interviews, giving her total run of their cozy home while he puttered inconspicuously in the garage. Everyone was instructed to not interrupt during my visits. Her sons, Alex and Joe, carefully followed the progress of her interviews and eagerly awaited the completion of the transcripts.

Margie suffered from a chronic, severe back problem. It was difficult for her to sit for long stretches, but she became so absorbed in her story that she forgot her discomfort. She enjoyed reminiscing, and much of her interview was punctuated by laughter—except when she spoke about the deaths in her family. Then she would drift into a melancholy reverie.

Born in New Mexico, the fourth daughter of a large family, Margie was an infant when the Salazars moved to

Los Angeles. When she was nine years old, her family was among the first Mexicans to move into the predominantly Jewish neighborhood of Boyle Heights. Margie's life revolved around her large extended family, the neighborhood, and the church school she attended. During her high school years the family moved away from Boyle Heights, but by the time of her graduation, her father had died and they returned to their old neighborhood, which by then was largely Mexican. Closely supervised, her social life revolved around the Mexican social club to which she belonged.

Margie went to beauty college and began to work as a beauty operator until she took her war job. By war's end, she had already made the switch back into the field of cosmetology, but instead of working as a beauty operator, she worked her way into a white-collar job. In 1945 she married Alex McSweyn, also a Mexican-American, despite the name. Margie worked until the birth of her first son, when she assumed she would retire from the work force. When Alex, Jr., was only a few months old, however, she and her husband opened a malt shop, which they ran for about two years, after which Margie returned to full-time homemaking.

When her sons were in grade school Margie again returned to work, at first on a part-time basis and eventually full time. She continued working until 1970, when her sons entered junior college. Since then, she has stayed home, initially attending sewing and other classes and more recently, since Alex's retirement, spending time with him.

Interviewing Margie was enjoyable, partly because I was getting a lesson in Los Angeles history and in the community and family life of a middle-class Mexican family. The changing ethnic neighborhoods of Los Angeles form a backdrop for her story. By the time the Salazar family settled in Boyle Heights, it had become a Jewish community—one step up from the original Jewish settlement in south central Los Angeles, which had by then become predominantly black. Gradually, the Jews moved out of Boyle Heights and into the Fairfax neighborhood, the next place Margie's father moved his family. By the time of his death, when the family moved back there, Boyle Heights had become a Mexican barrio.

Margie had no trouble accepting the closely supervised life of the Salazar daughters—a carryover from traditional Mexican, and especially Spanish, life. While some Mexican young people were sowing their wild oats and often flaunting their defiance by adopting outrageous clothing styles, like zoot suits and tight black skirts, the Salazar girls were going to formal dances and parties chaperoned by the sponsor of their social club. The Mexican youth clubs were an extension of the social networks established by immigrants. Logia Alma Joven (Young Souls Club), the group to which Margie and her sisters belonged, was the youth auxiliary of the Alianza Hispano Americana (Hispanic-American Alliance).

Margie's story illustrates how much the war altered the social world of many young women. Although the protective shell that had surrounded Margarita Salazar was beginning to crack even before the war, the changes brought about during the war hastened the process. Her world expanded beyond the pink-collar ghetto of the beauty shop and outside the Mexican community where she had both worked and played. At work in the aircraft factory she made friends with Anglos and even dated an Anglo man for a while. She dated servicemen and went to the Hollywood Canteen as part of her volunteer work with the Civilian Defense Corps—a far cry from her circumscribed prewar social world.

Despite this expanded world, Margie defined herself primarily as a family woman. Her work life was built around family needs, yet her story also reveals a great deal of ambition. Even before marriage, Margie viewed herself as a housewife type, in contrast to the businesswoman that her friend Molly was. Yet Margie resisted early marriage, unlike her sisters, and she wasn't just biding her time, waiting for Prince Charming. She made job changes when she confronted dead ends or saw an opportunity to improve her situation: the move from the beauty shop to the defense job; the transfer from production work to cleaner work in the tool shed; the shift from the aircraft plant to a clerical job in the beauty business.

Margie's decision to go to work in the 1950s, once her children were in school, was really an extension of domestic values, as it was for most of the mothers who were entering the work force. It was a way to help save money and provide for the parochial schooling of her two sons. During the period she stayed in the work force, she was a supermom-superwoman. She stayed up late at night, preparing the next day's meal, ironing the white shirts her sons wore to school, and baking cookies for school bazaars. All this was done lovingly and without complaint, although today she marvels at how hectic her life must have been. It was not the strain of the double duty that led to her leaving the work force again, but an odd combination of two contradictory needs: domestic values and personal ambition. On the one hand, she felt that her sons needed more supervision as they began junior college and were beginning to see girls. On the other hand, it didn't seem to her that her job was going anywhere.

Margie herself was not troubled by the conflicts between her domestic values and her personal ambition. In fact, she was probably not even aware of them. It is my contemporary feminist perspective that highlights this dilemma. Margie, on the other hand, had figured out a way to express her talents within the cultural constraints she faced. Her finely crafted clothes and household furnishings and decorations—of which she is justly proud—are a testimony to this fact. Margie continued a family and cultural tradition that was passed on to her by her mother when she was a young girl. Yet her story also reveals that she made other choices along the way, choices that constantly expanded her world.

My mother's parents were small-town farming people from Silver City, New Mexico, near Albuquerque. Maybe they came from Mexico; they've never denied it. But my dad's family always said that he was from Spain—and his mother was French. And they let you know! They were uppity. In those days it was something to come from Spain. Even to this day we'll see cousins and they are so different from mother's side of the family. They are more sophisticated and the other ones are more friendly, more family.

We weren't called Mexican, 'cause we weren't real Mexican. We were called *manitas*, little hands. Why that name was used or where it originated, I don't know. [This word is apparently derived from the word *hermanito*, little brother, an expression used by the New Mexi-

Margarita Salazar (McSweyn) with her brother, 1944.

can Hispanic settlers.] But I know that we were looked down on by the Mexicans. We were in between: we weren't really Mexican and we weren't really Spanish.

Anyway, my dad's family moved into that area. He started courting my mother when she was only thirteen. Her brother married my father's sister and that's how they got to know each other. He always said that since he first saw her he loved her and he wanted that little girl. But he was twelve or thirteen years older than my mother, and her parents would keep him away 'cause she was too young. Finally, when she was fifteen, they got married.

My mother had eight children. Nancy, Grace, Rose, and I were born in New Mexico. Then when I was about four months old they came here to Los Angeles. My dad came ahead and he got a job. He talked of working in pictures, but that wasn't for him because of the uncertainty of the job. So he started working for the city. When I grew up, he was surveying streets.

My mother became a nurse of sorts. We lived on Ann Street and there was a clinic about a door from us. She helped out there, part time. I was very, very young and she used to take me with her and leave me in a special room. I used to hate to be alone in a room from then on. But my mother was very, very active there, and she learned a lot of things about health that benefited her later in life. All the neighborhood used to come around and ask her what to do for this, what to do for that.

I was the most delicate in the family because I had double pneumonia when I was about three or four. In those years that was pretty fatal. I had to learn to walk again. But then I went to the Ann Street School and I recall being just like any normal child: going to school, coming home, help with the housework. I guess we played the normal baseball, hopscotch, jump rope.

My dad was very active. He used to take us roller skating a lot when we were little. He always wanted boys, but he still was close to the girls in sports and stuff like that—until he got his boys. In fact, my dad was very playful. I recall when you're eating watermelon, he was the first one to get one of those seeds and try and hit somebody. He was strict as anything, but he was fun.

I guess I was closer to my mother because we inherited so many of her ways. She was good at sewing, crocheting, knitting, housecleaning. She did a lot and she taught us. As far back as I can remember, I've known how to sew. It wasn't a matter of whether we liked to do it or not. We were supposed to do it. And from a young age we were taught that if we were going to have our friends over, you had to clean house. And when they left, we picked up after them.

My sister Rose and I were always very close. We used to go to school together and come home. We *had* to be together. That was a cardinal rule. She took care of me, I took care of her—until she got married. I was twenty-one when I went out alone with a boy.

But we had a beautiful, beautiful family life. I hear children that talk of a bad life and I say, "God, how lucky we were." My dad was a family man and so was my mother. They loved their children and gave us the best within their means that they could.

Margie's father managed a great deal within their means. By the time there were six children, he bought land in Boyle Heights on Marengo Street and built their first home.

We were the last house on the block and there was plenty of place to expand, and my dad kept adding. It was two-story, and the top had a porch all around the front of it. When my sisters were growing up, they'd have parties and dance on that porch. It looked way up to the Ascot Speedway and you could see the races. Downstairs, in the beginning, it was just a workroom, but later on he built two more bedrooms down there. Then we had a front porch and the steps going all the way down—'cause this was up on a hill—and he planted all the way down there.

My cousins lived across the street and three blocks down more cousins. Next door, the Calderons, they had a huge family, about thirteen or fourteen kids. Then all the neighborhood kids. The Jewish kids would come over to the house; we'd go over to their house. I don't think it was so much of a distinction in those years, there. We were accepted because we came with the idea of being accepted, of assuming the same likes and dislikes. We didn't think anything of eating sour cream and eating fish; the same as eating beans or eating tortillas. We blended in, shall I say. We didn't try to keep over here with our own ideas.

I had a very close friend, Ruth Silverstein, that used to come over. She lived on Evergreen and she'd walk over and holler at me from way down the bottom. I'd say, "Rosie, hurry up, Ruth is here."

My sister—we call her the "piddler"—she'd exasperate me. She had to do something to the last minute and I wanted to go.

When we were growing up, our door was always open. You never knew what it was like to lock a door. All the boys, the friends of my brothers, they knew they could come over, and if we had something they were welcome to eat. They'd call my mom "Mom." My dad had a truck and he'd load it up with the family, and we were allowed to invite one friend each. He'd take us to the mountains. The boys were in a tent with him and the girls were with my mother—well supervised. My dad supervised making the fires and picking the wood and we'd all join in the cooking and cleaning and putting up the tents. My dad would get his guitar and sing around the camp fire at night. We'd have a ball. They seemed to enjoy spreading what they had to everybody.

This segregation of the boys and girls on camping trips also carried over into other aspects of young Margie's life, including school. After the family moved to Boyle Heights, Margie, her sister, and her brother Leo all started attending Our Lady Queen of Angels school, where classes as well as playground activities were sex-segregated.

Sister Joseph was my favorite teacher. She was actually a friend of my oldest sister and had become a nun. From the beginning, we liked each other very much. In fact, I recall wanting to be a nun, but the priest told me that I was too young to make those ideas. Maybe it was just the idea that I admired the teachers. They were strict, but they were dedicated to teaching us correctly. Also, I think I saw my family life so sheltered and so together, I figured there I would go into the same role—live in that sheltered neighborhood, a convent. They seemed so happy and so serene. But I didn't follow it through. It would have been the happiest thing for my mom, that one of her children would have been a priest or a nun.

But I was active in the church groups, especially Children of Mary. It was very strict and very difficult to get in. You started out with a pink ribbon, then you graduated: pink, green, white, and then blue. When you got the blue one, you were "Miss Goody-Two-

Shoes." You'd better not stray. They would teach other kids cate-
chism; help in the church and the bazaars.

The Catholic school only went until ninth grade, and I guess my
parents couldn't afford to send me to Catholic high school, so I started
at Roosevelt High. I felt very smart. I went from the ninth grade to
the eleventh grade. I thought I had everything in hand, but it was
hard for me, because they were older girls, older boys, more liber-
ated. Especially at Fairfax High.

We moved there to Fairfax when I was fifteen. My dad wanted
to expose us to something else. He probably thought that there was
more out there than just this small little place that we were living in.
So he bought this huge empty lot across of where the Farmers' Market is. We owned all that land there and there was just one house
near the corner.

That's when I started going to Fairfax High. I could do the work,
but I found it very hard to communicate with the older girls. They
went to parties more often; they had more liberty to stay after school,
join GAA, and all those things. I took archery, but there was a lot of
meets after school and I had to be home by a certain time. And being
that I was coming and going by myself—I don't remember if Rose
was working or what, but she didn't go to school there with me—I
guess it was all the more reason that they had to be that strict.

I don't recall having a close friendship with anyone or having any
boyfriends. Probably walking to school, but not going dating. I know
I didn't go to my senior prom. At the time I didn't care that much. I
was so used to it. It was a way of life, like missing the baseball games
or the football games. We could hear them hollering, but it didn't
bother me that I couldn't go. I just took it all in stride.

We were such a large family that there was always some sort of
thing going on. The whole family would go over and visit the Calderons, and they'd be having a birthday party or whatever. In fact, years
went by and I still was the maid of honor to one of the girls. The
same with the cousins. And going to church. We still kept our religion, so I think that that was like a holding thing for the family.

Margie's father died during her senior year in high
school. The family was able to manage financially as a result of the city pension and the two pieces of property he
left them. But it was a difficult time, particularly because
they were so far removed from the extended kin network

in their old neighborhood. As soon as Margie graduated from high school, the family moved back to Boyle Heights. Her mother buried herself in the church.

When Margie started talking about this period in her life, she became sad. Lost in her own thoughts, she seemed to forget my presence. Then, as she began to reminisce about beauty college, her voice lightened and she became engaged again.

Well, I always wanted to be a beauty operator. I loved makeup; I loved to dress up and fix up. I used to set my sisters' hair. So I had that in the back of my mind for a long time, and my mom pushed the fact that she wanted me to have a profession—seeing that I wasn't thinking of getting married. I saw Nancy and Grace having it rough, and I didn't see any hurry to get into the headaches of that. Rose wasn't in a hurry to marry, either.

So I started going to Sullivan Beauty College. It was expensive, even in those years. The course was 360 hours and it was three or four hundred dollars and you had to buy all your uniforms and all your little extras. You were supposed to go at least four to five hours a day, but I couldn't afford to. I had to work. Rosie heard of a friend of hers that was working in a place, spinning yarn, and they needed workers, so I went to work there. I would go to school only on Saturdays. But then they told me that I would have to put more than those hours. So in the summer, I quit the other job, and I concentrated on beauty school.

Well, you'd think you were becoming a nurse or a doctor. That was how technical everything was. You had to learn all about the bones in the head; how the hair would grow; which were the finest, the tender points. And we had to learn facials; hair styling; how to iron hair. And then they were just starting with the permanent, the spiral, and we also had to learn marcelling, with a hot iron. Oh, it was really, really a very intensive course. Then you took a state exam. You took a model in and you gave her a complete facial and hairdo, the whole thing. Then they gave you a written exam. You were notified by mail if you passed, and you got your license.

My first job was just a local beauty shop. I don't think it was a bunch of money. To make money in those years you almost had to own the shop and work morning, noon, and night. It was only about fifteen cents for a rinse, and some women, you had to talk them into having a rinse for their hair. They wanted to wash their hair at home, come in and have it set, and go home. Well, they had to cut corners, too. But that made it harder on the operators. It wasn't a get-rich scene. You were on a weekly salary, and it was a very rare person in those years that gave a tip. Maybe around Christmas they'd give you a gift, but everybody was so hard up they couldn't afford to do those things.

I worked in a couple of neighborhood shops, and then I found my girlfriend, Molly. We were friends from when I went to Catholic school. I don't remember where we found each other, but it came up what a coincidence—she owned a beauty shop. I guess she got a little help from her sisters and brothers, and she bought this property and built the shop in front.

So I went to work for her. It wasn't far from where I lived. It was just the two of us. Molly's a businesswoman first, where I was a housewife first. I loved cooking; I loved all those things. So she'd be slaving away up there in front and I would have a break, and I'd run to the back and make us some lunch.

Molly and I were like sisters. She would take me to all her family gatherings and she'd come to mine. We started going out, my sister, Molly, and I. My mom started taking us out, but then it got too much with the boys at home and having Grandma come over or my aunt come over, so she started trusting us—as long as we went together. Then, Grace, the oldest, she got a divorce and she came back to live with us. My mom made the rule: three girls together go, three come home. We did that until Gracie got married again and Rosie started going with Eddie.

There was about five social clubs in Los Angeles: Superba, Imperior, Alma Joven. Ideales Señoritas was strictly a girls' club. The club we went to, Alma Joven, met at our sponsor's, Mrs. Martinez. She was like our chaperone. She had a huge two-story house and we met there on Sunday afternoons. Then, as the membership got established, we used to rent a hall. We had thirty or thirty-five people, a mixed group: two or three of the girls worked at the City Hall; some worked at the May Company; a couple of girls worked at Mission, packing dried fruits. One, Carmen, must have been involved in education, because to this day, she is here teaching at East L.A. College.

At the meetings, we'd make plans for the next activities, report what was made in the last dance. We'd send notices around that we're having dances this-and-this date or we're having parties, so as not to conflict with the other ones so we could all share the activities. Everybody would make different dances. We had formals at least three times a month and we'd wear long dresses. Really, really nice affairs and we usually had them in rather nice places.

The clubs had been around a while, but we actually didn't get into them until I was around nineteen. I think we were feeling our wings, shall I say. We were so sheltered and so kept at home, and we were beginning to make our own friends. Mom saw how they were and approved of them.

See, when I turned eighteen, my mom gave me a party, a surprise. That was really the party to end all parties. It was at Evergreen Playground and all the men wore dark suits and the girls wore formals. We gave all the boys a little boutonniere of ciciel bruners and the girls got little boutonnieres of four or five of them to put either on their wrist or in their hair. At that party my mother got to meet a lot of people and see the way they acted and she started trusting us more.

Still, I didn't go out on a date alone until I was twenty-one. This fellow, Rudy, we used to go out, my sister and I and her boyfriend. My mother liked him. He was a very, very nice boy. He said, "I'll ask your mother. I'm not afraid." So he asked her and she said, "Why do you want to go out alone?" I told her, "I'm tired of tagging along with Rosie and Eddie. They're engaged; they want to be by themselves." So then she let me go out with Rudy.

That was our whole ritual: going to work, being in the clubs. It was really a question of thinking: "Tomorrow, it will take care of itself."

This carefree period was interrupted by personal tragedy and by the war. When Margie spoke of her brother Joe's death, she was choked with emotion and tried to hold back the tears by rummaging through her papers, looking for the newspaper accounts. She frequently called her sister to get help in reconstructing events. Although no direct link was ever made to the gangs that were beginning to surface in the Mexican community, Joe's death did occur in the context of increased rebelliousness among many Mexican-American youth. Occasionally violent, most of these youths' defiant behavior was harmless and largely symbolic, like the Pachucos with their draped pants and zoot suits. These styles originated among black youth in Harlem, but the so-called zoot-suit riots in Los Angeles—when Anglo sailors attacked Mexican youths and stripped them of their zoot suits—has led to an almost mythic association between the zoot suit and Mexican-American youth.

The only thing that we recall as a family is that Joe came home and told my mom that he was going to go to confession. He said, "I'll be home early, 'cause I have to get up early to go to mass, but I'm taking the candy." He had bought a box of candy to take to this girl. He left and he went to her house by Hollenbeck Police Station. She verified the fact that he had been there, and the police had a report that he had been at the police station asking for protection and that they had looked out the door and there was nothing. They told him to go on home. That was the last we saw until they found him under the First Street bridge, there on the railroad tracks. The report said that he was beaten, then thrown over the bridge.

There was all kinds of reports, but they never, never, really found out what happened. They had the idea that there was jealousy about the girl, but she denied that she had any connection. She was a very nice kid. I think the police didn't want to admit that this gang activity was coming up and they would rather say that it was more personal.

My brother Eddie came home one day and told my mom that he had heard in the lunch hour gossip where he worked that some fellow he knew had been involved. That was just a bunch of baloney—to say that Joe was in one gang and this was another gang. Because we weren't mixed up with that. We were separate and Joe started going to the clubs with us.

We actually started seeing the drape pants around that time, but we didn't approve of it and we didn't dress that way. I've got pictures galore of my brothers and none of them have anything like that. And we never went for that excessive makeup or the tight skirts. They were really, really different; more dropouts, shall we say, with time on their hands. We kept away from them and they never tried to go to our dances or to our parties. We figured it's an exaggerated style of dress that's going to come and go away, never expecting them to take over as much as they did eventually. You saw them all over, but they weren't belligerent; they weren't that way yet.

Margie's mother became even more deeply engrossed in religion after Joe's death. Having lost one son, she reluctantly agreed to let her other sons join the armed services after the war broke out. The oldest daughter, Nancy, had died almost ten years before; Gracie and Rose were married. Margie was still at home and also wanted to join the war effort.

I quit Molly and went to work for defense. I could make more money. I could see that I wasn't going to make that much money working as an operator and the money was in defense. Everybody would talk about the overtime and how much more money it was. And it was exciting. Being involved in that era you figured you were doing something for your country—and at the same time making money.

There was ads all over. I thought I would give it a try and see if I could do it. There was so much talk about it being such hard work, and I had never done hard work. The ads, they'd talk about the riveting and running some sort of a machine—dimpling, I think they called it. It wasn't for the glamour. You weren't going to meet all these guys; you would be working primarily with women.

My girlfriends used to tell me, "Why are you going to try that when you have this nice, clean job here?" I thought it'd be a whole new experience. Find out if it was as lucrative as they said. And then being that my brothers would talk about going in the navy, I guess I felt it was something new, why not try it. I knew I could always come back to what I was doing as long as I kept my operator's license.

They checked you out, your American citizenship and stuff like that. They told you what to wear: pants and a hair net, always. Makeup, they didn't care, as long as you wore your pants and wore sensible shoes and kept your hair out of the way.

That first day, when I went, I was startled. That building is pretty large and each floor had something different. I think there were six or seven floors. It was so huge, I used to get lost going from one department to another, till finally I got to know the other girls and I'd go in and out with them.

You didn't know what your job would be. You walked in and went to the Personnel Office, and they had somebody that would take you to where you were going to work. The leadman who took care of that section, he'd say; "Okay, Mary Jane, you break her in. She's going to do this and that, and since you've been doing it you can more or less supervise." Jeanette broke me in. That's how come we got real friendly. Mainly they put you to do those holes perfectly straight until you could control it. Then they'd start breaking you in on drilling the wings. That steel was so thick that it was very easy to get your drill on an angle.

I don't think I found it so hard or that it made such a big impression on me to say that oh, my arm was breaking off. If I was willing to work overtime, it must have been possible. I did the same thing for about a year: drilling, drilling, always drill work.

In our crew of twenty or thirty, there were about four men. They would put the wing in its proper place so you could work on it—moving things and doing the heavier work. There were some older women we assumed were married. There were other Mexican women, but I don't recall too many colored girls, not in our little section there. But when we'd go to lunch, I'd see a lot of them. We all blended in—men, women, Mexican, Italian.

Jeanette was Italian, about my age. I just happened to hit it off with her. I recall two or three other girls that we were friendly with, the ones closest to you or that you would go to lunch with. But Jeanette and I used to stick around together most of the time—she was quite a card—but we didn't go out together after work.

The men, we always wondered if they were married. I know the one I went out with, Pruitt, that was one of the first things we found out: "Gee, he's such a nice-looking guy, is he married?" We found out he was divorced—or so he said. Jeanette had a party at her house and invited him. He took me to the party and then we started dating. He was a pretty good dancer and we'd go to the afternoon dances. He also liked the show a lot—I remember going to see *Fantasia*. And he was a good swimmer.

So I experienced more mixture with others. There was always a little bit of that, here and there, but I think as I broke away from the clubs, more so. During the war, that's when the clubs just went down the drain.

Margie's social world shifted even more as a result of her volunteer duties in the Civilian Defense Corps. Because of the outpouring of patriotism and the fact that almost all families knew someone in the service, there was tremendous sympathy for the boys away from home. In that period of relative innocence, GIs were respected and trusted and social activities with them were permissible. The resulting social climate often led to increased independence for young women.

While talking about the Civilian Defense Corps, Margie became much more excited than when she described her aircraft job and she proudly displayed her corps badge and photos. In one, she is seen in her corps uniform, standing proud and tall next to her brother who is in his navy uniform.

Even before I went to Lockheed, I remember a couple of our customers were talking about the Citizens Defense [*sic*], that they were going there. Two Jewish girls. They were trying to get Molly and I involved in it. We both went in at the same time, but it wasn't until after I started at Lockheed. I got off work 3:30 and then that duty was from 8:00 to midnight, four hours. I'd get home between 12:30 and 1:00. It wasn't that far and they had like a small station wagon and they'd drop us off.

The idea of the thing was the danger of us being attacked by plane. We would help by being there, communicating. There was a huge hall under the police station with phones and switchboards. We had a certain section of the city, and in case of attack we had certain air raid wardens that we had to call and tell them what to do. There was eight of us on duty every night, and if we were tired, four would go and relax—there were bunk beds where we'd lie down for a while—and four would stay there. Sometimes you were exhausted. It was more like a stand-by. They didn't keep us awake all night.

We also had servicemen clubs, sort of the USO deal. We'd entertain servicemen; give them coffee, doughnuts, make them feel at home, especially men that were far away from home or lonesome. We'd have dances for them downtown and we'd go over to the USO Club in Hollywood, too, the Hollywood Canteen. And we'd visit

Sawtelle Veterans' Hospital, a lot of little activities like that. But it
was stressed, you couldn't date them.

My mother thought it was all right, because her sons were in the
service. She was so wrapped up in missing her boys that she didn't
see anything wrong with the servicemen. In fact, a lot of us had boyfriends in the service and people we'd write to. I'd write to three or
four different fellows. It was so funny, like when we were working
over there at the Citizens Defense Corps, the girls would laugh because I'd get the typewriter and I'd put carbon in and type three or
four letters at once. "Shame on you, Margaret." But I was just exhausted. And what was I going to tell this one? The same thing I was
going to tell the other one. I wasn't going to get personal with any of
them.

Once in a while I'd meet a boy that was in the service; or boys
that had come back; or boys that were getting ready to go. Some
would be Seabees [C.B., Construction Battalian] or sailors, like two
boys in particular I knew from the clubs. Like Rudy. He was a
Seabee. He was stationed up at Point Hueneme and he'd come in
quite a bit. There was a lot of afternoon dances at the Palladium, at
the It Club up on Hollywood, at Earl Carroll's. That would be from,
oh, 2:00 in the afternoon to 6:00. Actually the dancing was what
called Molly and I, 'cause she loved to dance as much as I did. We'd
go to Hollywood on Sunday or Saturday afternoon and we would
teach dancing there. And we'd do a lot of bowling. That was about
it. Maybe go to the mountains when there was snow. But, mainly,
they'd have these short leaves, so we'd concentrate mostly on what
could be done like that. I actually didn't tie myself down in the sense
of the word until I made up my mind with Alex, when he came back.
I wanted to get married someday, but I wasn't in a hurry.

I was still working for Molly when I first met Alex. She had a
party for her birthday, and her girlfriend invited him and his friend.
It's kind of cute. He spotted me across the room and he told his
friend, "You see that girl over there, I'm going to marry her." He
came across the room and asked me to dance. He says, "Oh, you
were so snotty." He claims that I said; "I have the next two; do you
want to wait for the third one?"

He wanted to get married right away, but I wasn't ready for it.
We would see each other and he would pressure me to get married.
Then I wouldn't see him and I'd see other fellows, and he'd see other
girls and he'd go his merry way. I didn't actually promise to marry
him until he went into the service. He told me, "Let's get married,

'cause I'll come back and you'll be married." I told him, "If I do, I'll wait until you come back. I won't send you none of those 'Dear John' letters." I never used to brag to him about all the boys I was dating, but other people would write to him: "I saw Margie in this and that place with so-and-so." He knew that I was going out, but he also was doing it, so why not?

The name McSweyn came from Alex's grandfather, who was Scottish and went to Mexico and married. Alex was born in El Paso and moved to Los Angeles when he was ten years old. When he finished school, Alex started working as an extra in movies. During slack time, at the same time Margie was working at Lockheed, Alex worked for a steel company. When he went into the service, Alex first worked as a clerk and was then sent to the front lines. He was taken prisoner in Germany and held for about one month, until liberation. Margie received the news of his release during the special mass she was having said for him. Margie was still working at Lockheed when Alex was taken prisoner, though by war's end, she had left the plant. Because of the shortage of workers, defense workers were discouraged from quitting and had to be given a release before they could take another job.

I started complaining about my legs, but you didn't change jobs just because you had a whim. You really had to have a reason, especially if you were a good, steady employee that they could depend on to work overtime. I had gone to the doctor and gotten shots for my legs, for veins, so I actually had a good reason. Still, it took a while. I had to go through an interview with a lady there and express myself why and bring in my proofs.

I wanted to work sitting down. They asked me if I would like to do office work. I said, "I don't care, as long as I'm sitting down." They figured that the toolshed would be the best, because I wouldn't have to walk so much. I'd help the man that was in charge. There was just the two of us there. It was hectic when they'd come in with bunches that wanted tools, but it was much easier for me. And

cleaner because just your hands got dirty, nothing else. And you
didn't have to wear a hair net. You'd just dress in pants.

But after I started working there at the toolshed, I kept thinking
of getting out of there. Molly had sold her beauty shop and was working as a salesgirl for this man that owned two wholesale beauty supplies and a string of beauty shops. He hired the first woman to be a
saleslady, which was Molly. She told me that Mr. Allen needed a girl.
He was opening this budget shop, Eastern Columbia. She said,
"Make your break now." I went and applied. I guess I hit him right
and he hired me. When I went back to Lockheed and told them I
have to quit my job, I had to get a doctor's certificate and prove that
I was getting shots and that he felt that I should do a little less walking. And then I had to go to the counselor and get a release. I recall
her making a big issue of the fact, of walking from one office to the
other, and she told me, "Would you like a wheelchair?"

Margie was not unusual in her desire to leave the aircraft
job. Public opinion polls during the 1940s consistently
showed that younger women preferred white-collar work,
even if it paid less.

I started as a desk girl. I know that I took less money, but I always admired beauty work. I was trained for it and it was more my
type of thing. I got to dress up entirely different, working more with
women. Also, I figured, the war was just about over. Make your break
now before all the girls will be looking for jobs. And it was a good
chance. At Lockheed I saw where I was going to stay, whereas over
here I had a chance of good opportunities to advance. But I think in
a way the job at Lockheed did have an impact because I got to know
about tools, which I never did before. I could clean something or go
back there in cracks and drill a hole. Not that I'm mechanically inclined, but I was able to do it.

Anyhow, Molly being in the executive end, selling and all that,
she told me to try and get into that end because there was a lot of
money to be made. She wanted me, really, to go in as a saleslady,
but I never did like to go from shop to shop. But I had plans to advance myself. I hoped someday to work myself into the wholesale
end. I didn't know how, because I just started as a desk girl. But I
knew that I could learn the products from the bottom up. As the stock

would come into the beauty shop—well, I knew what this was and what this permanent was sold for.

Then the owner said he needed a switchboard operator and a receptionist—would I like to try it? I said, "Sure, why not." He said, "Well, you'll get a little more money." Then it was almost equivalent to what I got at Lockheed. In the long run, that training at the desk really helped me a lot for my future because I could relate to the salesmen what the girls actually liked, as far as the products were concerned. The only thing, I really felt I needed some bookkeeping, so I went to night school. That was after we were married.

I was taking one day at a time. I knew I wanted to get married. But I wasn't positive as to the role I would accept afterward, whether I would keep on working or whether he would come back and we'd get settled or what tomorrow would bring. It was such an upheaval that I didn't know.

Margie and Alex married in September 1945. It was a period of emotional extremes, and as she talked about her wedding and her mother's death, she was still torn between sorrow and joy.

We were sitting around—Rose, my mother, and I—and my mother said, "I don't feel good. I've got a headache. I think I'll lay down for a while." And that was it. It was a cerebral hemorrhage and a heart attack.

She made it clear to me—as if she had a premonition: "If something happens to me, don't postpone your wedding." Since Alex was going to be in Santa Barbara for a while, we discussed it. I could have a couple of weeks from work and I could spend it there.

We didn't want a celebration. So it was just a very quiet wedding, at a chapel there at the Biltmore. A captain gave me away and the priest there married us. My husband's friend there in the army was the best man and my sister was my maid of honor, Gracie. We went a week in advance, Gracie and I, 'cause we had all that mess to straighten out. Then I stayed a week after we got married and Alex got a week's leave. We'd sit out there on the grass—Alex found this place across from the barracks—and he'd sit there with a highball and taunt the guys, especially when they'd come out on formation.

I think he got out a month or two months after we were married.

I was living in the house on Fourth Street with Rosie, and we stayed there. I knew I would keep on working, 'cause he had to support his mother. My father had left us, and mother had left us enough, so that we each were entitled to ten thousand dollars, but I wanted it toward a house. Naturally, we wanted to save on our own and to have a family. But we wanted to get to know each other, 'cause girlfriend and boyfriend and husband and wife is an entirely different deal.

We weren't ready to buy a house and we didn't know where we wanted to live, so we stayed there at the house on Fourth Street. It was a large house and it had a huge back porch; just like a room. Alex divided that in half and built me a little kitchen back there and we had the bedroom. It was nice, because this way I cooked when I wanted to. He'd come from work, being that he was working in pictures, and he would go in there and start messing around the kitchen. We shared the front room with Rosie and her family.

Alex stayed on in pictures. He didn't quit until my son must have been about three or four months old, when we went into business. In fact, he wasn't here when my first son was born. He was away on location—*For Whom the Bell Tolls*. He made quite well. As a bit actor, he did a lot, but he never aspired to be a big-time actor. He played all kinds of roles, you name it. He'd be a savage one day, next time he might be a chauffeur. And he worked in those pirate pictures, Terry and the Pirates, and the one with Marta Torin. You see him dancing in the background. He wasn't picky. If they paid him, he'd take it.

Margie was almost thirty-three when she became pregnant with her first son. By that time she had become a bookkeeper and secretary to Mr. Allen, having taken a refresher typing course and some bookkeeping. She had had one miscarriage and the doctor warned her that she had to take it easy and stay at home. When she quit her job, she assumed she would remain at home.

Molly was into real estate by then, and she told me about this fantastic buy, a malt shop. She knew that my husband wanted to make a break from pictures. We were out together one night, and she says, "Why don't you kids do it? You guys have the personality, you could do it. Margie can do the cooking until you get used to it, then you can switch roles." I said, "But gee, Alex is so small." "Rosie is right there"—and Rosie was like his second mother. She always wanted a boy, and she had two girls. So I discussed it with Rosie. She said, "Do it. I'll take care of Alex."

So we decided to try it. We bought it and it was good. There was the Health Department right next door, the Hollenbeck Police Department, two banks, and the library. We attracted the people. It was more like home cooking and the prices were right. But the place wasn't large enough for us to really, really make money. How much could you make in a seven- or eight-stool place? And there was no room for expansion.

Anyway, my husband would leave the house at about 6:00 A.M. and he would get things going, and he'd take care of that early coffee-and-doughnut trade. I wouldn't come down until about 10:00 A.M. I would leave Alex cleaned up and I would take off. I would make the lunch and help with the lunch crowd and clean up afterward—until I broke my husband into doing the cooking. On the weekends we'd work late, 'cause there was a dance near there and we'd get that crowd, and the show would break. During the week, we used to close at ten o'clock. I'd stay as long as I could. I'd run back to feed Alex. He was only about three months old. I would walk from there at least a couple of times a day until he started taking the bottle.

When I realized I was pregnant with Joe—and I was very, very sick from Joe—my sister went to work there, Gracie, and I took over with her kids. So I had four kids, actually, to take care of. I had to take her kids to school, and then I'd go for them and bring them home and see that they would eat. Then their dad would come home. He had odd hours, too. He was just a rookie working on the beat.

I was busy, busy. I had a full grown family. The biggest relaxing time was when I put my kids in the playpen—we had a pretty good-size front yard with grass—and Gracie's kids would be playing out there, and we'd sit out there. Or else when we had birthday parties. That was our big thing, activities within the family. Rosie was living in the house, too, with her husband and two daughters, and Eddie stayed on until he married. And my husband's family was very close, too.

Alex and Margie decided to sell the malt shop after two years. Gracie had a freak accident, and they had bad experiences hiring "outsiders." Alex got a job as a fitter in the shipyards, which unfortunately resulted in his having asbestosis today. Margie stayed home at first, and her life continued to revolve around her children and her extended family. Then, like so many young mothers in the 1950s, she rejoined the labor force to help with family finances.

When we bought this place and moved over here, then I went to work. When you bite off such a large bill, you need a little help. So I decided to go get a part-time job. There used to be a great big market nearby and I'd take the kids to school and stop at the market. There was a small bakery, a doughnut place, and I got to know the man quite well. One day I was buying something and he said, "I lost my girl. If you know somebody that would like to work part time here, will you let me know?" I said, "Well, I'd like the job." So I started working a couple of days.

My kids were already both in Catholic school. I'd take a break and check that they were both home after school, and leave them doing their homework. My husband would be home at 5:00, so they were alone maybe an hour at the most. I've always had two dependable neighbors and they would keep an eye out. Then I got to know that I could trust them. No friends were allowed in the house and they weren't allowed to go anyplace for that hour.

I stayed on at the bakery until I met Desi again. He was a salesman that I broke into the business over there with Mr. Allen. He was a big talker, Italian, a very nice man; a little short guy. One day he stopped in there to buy doughnuts: "Margaret, what in heaven's name are you doing here?" He said, "I have a wholesale beauty supply. Do you want to come and work with me?" I said, "Well, not right now, Desi, because I can't work full time yet. I want to see how my kids are getting along." He said, "Well, I'll come back and see you periodically."

When my kids were in sixth and seventh grade, my husband and I discussed it and he said, "Well, it might be a good idea because with tuition it will be quite a bit of money, so maybe we should worry about our bank account." So next time Desi came around, I told him, "I'm ready to go to work with you." By then I already knew how to drive, and we had saved and I got myself a little car.

I went in just as accounts receivable, and his wife, she would do the books. I guess she had to feel me out. Then she broke me into taking trial balances. Pretty soon, she started taking a week off, taking two weeks off, or they went to Europe, and they left me in charge of the place. And the bank was just right next door, so I did all their banking.

I'd leave the house at 8:00 A.M. Alex was already gone to work. The kids, the night before I would leave all their clothes out, 'cause they wore white shirts and dark pants to school—and that was a clean white shirt every day! I would wake them up and they would get ready and I'd be getting ready. It was a madhouse. They would be eating and I would take off. My neighbor said, "I thought it was so cute, I could time it that it was fifteen or twenty minutes to nine, those kids were going to slam that door and walk past my house to go to school."

I got out of work at 5:00 or maybe 6:00, because it was after the traffic. My husband was already home. But I already had my dinner ready, and Alex would just come in and get the things started to be warmed up. I always got my things together the night before. I used to stay up until all hours. My husband did most of the grocery shopping because I didn't have the time. I had washing to do and I didn't have a drier and I had piles of ironing to do—I never saw so much ironing! The kids were brought up to help me. They would clean house. They would split it however they wanted. For a while I worked half a day on Saturdays until I told them that I couldn't hack it.

We went to church every Sunday, of course. And I was in Parents' Club. We were very active in that, and, oh, we'd have bazaars. And then the Mothers' Society, we used to have fashion shows and luncheons raising funds. Oh, and my kids volunteered me as a den mother: "Mom, you can do it. We know you can." Here there was four or five other mothers that stayed home that could have done it. No, I had to do it because my kids volunteered me. And they belonged to the basketball team and Joe was on the football team. There was always something to do. But we managed. The one day off I had, I'd spend it making nice fresh cookies for them.

I stayed on at Desi's until the boys started East L.A. College. I didn't see that I could go any further, not working with Desi, and we always talked of my staying home someday. It got to the point to where—one little girl that Alex went around with, she was going to the Catholic high school and she was a yell leader. The kids couldn't afford to buy lunch all the time, and many times they would come home for lunch. My neighbors would say, "You know, girls were waiting out in front for them." So my husband and I started talking about it. We can supervise our kids, but not the girls, whereas if somebody is here, fine. So that's what really brought it to a head.

But I didn't mind quitting. I liked it because I started taking up different courses in school: knitting, crocheting, more courses in sewing. So while the kids were at school, I was at school. So it worked out nice.

Margie's sons both went to nearby East Los Angeles College, a community college with a largely Chicano student body. They were there when the Chicano movement was gaining strength in the community, but neither of them became politically involved. Later, while attending California State University, Alex enrolled in Chicano studies courses and also went to Guadalajara University to study Spanish. He married a Central American woman. Joe, on the other hand, does not seem to have much Mexican or Chicano identity. Alex, Jr., completed a B.A. and then went to Stanford for an M.A., but Joe, the younger son, quit school after he married and had a son. Margie really perked up when she talked about her grandchild. It is not hard to imagine how crushed she was when her daughter-in-law moved away after she and Joe were divorced.

Margie's life still revolves around family. She is close to those siblings who are still in the area and talks with her sister on the phone frequently. She is still close to Molly, too, and sees her own children quite regularly.

When Alex retired, I retired, too. From school. We do a lot together. My husband is the type that wants me around. He won't come out and tell me, "No, you can't do it," but he wants me with him, more so now, with the sickness. He makes excuses so that we'll be together. Rose, oh, Eddie, her husband, he goes his way, she goes hers. Whereas Alex, he'll get up in the morning: "Come on, let's go for a ride. Do you have any shopping to do?" and we'll take off. Three to four days of the week. The other days we'll usually stay home. Saturday I generally give a good housecleaning, 'cause I know Sunday the kids will be here.

Every morning we play tennis together. I used to get up and go for this brisk walk all by myself. I used to take my dog on a leash, but she would pull me and it was bad for my back, so I started leaving her at home. I think he kind of worried about me going and he doesn't have the energy to walk that much. So he said, "Why don't we start going to the tennis court? We can hit on the backboard." I asked my doctor and he said, "Yes, as long as you don't do any running; leave the ball go." So Alex started teaching me how to hit the ball. In fact, he can be pretty snotty sometimes. We'll volley back and forth, but if he hits it extra hard—shows off, like I tell him—I just let it go.

The future? Take it easy and hope and pray that my husband will live to realize what they owe him in money, his disability. He'd like to buy a car. He loves to travel. We've been to Europe twice. If we could go away not once a year, maybe twice a year—let him enjoy what he can. God willing, maybe I'll go before him.

When I asked Margie if there was anything she would have changed, she spoke regretfully of never having adopted a girl. Now, given the changing opportunities for women, Margie said she might make other choices if she were a young woman starting out today. Margie supports women's rights, including the right of women to choose an abortion—a belief counter to her strict Catholic upbringing.

I think women have more opportunities than when we were young. There's so many other things that they can do now. It's more in the law. My God, in our day you hardly ever saw a woman lawyer, even executive positions. My God, I thought I was doing wonderful having attained what I did; to be there without the minimal of education. Girls say they haven't progressed, like my daughter-in-law, Cara. She feels that they're still being held back. I said, "But you still have a lot more than we had."

I've told my kids that I think I would go into public speaking of some kind; gotten involved with the public in some way or another.

Maybe in a political sense or maybe just organizing things. Like when I was in the clubs, I was always secretary or arranging affairs.

The women's movement is very good in one way as long as they don't . . . Be a woman. Push for rights, but be a woman first. Some of them think they have to be more man-ish to get where they want, instead of getting where they want to as a woman. Don't make yourself ugly; make yourself pretty. That's what I held against the girls when they went through that transition where they wore the Levi's and the hair and all that stuff. It's not necessary. You can get where you want to get as a woman. Fix your hair and fight like a woman— but get what the women should have.

PART III

Bewitching Though Begrimed
The New, Young Workers

American women are learning how to put planes and tanks together, how to read blueprints, how to weld and rivet and make the great machinery of war production hum under skillful eyes and hands. But they're also learning how to look smart in overalls and how to be glamorous after work. They are learning to fulfill both the useful and the beautiful ideal.

Woman's Home Companion, *October 19, 1943*

nized. Still, there were the telltale signs of a working
ist. In her workshop, pieces of glass were spread (
large table, waiting to be assembled into a stained-
composition. Out back, on the spacious lawn, the
sive sculpture she had completed for her M.F.A. wa
stalled.

Serious in her demeanor, Betty was anxious to
her story "well." Her belief that women's wartime e
riences were significant created an added burden
made her initially nervous. But her earnest recit
soon gave way to excitement as she resurrected her m
ories.

Betty spent most of her youth in the Pacific N
west. Although she was a very shy child and her mo
was extremely protective of her, one catches glimpse
an adventurous young girl. By the time she was thir
she already was dreaming of being a test pilot—dre
that were undoubtedly inspired by women like An
Earhart. When she graduated from high school at age
teen, Betty enrolled in the Jesuit-run Seattle Univer
with the intention of majoring in aeronautical e
neering.

Betty's studies were cut short when her father
transferred to the Los Angeles area shortly after the
break of the war. She planned on continuing her co
of study, but the Jesuits at Loyola University quickly
an end to that idea. So, instead of going to school,
went to work at Doaks, a small plant that manufact
parts for the C-47 airplane produced by Douglas Airc

After the family returned to the Northwest be
the war's end, Betty held a variety of jobs. Surroun
by young servicemen, her social life expanded grea
despite her mother's watchful eye. At war's end, B
returned to school, finally deciding to study science,
plans to be a lab technician. Her future husband, J
was also a student at Seattle University.

After they married, Betty and Josh moved first to
Lake City for a year and then to the San Francisco

Single women in their late teens were natural recruits for the new
jobs. Since they were usually short-term workers who would be employed only until they married, they presented little threat to the status quo. It was assumed that they would be willing to relinquish their
jobs at war's end to the returning servicemen.

Directing these potential new workers into blue-collar defense
jobs was not easy, especially if they were high school graduates. As
the wartime statistics show, high school graduates were more inclined
to take white-collar jobs. But, ultimately, almost one-fifth of all new
entrants into the war industries were young women who had been
students on the eve of the war.

For many of these recent students, like Betty Boggs, it was an
exciting interlude in their lives—one during which a new message was
delivered about women. For poor, uneducated women like Juanita
Loveless, the jobs seldom offered a promise of a brighter future. But
regardless of the specific meaning of the job, for many young women
who were just entering adulthood, the wartime experience was important in shaping who they became.

Betty Jeanne Boggs

Betty Jeanne Boggs, 1982.

*I think it showed me that a young
woman could work in different jobs other
than, say, an office, which you ordinarily
expect a woman to be in. It really opened
up another viewpoint on life in general.*

The girlish excitement in Betty Boggs's voice as she detailed her experiences as a seventeen-year-old aircraft
worker underscored the cool, reasoned assessment of its
importance made by the mid-fifties woman. Betty's story
gives us a glimpse of how conventional notions of womanhood ultimately prevailed and blocked an adventurous
young woman from pursuing the new vistas that had been
opened during the war.

It is hard for me to get a fix on Betty. There is a reserve about her—perhaps an adult extension of the shyness she refers to so often in the interview—yet she is incredibly open in talking about her life. The lack of
confidence she displays belies both the adventu[rous]
dreams of the young girl and also the accomplishment[s of]
the adult woman. At the time she was interviewed, [she]
had recently completed a master of fine arts degre[e and]
was beginning to plan her future as a sculptor.

Betty's large home in the hills overlooking [San]
Fernando Valley was very neat and incredibly w[hite]

Single women in their late teens were natural recruits for the new jobs. Since they were usually short-term workers who would be employed only until they married, they presented little threat to the status quo. It was assumed that they would be willing to relinquish their jobs at war's end to the returning servicemen.

Directing these potential new workers into blue-collar defense jobs was not easy, especially if they were high school graduates. As the wartime statistics show, high school graduates were more inclined to take white-collar jobs. But, ultimately, almost one-fifth of all new entrants into the war industries were young women who had been students on the eve of the war.

For many of these recent students, like Betty Boggs, it was an exciting interlude in their lives—one during which a new message was delivered about women. For poor, uneducated women like Juanita Loveless, the jobs seldom offered a promise of a brighter future. But regardless of the specific meaning of the job, for many young women who were just entering adulthood, the wartime experience was important in shaping who they became.

Betty Jeanne Boggs

Betty Jeanne Boggs, 1982.

*I think it showed me that a young
woman could work in different jobs other
than, say, an office, which you ordinarily
expect a woman to be in. It really opened
up another viewpoint on life in general.*

The girlish excitement in Betty Boggs's voice as she detailed her experiences as a seventeen-year-old aircraft
worker underscored the cool, reasoned assessment of its
importance made by the mid-fifties woman. Betty's story
gives us a glimpse of how conventional notions of womanhood ultimately prevailed and blocked an adventurous
young woman from pursuing the new vistas that had been
opened during the war.

It is hard for me to get a fix on Betty. There is a reserve about her—perhaps an adult extension of the shyness she refers to so often in the interview—yet she is incredibly open in talking about her life. The lack of
confidence she displays belies both the adventurous
dreams of the young girl and also the accomplishments of
the adult woman. At the time she was interviewed, Betty
had recently completed a master of fine arts degree and
was beginning to plan her future as a sculptor.

Betty's large home in the hills overlooking the San
Fernando Valley was very neat and incredibly well orga-

nized. Still, there were the telltale signs of a working artist. In her workshop, pieces of glass were spread on a
large table, waiting to be assembled into a stained-glass
composition. Out back, on the spacious lawn, the massive sculpture she had completed for her M.F.A. was in-
stalled.

Serious in her demeanor, Betty was anxious to tell
her story "well." Her belief that women's wartime experiences were significant created an added burden and
made her initially nervous. But her earnest recitation
soon gave way to excitement as she resurrected her memories.

Betty spent most of her youth in the Pacific Northwest. Although she was a very shy child and her mother
was extremely protective of her, one catches glimpses of
an adventurous young girl. By the time she was thirteen
she already was dreaming of being a test pilot—dreams
that were undoubtedly inspired by women like Amelia
Earhart. When she graduated from high school at age sixteen, Betty enrolled in the Jesuit-run Seattle University,
with the intention of majoring in aeronautical engineering.

Betty's studies were cut short when her father was
transferred to the Los Angeles area shortly after the out-
break of the war. She planned on continuing her course
of study, but the Jesuits at Loyola University quickly put
an end to that idea. So, instead of going to school, she
went to work at Doaks, a small plant that manufactured
parts for the C-47 airplane produced by Douglas Aircraft.

After the family returned to the Northwest before
the war's end, Betty held a variety of jobs. Surrounded
by young servicemen, her social life expanded greatly,
despite her mother's watchful eye. At war's end, Betty
returned to school, finally deciding to study science, with
plans to be a lab technician. Her future husband, Josh,
was also a student at Seattle University.

After they married, Betty and Josh moved first to Salt
Lake City for a year and then to the San Francisco Bay

area. Betty went back to school full time while Josh
worked; when she finally finished her course of study,
she went to work and Josh resumed his studies. Betty
worked at Sylvania Electric until the birth of her second
child; then she left the work force permanently, except
for a very brief stint at her children's school. Torn between the conflicting needs of her own career and the
responsibilities of motherhood, Betty stayed home and
devoted herself to her children. As they grew older, she
returned to school and eventually earned her M.F.A. degree.

Betty's story touched me deeply. Her pain is still evident as she talked about her dashed hopes of becoming
an aeronautical engineer and the dilemma she faced as a
young mother with career aspirations. Betty was born too
soon. Today, a woman with her aspirations might be an
astronaut, although she would probably still face the dilemma about combining a career and motherhood.

Betty was a dreamer, but not a fighter. Denied the
chance to follow through on her dream, she seemed to
lose a sense of her own direction. Her story of getting a
job after she completed her degree in 1953 also reveals a
certain lack of self-direction. Betty rarely sought out opportunities on her own, although she took full advantage
of any that came her way. And she certainly chafed at any
suggestion that she was less able because she was a
woman. But women like Betty have had few outlets to
express their anger. Their "premature feminism" could
not take root without a social movement to support it.

Sitting in Betty's living room and reviewing the transcript of her oral history with her, I happened to glance
out the picture window onto the lawn. There stood her
M.F.A. project: a group of life-sized stone figures, mute
and detached, staring past one another—a representation
of contemporary relationships. It is a massive ensemble,
drawing on the mechanical skills and abilities she first
discovered in a high school shop class.

At that moment, I understood the full significance of

Betty's comment about how war work had showed her that women could follow paths other than those to which they had been traditionally relegated. I realized that her job at Doaks Manufacturing had done more than just bring her out of her shell and expand her social world, as it had Margarita Salazar's. It had kept alive a dream.

I was born in Fort Worth, Washington, in 1926, an only child and spoiled rotten. My father was a career army man, so I was an army brat. My mother graduated from Holy Names Academy and I think she had some college education, like business school. She met my father at a roller-skating rink in Seattle and they got married there. She must have been about twenty-one and he was eleven or twelve years older. I was born within the year after they got married. In other words, I came along rather quickly.

Betty Jeanne Aldridge (Boggs) with her mother, ca. 1942.

He was in the infantry when I was born. Then he switched over to the Army Corps of Engineers, the Topographical Section, and we started into moving. The first time, I guess I was in the first grade. They were surveying a lot of different sections of the state of Washington. Sometimes we would really be out in the boondocks—I mean, way out.

We followed him everywhere, which meant a lot of packing up and taking off down the road. Sometimes the orders would come through rather suddenly and we'd be gone in two or three days, and sometimes they would get rumor of it. Oh, I went to so many schools! At first we were in the state of Washington; then we came down to Oregon. I was in the eighth grade for about a month and that's when we went back east. We were in Virginia, Georgia, and Louisiana, and then we came back out to the West Coast. So I had a well-rounded education.

By the time I graduated from high school, I was about the youngest one in my class. I was sixteen. So I wasn't held back—I just would have to work a little harder at times. I managed. But I think I would make it more difficult for myself because I was extremely shy. Just about the time I'd get over that shyness, then we would move again. When I finally did have a girlfriend, then I moved from the West Coast back to the East Coast. It was very difficult when that friendship broke up. She was about the only one I had known for any length of time and I was closer to her than a lot of my other friends.

Another thing that kept me kind of shy—during the winter, my mother insisted on putting me in these long brown cotton socks and it would just be, oh, humiliating! And when I was very young, because I guess I was rather rambunctious, instead of putting me into boys' pants, she would make bloomers out of flour sacks. I'd go slinking around the corners. Oh heavens, those long, brown socks and those bloomers!

My father had a terrible temper and a lot of times he'd argue with me. But she seemed to be the domineering one. If my father and I would get into an argument, she would go off into hysterics. If we were really arguing "vigorously," she'd always claim, "I'm having a heart attack! Oh my God, my heart, my heart!" And we'd stop. That went on for a while and pretty soon that didn't mean anything to us. We'd go ahead and argue anyway.

I've thought about it and I'll be gosh darned if I can remember what we argued about. It seemed like the arguments would always start at the dinner table. My father would roar up out of his chair, swearing at me. The worst argument I can remember—oh, it had such a demoralizing effect on me. I was about eighteen or nineteen. I can't remember what started it. I just remember as an answer to him I said, "Well, I'm just as good as anyone else!" And his screaming at me: "No, you're not as good as everyone else!" He started to hit me and I remember picking up the milk bottle, saying, "If you hit me, I'm going to hit you with the milk bottle!" He never threatened me again; everything quieted down.

My mother would do psychological warfare where I was concerned. She could always build up this big speech and sway me through words. And she kept me all to herself. If I talked to my father too long, she'd get a little upset over that. I can remember being aware that she was very possessive. You know how girls would have pajama parties, or a group going to a movie. Well, if I did things during the day, okay, but stay overnight, no.

She even treated the family cat this way. She kept the cat in a little harness tied to the back porch and then she'd bring it inside. I'd say, "Why can't I go stay overnight with so-and-so?" "Well, don't you think I think more of you than I do of the cat? I take care of the cat by not letting it run all over the place." Boy, when I was sixteen and graduated from high school and being kept so close to home, I just wasn't aware of a lot of different things. The fact is, I just dated two or three times in high school. It wasn't until I went back to college after the war and joined a hiking club and a couple of other clubs that my shyness started to dissolve a little bit.

We may have had our scraps and so forth, but I can remember going on family picnics. And whenever we moved to a new place, my mother was really great in making us see what was interesting, all the historical things. So we'd have our little tours, family picnics, and maybe we'd go to a movie together. But we also had our family fights together.

Social changes catalyzed by the war soon overshadowed the conventional limitations placed on young girls. As an abrupt departure from the earlier depression years when gender roles had become increasingly rigid, the wartime needs required new skills of women. Young women were introduced to the world of machinery. For some, like Betty, this exposure began with a special high school shop class.

They didn't force us to take it, just whoever was interested. It was the idea that you could get used to machines, used to the noise. Well, we were just going to go to work in an aircraft factory. I mean, what else are you going to do? You're graduating. This is during the war. Why, of course, you're going to go help your country and go into a defense job.

There were maybe twenty-five girls at the very most. It was amazing what was accomplished in the class. The ones that worked on the lathe, they just took to that like a duck to water. I remember one girl, she made several sandwich trays and bowls. They thought that was great. Some of them were so enthused, you couldn't get close to the lathe. This other girl and I decided we would make cedar chests. Nobody was close to the table saw. It was a pretty good-sized cedar chest: about thirty-six inches long and a little over a foot deep and maybe eighteen inches in the other direction. It was quite a big accomplishment. I'd tell people, "Oh, I made a cedar chest in high school." "You did what?" I guess it's just not done. That was the greatest class that anybody had ever invented. Oh, that was my cup of tea.

And I had a burning desire to fly—since I was thirteen. I thought, "Some day I'm going to be a test pilot." Oh, I wanted to fly in the worst way. And I did learn to fly. I had to sneak out to Boeing Field on Saturday 'cause my mother didn't want me to learn to fly. She encouraged me, up until I actually wanted to take lessons and then: "Oh no, my daughter in a plane!" I wanted to join the Women's Air Force Command [Women's Auxiliary Ferrying Squadron, later known as WASPs, Women's Air Support Pilots], but my mother wouldn't sign the papers for it.

So when I first started college, I took aeronautical engineering. "Okay, I'll do aeronautical engineering and I'm going to be a test pilot. Eventually I'll be out at Boeing Field." I was going along pretty well in that. I was going to Seattle University, and that was run by Jesuits and they encouraged me.

When we were transferred down here to California, I said, "Well, what am I going to do about a school?" They told me to contact some priest down at Loyola University. When I talked to him and told him what I was doing, he said: "No, women just don't do that sort of thing. You should be taking something that will give you education for the home." I was just completely crushed. So I didn't take engineering anymore.

My mother decided that instead of sitting twiddling our thumbs, we would go to work. It was something to do. I didn't know anyone and I didn't see any way of ever getting acquainted, because the kids that I would get acquainted with would probably be high school kids and I was already out.

We filled out the form. "Okay, you start next Monday." I was sort of scared. For some reason or another, they took my mother right to work. For myself, they gave me training. There was one little small area inside that big plant that was like a classroom, and you had drills and pieces of aluminum and rivets and they would tell you what they wanted you to work on. They had me for a week in the school, then: "Okay, time's up."

I was put out on the wing flaps in the smaller building. I was nervous to begin with, but then you get used to it: "Tell me how this thing works." So you get over that initial hesitation and it gets to be fun. You had a familiarity with it. Being young, of course, I liked to talk. That was my one problem. They would tell me; "Shut up and go to work and get these things turned out!"

We had to wear our hair in a certain way. They had hats for us. It had a brim on it so that in case you were near machinery, the brim would hit the machine first and protect you. Then if you had long hair, it was in this thing they used to call the snood; they had that net in the back. I used to think I looked dopey in that and I hated to wear it, but then that's the female point of view. And we had to wear either pants or overalls. We used to have a one-piece suit, too, that you could buy from the company. Pants were just becoming fashion for women and I felt like, gee whiz, it made me look like I was different. I was working someplace and nobody else was and people would look at me.

I worked at the beginning, where you start to put the framework together. Then, after about two months, I got to what I thought was the first section—on the other side of this rack where everything stood on end. I felt like I was more in an intermediate position. I guess Art, the leadman, thought my work was good enough that I could be moved on to that. This channel would go down the length of the wing flap, and every so often there would be these heavy aluminum pieces with a hole in it. The wire that would control the flap would go through that. My job was to put those things in there and rivet them, make sure that everything was all right. Once in a while one would crack and I learned how to drill out that particular-sized rivet and put in a bigger one to cover up that crack. So I could do my own repair work.

When I finished, I would take them off of my table and stack them in another rack. Then they would go further down and they would put the aluminum sheeting on it, the skins. The line was even longer past me, but I felt like I had a very important position because I'd be the only one doing that particular operation.

Occasionally, there would be days when I worked very hard and I'd get a bunch of these frames up to a certain position and then I couldn't work on anymore. They'd put me off to do something else temporarily. I had to be on one side of this thing and either rivet or buck. You'd get used to your partner, and you'd have signals to go back and forth because you couldn't holler over it and you couldn't walk around. So there would be some good teamwork. That was kind of fun. I'd be kind of disappointed when I went back to my own job, because I'd think, "That's even more fun."

After a couple of months, Betty's age caught up with her. At seventeen she was not old enough to work a full eight-hour shift and was required to punch out an hour or two before the shift ended. Though she was younger than most of the other workers, Betty enjoyed their company and blossomed. Like Margie Salazar McSweyn, Betty also was given much more latitude in this period of heightened unity and trust.

People were very friendly and I could get over my shyness a lot easier. We'd talk about our families and maybe that we'd gone to a movie or what we did on the weekends. We did an awful lot of joking back and forth. Oh, one girl was engaged and she would talk about what she was going to do when her fiancé came home from service. It was a lot of female talk.

I knew the people I worked with, but my social life was still zero until I became acquainted with a fellow who worked at that same place. He was a welder. I would walk past his area to go over to where my mother was. I was seventeen and he was thirty-four. There was something wrong with the hipbone and he used to walk with a horrible limp. But I had a great time with him. He could get gas for the weekends and he'd take me any place I wanted. So I took the AAA book and I saw all the tourist things of Los Angeles. Every weekend I was out with him. We had a heck of a lot of fun.

I don't know what my mother thought about me going out with such an old man. Of course, she would see him at work, so I guess he couldn't misbehave too much. But I don't think she was aware of half the things I did. Gee, there was some nightclub we went into and they had a striptease. I was embarrassed: "Oh, she's got all her clothes off!"

I didn't pay room and board, nothing. So my only responsibility was just to take care of myself. I would buy everything: my shoes, lingerie. The more I worked, the more clothes I bought. I could go out and blow my whole pay in one day if I wanted to. I remember I bought myself an accordion—it's only a few years ago that I finally got rid of that—and I bought myself a bright red coat. And then I bought a black dress with a low neckline and it had some black lace. Boy, I must have been a smash in it. My mother let me wear it, so I guess it was all right.

I didn't save anything. My parents let me spend it in any way I wanted. When I look back, I think it's kind of sad but that's hindsight again. Maybe at the time I would have rebelled. I just felt: "Oh, goody, I'm having fun today and this is fine."

But I felt like I was glad I did it, that I'd done my part. I worked in a war plant and it was one of the things you did when your country was at war, and it had been an enjoyable experience. Even today, I'm very proud of that job. I can always say, "Hey, I was a riveter during World War II!"

Betty worked in her war job for a little over a year. Then the family moved to Portland and later returned to Seattle. In the spring of 1945 she reentered Seattle University.

The job I got after that, I was working in downtown Portland, like a file clerk. Office work—you had to dress up, you had to behave yourself in a certain way, and it just didn't seem to be as productive. I liked working with my hands, and I didn't mind dressing in pants and blouse or shirts or overalls or jumpsuits. But that office, oh, a total bore!

I would much rather have worked in a factory. There was a ship-yard, I remember, and some small companies, but I wasn't given the chance to think about it. My mother made me quit that job. She was trying to have me where she could watch me. See, when I was work-ing down at that office, I would meet a lot of "boots" who were get-ting ready to get on the ship that was being launched there at the shipyard. They would be in town for maybe two or three months. I didn't see any sense in rebelling. So we went across the river to Van-couver Barracks, which was an army post, and I went to work as a dental assistant.

When I went to work there, I went from sailors over to meeting soldiers. Gee, there was no lack of knowing men, for goodness sakes. I was right at the source of supply—and whoopie! You'd wade in bare-foot and have a great time! It was always movies and there was a roller-skating rink in Portland. If you didn't like roller skating, okay, then there was ice skating and there was hockey we could go to. We'd go sight-seeing a little bit and we could go on picnics. There was a lot of recreation.

We left the Portland area because she thought I was dating too many servicemen. But what I could never figure out, what was her reasoning in having me work there at Vancouver Barracks if she didn't want me to date servicemen? That put me right in the lap of the whole works.

I started to major in math, and you know how people'll ask, "Well, what are you going to do with it? Are you going to teach?" "Oh, is that all you can do, is teach?" "Well, there's not much else you can do with it because you're a woman." Always this—"because you're a woman." So I thought, "Teach? I can't imagine me being up in front of a class trying to teach kids." Still there was this shyness. So I think I finished calculus and also got through physics.

I was working part time at a scientific supply house. They brought in an auditor and his desk was next to mine. Naturally, you get to talking. He told me that at Stanford University they had a test which you could write for. You answer all these questions: "What are you best suited for?" So I wrote for the test. When the results came back, the two top things—it was equal—was either an artist or a labo-ratory technician. I had never given either one of them any thought. In fact, a laboratory technician—I'd never even heard of it. Then it went down to a dentist, a librarian. Oh, I think even an engineer was kind of high. Anyway, it introduced new ideas.

So I thought, okay, look into a laboratory technician. That's when I changed my major from math into biological science. That made a big difference because before, in math, I just couldn't figure out—what am I going to do with it? Also my social life sort of got in the way. I knew a fellow at that time, and he kept telling me he couldn't figure out why I was taking calculus. He was in one of my calculus classes and his presence bothered me. I just didn't quite get a hold of the idea of calculus as well as if I'd been in there by myself. In the engineering classes, I may have been the only girl but I wasn't going on dates with them, and I seemed to get those subjects a lot better. Anyway, in chemistry I felt, "This is my place." It has that nice feeling to it.

Oh, zoology, when I took that, now that was a different experience. That was about the time when there was a lot of vets coming back to school and the classes would be huge. A lot of them had come back to major in medicine, and the courses that I took would be courses also taken by premed students. Zoology courses were about three-fourths men. And, of course, the vets coming back, they were a little rowdier. Being in war had taken off some of their finer points.

Betty became involved in various campus activities and began to meet more people. A heart-to-heart talk with one of the Jesuit sociology professors helped her overcome her shame for thinking about sex, and she began to relax more in the presence of men.

My girlfriend, Shirley, was in a couple of my classes and we would do things together. Pretty soon she started talking about this character she met in one of her classes, and his name was Josh. Being a lab technician, there was a club that you joined, and she and I would go to these meetings. Josh was there because he was going to be premed. He would take us both home from these meetings, and I gradually got acquainted with him. There was nothing going on at first, except that he had such a terrific sense of humor that I just really was quite fascinated by him.

I didn't go out with him until February. It was one of these dances where the girls ask the boys. He will deny it to this day—I'm glad he's not here because he can't argue with me—but I stopped to talk to him in the hall and he said something about going to that dance, and I said, "Well, I just hadn't thought of who I'm going to take." And he said something like "I think it would be nice if you took me." So that was the first date with him, and from then on there wasn't anybody else. We got married September the first, and so here we are a hundred years later.

When he came to pick me up, of course, I was just thrilled to pieces. I was so infatuated and just head over heels. I think my mother must have realized it because from then on Josh was no good. Didn't I see what a bum he was? And my father, he would have a fit because if Josh was going to take me some place and he dressed up, he only had one suit. Well, I think he only got sixty-five dollars a month from the GI bill. He was working part time and he just didn't have money to buy another suit.

I was working part time at the school for seventy-five cents an hour. I would be paying for most of the dates, because Josh would be giving all his money to his father, who immediately drank it. Between the two of us, we'd get a payday and we would immediately splurge— we'd go out to dinner or something—because we knew we wouldn't be able to the day after that check.

Betty and Josh moved to Salt Lake City after their marriage so that Betty could begin her internship. When she realized that she was short five units in chemistry, she went to work instead. They stayed in Salt Lake City a year and saved money to return to the West Coast. It was another three years before Betty returned to school full time.

Josh said, "I want you to finish school, and then I'll go back and won't have to work because you'll work full time. We can live better off of your salary than we can this other way and I can get through faster."

California, having different rules and regulations as far as lab technicians go—you had to graduate and then you intern and then you take the state test. There was just a lot of other classes I had to take. It was almost like starting school all over again, because it was more bacteriology and more chemistry, parasitology and embryology. Finally I graduated from San Jose State in 1953.

I was going to intern at the County Hospital in San Jose. I just about had that lined up when one of my friends in class says, "Betty, I got a job through the Sylvania Electronics Company and it's right near where you live. I'm going to get married and I'm not going to take the job. Why don't you go over and talk to them? That way I don't have to face them and tell them that I'm getting married and leaving them in the lurch."

So they hired me. It was only like two and a half miles from my house, and it was working in a chemistry and plating lab instead of a medical lab, which appealed to me even more. I would test the plating tanks and make sure that all the chemicals were made up. If we had to have a new tank or if one had to be emptied and cleaned out, I would make that up. As far as the plating, I would do a lot of experimenting. We were doing little, oh, klystron tubes and traveling wave tubes. It was a hush-hush thing. They had a jet that we were working on and a lot of test equipment for it. The engineers would bring in something: "I need just a little tiny gold plating on this little mark right here." We had two or three different types of plating: the copper, nickel, cadmium, silver, and gold. I took care of all of that.

I started out at two hundred dollars and something. I remember I got a raise to three hundred dollars, and there was some other engineer that was provoked because he didn't get as big a raise as I did. About a year after that, they transferred my boss to another part of that lab. I was then supervisor. Because I had a degree and was a white-collar worker and working out in the plant, they gave me the title of engineer. There was a couple of girls under me, maybe one or two. The most I had reporting to me at one time were ten girls. They had leadgirls, but as far as being a supervisor, I think I was the only woman. From what I've been told, I was supposed to be the first woman engineer, which naturally was very thrilling to me.

When they talk about women's lib, boy, oh boy, this is where the whole darn thing came in. If I'd known then, I really would have told the son of a gun off and I really would have run him right into the president's office. He was the production manager, and I think he was one of these people that came out of the plant back in West Virginia. He didn't have a college education but was one that came up through the ranks. Not that there's anything wrong with it, but when it affects the male ego, then there's a lot wrong with it. He could not stand to think that there was a woman white-collar worker, and he didn't like it one bit. He thought that I should be at home, and he hassled me every way he possibly could. He hassled me right up until practically the day I quit.

Betty worked up until one month before the birth of her
first child and then took maternity leave. She came back
to her job when her son was three months old.

When we married, Josh's health wasn't that great and we got a
sperm count. He was just so sterile at that time, we just sort of figured, okay, kids are for everybody else. We didn't do anything for or
against. I don't think we even gave it any thought like "Well, are we
going to adopt later on?" It was like "Oh, I guess kids are for everybody else, and maybe one of these days we'll sit down and think
about it seriously."

Then when I did get pregnant: "Wow, I'm pregnant!" It was be-
wildering, in a way. Like "Oh, for heaven sakes!" So I will jokingly
say to this day, "Well, shrugging the shoulders did it."

Then I was really torn up. For one thing, I wanted to stay home
with the baby; two, I wanted to help Josh get through; three, I really
enjoyed that job. I just didn't know what to do about it, because I
enjoyed working and yet I thought I should really be home with that
baby. My mind was sort of made up for me because Josh kept saying,
"I've got to get through school. It's better that you work. I can spend
all my time studying and get through engineering. When I get
through, then we'll take it from there."

We kept trying to find baby-sitters and I think I went through
five of them. That was a chore because you just didn't want any old
body. At that time there weren't any of those places where they have
preschool—which would really have worked out nice. So I'd find
somebody that could take him for a while. I was paying ten dollars a
week at that time for child care. Then the last one, oh gad, she was
taking care of some other little baby about the same age as my son.
She caused more trouble than any of the others put together: "Don't
do this, don't do that. No, no, no."

When I stayed home with Tad when he was a little over two
years old, his attitude was rather antagonistic. I'd go to be affectionate
with him and he'd just kind of close up. I thought, "Okay, doggone
child, you're going to love me and you're going to be affectionate. I'm
just going to keep working away at you."

Josh had a good relationship built up, because he'd have Tad to
himself. Sometimes he'd be home earlier and then he would pick up
Tad, or he'd have a day off and he'd keep Tad with him, or if he was

out working in the yard, he'd have Tad with him. And he took care of him. He never once hesitated to change diapers or to feed the baby. Absolulety no holding back as far as caring for him. The only thing I think that held him back was if he had a lot of homework.

Betty continued to work at Sylvania Electric until just before the birth of her daughter in 1957. Josh was scheduled to graduate the following June and to start to work as an industrial engineer. In the meantime, they lived on savings. Betty's third child, another son, was born in 1959. Two years later, the family moved down to southern California. Most of Betty's activities revolved around the family for the next fifteen years. Her dilemma about quitting work during her second pregnancy is still very fresh in her mind.

I felt terrible—terrible, because I really enjoyed my job; good, because I could be at home. It was really a mixed emotion. You wanted to be in two places at one time and how can you resolve that? So in one way it was resolved for me, because then I didn't go back to work. I was at home with the kids all the time.

We took them everywhere. We never went on a trip that we left them at home. We didn't do any camping at that time, but we'd go to parks, we'd take them to the city—San Francisco—we'd picnic. Of course, Josh and I always did a lot together right from the time we got married. In fact, people are going to think I'm archaic when I mention this, but I would never go anywhere unless he could go. We always had the philosophy, "Well, why should I go enjoy myself when you're not here to enjoy it with me?" I think we've carried that out even today.

I gave it some thought that maybe someday I would go back to work, but I didn't really think about it too much, 'cause my time was taken up pretty much by the kids. I don't regret one moment of ever staying home with them, because to me, it's very important that I was there. I think it has paid off. My daughter has told me, she's glad I didn't work. I think it's important for a woman to do something, 'cause I think she's got a brain, the same as a man. But I can't quite come to grips with women working full time and having children. It's either one way or the other, 'cause I feel that there's a lot of problems nowadays that are caused by women working and you've got everybody else raising your kids. I think a mother should be there the first couple of years of a child's life and, like high school, I definitely think that she should be there. I know they're old enough to take care of themselves, but it seems to make a difference. You just sense it: a parent cares, they're there.

Betty began taking night classes shortly after the family moved to southern California. Later on, in the late 1960s, she took art classes at the local community college. She then decided to return to school in earnest and carefully looked around for a university program that was hospitable to the older returning student.

I told my family one night, "I'm bored, I'm going to go back to school"—which they all cheered. Then I began to take school a little more seriously. There was this woman I had met who lived across the street from us in San Jose. She had three girls, the same ages as my kids. When the oldest one graduated from high school, that just destroyed her: "What is there for me to do?" I thought: "I'm not going to be that way. I'm going to have another interest."

As I was getting near the end of the bachelor's, I kept looking at what everybody else was doing. I thought: "Well, if that person can get a master's, then why can't I? I'll never know until I try." I went back with the idea I would go until I either fell flat on my face or someone said, "You're lousy; quit school, for Pete's sake!"

When you're working on your master's, you get things half done, and you have to go in and get an okay on it. Then you continue and you finish it, and then it has to be okayed again. The first time around, it's interesting to stand there and listen to people criticize your work. You have a counselor and an adviser. Mine happened to be kind of egotistical, except that I thought he was very good, and he taught me an awful lot of discipline, which I appreciate. He would sit in and he would defend my work. Then behind the scenes he and I would get into a hassle.

Being a female into sculpture, you also get it from a male standpoint: women just don't sculpt. There's still a deal on that. Agewise, there's a little bit, too. But I can point to Louise Nevelson. She's older now and she still produces, and, gosh, Georgia O'Keeffe is in her nineties and she still does beautiful work and she's looked up to [Georgia O'Keeffe subsequently died in 1986]. I feel like: okay, if somebody else can do it, then I can, too.

I stick to stone and wood. I haven't gone into clay—making a figure out of clay and then having it cast. I feel like I've got to learn to do these other two things well. The reason why I picked up the stained glass is that it's a good thing to turn to when I've got a problem trying to create something in stone. All of a sudden something becomes clear in another field. I'm still being creative, and it's helped me over a bump.

Betty's new career as an artist harked back both to her high school days and to the results of the aptitude test she took in college. She had scored equally high in the occupations of lab technician and artist. As she talked excitedly about her new "toy" and the rediscovery of her mechanical skills, Betty's voice rose in pitch and her speech speeded up.

Way back when I was in high school, I'd worked in that shop and I enjoyed that. That sort of sat there dormant for a while, but I think I tend to be a little more mechanically minded than the average woman. Anyway, one of the classes I had when I went back to school was called Tools for the Artist: welding, electrical work, table saws, drill presses, and sanders. It was down in the Industrial Arts Department. That was my cup of tea. I could almost switch from an art major right over to industrial arts, for heaven's sakes! I just thought, "A table saw. Oh, I've got to have a table saw." I also bought a joiner at the same time, which smoothes down the wood and evens it up. Now I think, "What other tools would I like to have?" See, in getting this, there's a method to my madness. My husband likes to work this way, and if it happens to be there, it gives him an idea for retirement, too. Also, if we have it now before he retires and the money drops off, then we don't have to ever worry about buying it.

It will be two years in August since I got my master's. Now it's another thing that I have to come to grips with. Discipline plays a big role in this. I've got some sketches and I've got some stone and I've just made up my mind—okay. I want to get the house in such a way that it doesn't take anything to clean it up. I allow myself two hours a day on that. I take two hours a day and I work on my art, whether I just look at something and get an idea or if I sit there and doodle— as long as it's art in some way, shape, or form.

I want to pursue this art thing to its fullest. I want to be able to sculpt. I want to be able to work in stained glass. I want to be a creative person for the rest of my life. If I could sell something once a month or once every other month, I would be successful. There's a gallery in Pasadena that every once in a while will take just three or four pieces and that's all you have to work up. I'd like to think of something, say, like a small business—if I could produce sculpture for an interior decorator. Just as long as I don't sit still.

> Betty's children are all grown now. Her daughter, whom she always encouraged to be independent, was a marketing major in college and is now working for an advertising agency. Betty is very proud of her children and has no regrets about the years she spent at home. She laughed nervously when asked her feelings about the women's movement today.

Oh, oh, you're really going to have me hang myself, aren't you? Well, I think it's great that women fight for their rights, because I could really get out there and I could fight even more enthusiastically than all ten put together. Who is it, Gloria Steinem and Gloria Allred—she's a lawyer and has been the president of National Organization for Women in L.A.—when she fights for things like that, I think that's terrific. I think it's terrible when a woman does the same work and doesn't get the same pay.

I think it's very necessary that women do something. Of course, there are old women who stay at home and aren't good for much else—I mean, as far as going out and going to work. Boy, that sounds terrible! Anyway, there are some women who are just inclined to stay home and that's it, but there are women who really want to do something and I think they should.

But women have a very difficult position, because there they have a head on their shoulder and they have a brain and if they're goal-oriented, they have to hassle so much. What I've said about women having children and being home with them—what do you do in a case like that? I've never really thrashed it out in my head. Just that I'm glad I stayed home with my kids.

Anyway, I do approve of ERA, 'cause I think women really get taken advantage of. Switching over to abortion, I know this is really going to bring down pains around my head, but I approve of abortion. The first three months. They say, "Well, it's a life right from the very beginning." Yes, it's a living thing, but it's not a human being per se, it's just a bunch of cells that are dividing. These people who feel that it's murder—now wait a minute, you're telling me what I can do with my body? And what about that child's life after it gets here?

Reflecting back on her life with the hindsight of a contemporary perspective, Betty thinks she would have been less passive—that she wouldn't have taken no for an answer.

If I had known then, I might have finished engineering. I wouldn't have listened to someone say, "Well, a woman doesn't belong in that." I would have said, "Oh well, the heck with you, I'll go someplace else." I just wouldn't have taken that. And I think that I would have designed planes or something like that.

But the war work, I think, showed me that a woman could work in different jobs other than say an office, which you ordinarily expect a woman to be in. You know, they don't expect you to be out in the plant wearing dungarees or anything like that. I think it just showed me they're capable of doing that type of work; they have a brain just as much as a man, and the man is not the only one who can think. It opened up another field of thought, another viewpoint on life in general. You don't sit around and do nothing. You can produce just as well as anyone else.

CHAPTER 6

Juanita Loveless

Juanita Loveless, 1986.

Actually what attracted me—it was not
the money and it was not the job because
I didn't even know how much money I
was going to make. But the ads—they
had to be bombardments: "Do Your
Part," "Uncle Sam Needs You," "V for
Victory." I got caught up in that
patriotic "win the war," "help the
boys."

Juanita was no ordinary teenager when she was recruited from her job at a gas station in Hollywood to work at Vega Aircraft, a division of Lockheed, in early 1942. A child of the depression, Juanita had been educated in what used to be called the "school of hard knocks." At seventeen, she had already been on her own for four years. Spunky and resourceful, Juanita was a peculiar blend of country girl and urban sophisticate.

Now, more than forty years after Juanita settled on the fringes of Tinsel Town, there are few signs of the barefoot country girl who stayed in an Oklahoma community camp during the depression. The images conjured up by Woodie Guthrie songs might have described Juanita's life in the 1930s, but today, trim figured and dressed in smart, casual clothes, Juanita appears to be a sophisticated observer.

Juanita Loveless, ca. 1943.

On my dad's side, my ancestors came from Bohemia—Czech or German. They came to Alabama, Georgia, and Mississippi and then migrated to Texas by covered wagon in the 1860s. They were farmers and my grandfather was a preacher. My grandmother was of Cherokee Indian blood. I remember her very well. She lived to be eighty-three. On my mother's side, some were artists, opera singers, musicians. My grandfather was a teacher and my grandmother, I do not know, she died when I was four months old. So my mother's people were educated but by circumstances had to become farmers, too.

My dad was born in Texas in 1896. He met my mother when he had come back from the war. She was fifteen or sixteen, still in high school. I guess they had a forced wedding. My oldest sister was on her way when they got married. Vets were heroes, coming back in uniform. It was a repeat in the Second World War, except during the First World War, if a girl fooled around or didn't come home on time, the guy had to marry her. Actually, they met at a church dance.

When my dad came back from the war, he was a wreck—totally shattered by thirty, physically and mentally. He was gassed and had shell shock. He got along fine until the thirties and then any noise or any aggravation could set him off. He moved to Childress the year I was born—for his health.

I saw lots of old soldiers there. Actually, they were young men. Some of my earliest memories are of those vets from World War I without faces, arms, legs, ears, no noses. It was awful. They were then called hoboes. They'd come down in and around Childress because of the air, plus the lakes there, especially on Poppy Day and Armistice Day—now called Vet's Dày. We would see them on the streets. My dad told us to stay away from them: "Run, don't go near them." It was some sort of an obsession with him. I asked him once, oh, twenty years ago, why. He told me that he saw soldiers raping girls in Europe.

As far as those men were concerned, most of them rambled and were disconnected; they shuffled. They simply were like vegetables. Now my uncle Jim came back without a leg and he resumed farming, so I think that what we got down in Childress were the real misfits, the shell shock and gas victims. Like in my dad's case, his shell shock had damaged his nerves. He had attacks of palsy; a loud noise or a gun could set him off. One time he had to go out and shoot all of our dogs. They got into a wild dog pack and killed some of our calves. He came back and he went into a rage. We had to tie him down and go get the sheriff. The next day, he was perfectly harmless.

There were eleven children, one right after another. I was the third and I was born in 1924. The last one was born in 1935. My mother was always pregnant. Always with a headache and always with a baby one in the arm and one in the belly. In all fairness, there was no access to birth control, not in a small farming community like that in the heart of the depression.

We lived in a ramshackle frame wooden farmhouse; no wood floors, homemade furniture. My father was a dirt farmer. He hired out and got the shack in exchange for working the land. This must have been at about the end of '24. Just after that, he got his job on the railroad and in 1929, we moved to a better place. It was a doctor's home and it was beautiful: two story, two bedrooms up, two bedrooms down. I think my dad paid two dollars a month rent in exchange for keeping it up and giving the doctor vegetables from our garden. We had grapes. That's how I got hooked on smoking—smoking the grape leaves.

During the depression he was one of the very last to be laid off, so from railroad shop man, he went to digging trenches and planting trees, scab labor picking cotton, things like that. In '32 he got a bonus from the government. He went to Washington on that march for the veterans, where Hoover had the troops fire on them. He was in that tent city there with the mud and the dirt and the flies and disease. He never forgave Hoover. In fact, I don't think he ever cared about this country anymore after that, except during the second war.

In '32, '33, '34, those real rough depression years, my dad would
hire out to pick cotton, to pull bolls. That's the word—I haven't used
this language in years! They hired us out, too, at fifty cents a day.
Those are some of my early memories. They'd go from farm to farm
and pick up the man and his children; they'd hire for so much a day.
In later years, when things got a bit better, we would get paid by the
sack. In the real tough depression days, that actually kept us from
starving to death. As poor as we were, we weren't the only ones. The
only person with money was the man who owned the ice plant.

I was only seven or eight and do I ever remember it! But that
passed. That will never happen again because of child labor and
school laws.

The children attended a little brick schoolhouse about
three miles from their home. Those were still the days of
corporal punishment in the schools. That didn't set well
with Juanita. After challenging a teacher who boxed her
little brother's ears, she quit school at the age of ten.

The only thing I really wanted to do in school was study music.
I had one teacher that was interested and she begged my dad. Even
put up a few pennies for the music sheets. My dad said, "I can't afford it. I can't give her time for lessons." I don't remember anything
else about the school. In those days they called you up to the front
desk, slapped you or hit you with a ruler or a stick. The more they
hit me, the more quiet I got and the more sullen I became. I just sat.
Or I'd wet my pants. Then I'd be too embarrassed to move. I didn't
learn in school. I learned at a kitchen table from my dad, my aunt,
and my great-grandmother. Later, out here, I went to Hollywood
High. I tried to educate myself in later years.

Our play was when we were slopping the pigs. And when it
rained in the summer, it would pour warm, sultry rain and we'd run
out in it and throw our clothes off. Oh, we got a few beatings for that
until we learned—the girls especially—that we had to keep our un-
derclothes on. In the winter we did play, but we had to work inside,
too. We helped my mom can; we stripped the beef in the smoke-
house; we sewed quilts. The girls had to sew. And we heard stories.
Our grandparents, the old townspeople, and the aunts and uncles
would come to visit and we would listen. Then you just sat and listened. You spoke only when spoken to.

At Christmas time, my aunt would give us jacks, balls, baseball gloves, and china tea sets for the girls. She gave me a play store one time: a box that made into a store and it had shelves with little tiny boxes of cornflakes. Once a year, she would give us something and that's all we had. But we played store and we cut pictures out of the Sears and Roebuck catalog. We'd fight over cutting the pictures, boys and girls alike. The boys made whistles and slingshots. We had the Dionne paper dolls and Princess Elizabeth and Margaret paper dolls. We were all cramped in the kitchen. We had a table with benches, and then we had the family table for the parents.

I was the one girl among six because my sister never played. She was actually the mother of ten kids. At eight, nine, ten years old, we went to her when we were sick; we went to her with our problems. She never outgrew it. When we grew up and moved away and became adults, she could never relate to us. She hasn't been friends with me for twenty-five years, but she was my mother!

I walked in my sleep when I was a child, and I started my period when I was walking in my sleep. I might have been eleven or twelve. I woke up and I was down by the lake—from where we lived it was about six hundred feet, across the gully—and I had blood all over me. I was scared to death. I didn't know what had happened. I was afraid to tell Mama; I was afraid to go to my sister; I didn't know what to do.

My dad came down to milk the cows, and he found me and asked, "What's the matter, child?" He said, "Did your mammy ever tell you what happens to girls when they get to be about your age?" I said, "No, what happens? Will I stop walking in my sleep?" He said, "Well, I think you'd better go up and have a talk with your mammy." He didn't get mad or anything.

Viola told me: "Well, it's time for you to get the rag." That's how I learned. Now, we knew about VD because my dad told us about how girls had to be careful and men had to be careful. One time we found his prophylactics up on top of the clock, and we didn't know what they were. We blew them up. We thought they were balloons. He sat us all down, boys and girls alike, and he told us a lesson.

Juanita's childhood ended abruptly. It was the mid-1930s, and although the full effects of the depression might have been blunted in some northern industrial areas, there wasn't yet much hope for the people in

Texas and Oklahoma. Some WPA projects offered only minimal employment to women, usually sewing. There was no public housing, and Little Hoovervilles, the temporary shanty towns erected by the homeless, still dotted the land.

My mother left my father in '36, after the last girl was born. She moved from the farm to town and taken some of the kids and left some of them out at the farm with my dad. She went to work for the Sewing Room, a project that they had during the depression. I was out on the farm with all the boys. Some boy in town was coming out and was fresh with me. When I told my dad about it, he said, "Well, I guess you'd better go in and live with your mother. You're getting too old to be around all these boys."

My mother wasn't too square then, wasn't too honorable. She had some guy move in with her, a young kid almost half her age, and it just seemed like she went bad. She was having men coming and going to the house all the time. My dad came around a couple of times, and I guess she got scared. Once he came over with a shotgun. He'd heard about her partying, and he came over to get the kids.

Then she took us all one night. I don't know how she did it. I went to sleep in Childress and woke up at 3:00 or 4:00 in the morning at a truck stop with music blaring, in Oklahoma. I'd never seen neon lights. Hell, in Childress we had little lights strung up with bare bulbs, and that was only on a special occasion—for example, when Roosevelt was relected. And I'd never heard jukebox music. I said to myself, "My God! What is this?" That was the spring of '37.

My mother moved into the community camp in Oklahoma City, like a refugee camp. They took old cars and old pieces of cardboard and wood and they built shacks. They got their water from the faucet at the city park, and they camped under bridges like hoboes. Hobo camps is really what it was. She was working for someone who was making bootleg whiskey. She would give me and one of my brothers a certain amount of bottles, and we packed these pints in a satchel and made deliveries.

I was in what they called a honky-tonk, a beer bar, making a delivery when this woman saw me. She started questioning me, "How old are you?" "I'm thirteen." "Well, are you working?" I said, "Well, I work for my mother." Then she said, "I am a police officer. You tell me everything."

She was a big heavyset woman with authority like a big bull. I'm young and I didn't know the difference and I don't know Oklahoma. All I know is the community camp and a few slummy honky-tonks around it. So I take her down to this camp. She says to Mama, "Well, I want to hire your girl off of you. My daughter is having a baby and she's got a couple little kids and she's married to a lawyer. We live on the north side of town and we need the girl to do the housework." Mama said, "Take her." Just like that.

I walked out of there with a ragged pair of my brother's overalls, no shoes, and one of my brother's shirts. The first thing she did was cut my hair and de-lice me. I walk into this beautiful home and I can't believe it. It's a home with rugs and a radio. It was a mansion to me. But it didn't remain a mansion very long because the first thing she did was tell me what I had to do.

I washed and ironed and cooked and sewed. Then they would wake me up in the middle of the night right after she breast-fed to put the baby back to bed. Then the mother-in-law would come over when it was supposed to be my free time, and she'd say, "You can't sit around. Get those cabinets washed." I wondered what the hell is this? I was with those people six months. But, oh, my god, they almost killed me. Day and night. There was never any rest.

Juanita left that job when she met another family who took her in and found her a job as a carhop. They bought her clothes and taught her how to spend money. In 1940, she came to California with another Oklahoma family and worked in the fields picking dates, oranges, and avocados. At the end of the season, they all returned to Oklahoma, and Juanita went to Fort Sill to join the friends with whom she had lived earlier.

I got a job in the post exchange. That was in 1941. I was there about six months before the war started. All hell broke loose on the seventh of December. We were told to evacuate the barracks and find quarters in town. It was general confusion. Everybody was leaving to go to Seattle or California.

I came out here. In those days they had drivers' cars who came back and forth. You'd pay something like ten dollars or fifteen dollars. There were six or seven passengers and we were stacked on top of each other. They dropped us off in a hotel downtown and we were to wait in the lobby. We waited and he never came back. I had four or five dollars, a coat and the clothes on my back, and that was it. He took my luggage, my pictures, everything—the little souvenirs a young girl has. But every place I'd turn, someone was there to help me. Maybe it was my youth.

I came to Hollywood and got a room. That first time I was in California, when we were working in Indio, we came into the city a couple of times, and to Hollywood. Real tourists. I liked the weather and the smell of orange blossoms and gardenias. The palm trees impressed me. So it just seemed the logical place for me.

The name of the hotel—I'm sure it will bring back a lot of memories to anyone who was in California in 1940 or '41, or even before—was the Studio Hotel. It's in Hollywood, nestled almost within two or three blocks of Hollywood and Vine Street. It was a small hotel with three floors, nice little singles with a bath. Prior to the war it had been for studio people, actors and actresses. The manager was a lovely woman. You could only stay in a hotel for X amount of days and you had to move. This was a wartime thing. So she'd put me on the first floor, then she'd put me on the second floor, then I'd go to the third floor, and I'd register each time.

I sent my dad a telegram and told him I was in California, and I was going to get a job but I don't have any money. That was the first time in my life I ever asked him for anything. He sent me a blank check. I think I wrote a check for seven dollars. My landlady accepted it and that was my week's rent. He sent me another check about a week later, a blank check again, and he kept doing that for about three months until I told him I didn't need money anymore. A year later I sent him a couple of hundred dollars. That is one memory I have of him. Although I never asked him for anything before or after that again, I never forgot that.

So that's how I really got started in that first crucial two weeks. Then for food, I went to Thrifty Drugs and got a grilled cheese sandwich and a Coke for a dime, or an egg salad sandwich and a Coke. I lived on one meal a day for a week. That's my first early memory of being totally and completely alone in California.

I didn't know what to do: no experience and I was under age. So I walked to the bowling alley and I got a job as a pinsetter. I was working for tips, setting up pins, but I couldn't take that. It was too noisy. I stayed two days. Then I went to work at a gas station.

The first gas station I worked at was paying me sixteen dollars a week, Mueller Brothers, on Sunset Boulevard. They had a black co-median who greeted everyone. It was a gimmick. I walked over there and said I was interested in working. Fifteen minutes later I was filling tanks with gas. I had no experience, but I learned as I went along. They didn't want to pay me very much money. Then someone came into the gas station and recruited me: "Look, we'd like to have you. How much are you making here?" And I said, "Sixteen dollars," and they said, "We'll give you eighteen dollars. Come work for us."

So I went to work for Kreager Oil Company, which was better. They gave me a uniform everyday and soap to wash the grease off my hands, and they taught me how to do batteries. It was very simple, very easy: check the oil, wipe the windshield, put the gas in, get the money, get the coupon.

I worked for six months and everyday someone came in saying, "Do you want a job?" My head was going crazy. They were recruiting for any kind of work you wanted. Newspapers, just splashed everywhere: "Help Wanted," "Help Wanted," "Jobs," "Jobs," "Jobs." Propaganda on every radio station: "If you're an American citizen, come to gate so-and-so"—at Lockheed or at the shipyards in San Pedro. And they did it on the movie screens when they'd pass the collection cans. You were bombarded.

They were begging for workers. They didn't care whether you were black, white, young, old. They didn't really care if you could work. It got even worse in '43. I worked two jobs for a long time. I had so much work offered to me and I was not even qualified—I just had the capability of learning very fast. Within three weeks of coming to California my mind was dazzled with all the offers I had. Before the war, in Oklahoma City and in California, I'd ask people if I could get a job and they'd say: "Well, you're not old enough." But here I didn't even have to look. I was having people approach me six to ten times a day—RCA Victor wanted me to come work for them; Technicolor said they'd train me.

Actually what attracted me—it was not the money and it was not the job because I didn't even know how much money I was going to make. But the ads—they had to be bombardments: "Do Your Part," "Uncle Sam Needs You," "V for Victory." I got caught up in that patriotic "win the war," "help the boys." The patriotism that was so strong in everyone then.

Anyhow, Vega Aircraft was the first one I learned about. Someone came in two or three times to the station to get me to come to the application office. One day I said, "I'll be off tomorrow and I'll go and fill out papers." I called this girl I had met and we went together. We both went for the same job, but she was immediately hired for a more educated job because she had finished high school. I went on the assembly line.

I already had something to wear. When I was recruited for Kreager Oil Company, they made me a jumpsuit which was absolutely stunning. It was in khaki color, made of gabardine or wool and cotton. When I first went in, I wore that. Then went into boys' blue jeans and a plaid shirt. Jeans were sturdy and their little shirts were made of a heavy, tough material, and the heavier and tougher the material the better for me, because it kept me from getting hurt.

I wore some kind of a cap that had a net and a bill and you put your goggles on. Some women wore bandanas. Most of us eventually ended up with our hair cut short. That's another reason they say the women became very masculine during the war. I disagree. Your hair would slip down and you'd try to get it up, and your hands were filthy with chemicals and little bits of metal. It was like rubbing salt into a wound. We didn't wear earrings or necklaces or rings, obviously, because we were working with tools.

Let me see if I can describe my first impression—which later wasn't the truth. It was like you were walking into a big, huge cavernous barn, just like a huge hangar; dead white from the huge, tremendous lights. On platforms—saw-jacks I would call them—they had poles and shelves and pieces and parts of planes. The first thing I noticed was that all the men were instructors. Most of the workers were men. I saw very few women. Even the bench I worked on, there were six or eight young boys, eighteen or nineteen years old, and myself, and two or three middle-aged women.

It was very dull, very boring. The first day I thought, "Oh, this is ridiculous. I have to set here for three weeks on this bench?" What we did was we learned to buck and then we learned to rivet. I set there for three or four hours that first day and I picked up the rivet gun: "You show me once and I'll do it for you." The bucking, you have a bar. I said, "What's to learn here? Look at my hands. I've been working as a grease monkey. I could do this. I don't have to set here and train." I learned very fast.

I went into the shell the next day. First I went inside and I bucked, and then I went outside and I riveted. I was working with real seasoned workable men and it was so easy. We did strip by strip, the whole hull. We used strips of like cheesecloth and paste that had to go on the inside and across the seam. I had to do that. Then, as the riveter outside riveted, I was inside bucking. It would be like a sewing machine, you just sort of have to go along with them.

I stayed there maybe six weeks, and I worked on all parts of it, up in the wings. One by one, day by day, new faces. I would say within six months there were maybe twenty or thirty men left in Department 16 where maybe there had been fifteen hundred. One by one they disappeared. I'd have a group leader one day and two or three days later he was gone. Leadman, two or three days later he was gone. There were men in the tool crib and one by one they disappeared.

As they recruited more and more women, men with deferments were the ones that actually remained to work. Even a lot of the young women working would disappear, going into the service. I made friends with four or five girls that became WACS and WAVES and nurses. It was very more difficult to keep friends, because they came and they went so fast.

By late '42 we had very few men left. They were gradually replaced by women and blacks. When the blacks started coming in, suddenly I was jerked off my nice little wing section and I was sent over to the training area, which was at the far end of the huge plant. The first day I picked a young man who was nineteen years old, Stan—I can't remember his full name, but today he is a musician and you see him on television in the Les Brown Orchestra—and four or five other blacks, men and women. I worked with training them the first day, the second day, the third day. They just couldn't get it. Stan, he'd fall asleep, he wouldn't work. I gave up. I went to my group leader and said, "I have to either transfer or I'm quitting."

So I got out of that assembly and went into final assembly, thank God, or I would never have stayed. I thought, "I really have got it made now." Only it was just as bad or worse, in a sense, because the heat and my getting up into those wings. I used to carry a crawl light with me, and I'd lay up there and I'd wait and wait for my partner on the outside. I had no way of knowing what's going on outside. I can't tell you how many times I'd lay there, and a drill or something would come through and nick me in the leg. Carelessness on the outside part and they'd missed the mark. Two or three of my very vivid experiences was climbing out of the wings of those planes, sweating, hot and dirty, finding whoever was supposed to be working with me sound asleep. I'd give them a good kick in the ass.

Then I transferred again. I went into the wiring and cockpit section and I loved it. But sometime during this work with chemicals and metals I got a skin disease. It started out on my arm.

The war activity transformed communities from a relaxed, small-town atmosphere to frenetic, bustling centers. Where jobs and money had been so scarce just a few years before, they were now plentiful. Because of the wartime shortages, war workers were often earning more money than they could spend. It was a time to recoup from the hardships of the depression, and many civilians held several different jobs. Businessmen left their white-collar jobs at five to put in a half shift at the local war plant; high school students spent half days in school and half days assembling planes; even servicemen on leave often put in half shifts at the defense plants.

The daily pace of life was hectic, but there was also time for play, especially among the young single war workers. The excitement of the period, the activity, the social interactions were the up side. But there were also bitter reminders of the war as casualties mounted.

At the same time I worked in the aircraft, I also worked for a record-cutting company; we'd cut records and make tape recordings for the servicemen to send back home. I also worked for a fellow in Glendale who had a storage garage. As the young men were going to war, they would store their cars with him. He hired me to come over and take each car out every other day or so and put a few miles on it to keep up the engine, and I'd check the water, check the tires, check the oil, and sometimes lubricate them. He wasn't paying me very much, but I got gas coupons and I'd take a car occasionally to work.

I had so much work sometimes, I wouldn't even go back for my money. Sometimes they'd just mail me a check and I'd think, "Gee, now where was this?" At one period of time I had six or eight checks laying in my dresser drawer that I hadn't even cashed. I simply didn't know how to handle money. The first paycheck I got in aircraft was more money than I'd ever seen in my life. I didn't even know what to do with it. I didn't have a bank account. You couldn't buy anything much.

But we'd hang out in drive-ins or the bowling alleys. And we went to places like the Hangover, Tropics, Knickerbocker Hotel, Blackouts, Garden of Allah, Har 'O Mar, the Haig on Wilshire. I was going into bars and drinking. One of my favorites was the Jade on Hollywood Boulevard. Another was the Merry-Go-Round on Vine Street. When Nat King Cole sat at the piano and sang, he wasn't even known and the piano bar went round. This was long before I ever reached twenty-one.

We found places like the beach, the pier, on our day off. I think that was on Sunday, 'cause some of us were on a six-day schedule. But we hung out, we read poetry, we discussed books that were current and popular. One book was passed from one to another. It was word of honor, really; you'd pass your book on to the next person and it would eventually get back to you. And movies, mainly movies. We'd sit in the lobbies.

Young people got together in harmless, easy companion ways. Dancing was great. You got rid of your energy by dancing. You'd get a little radio and put it out on the back porch or the lawn where you were living and had everybody come over. That was it. There were no cars racing around. We had a lot of blackouts so you couldn't have outdoor picnics or beach parties.

Oh, I'll tell you where we met, workers and their relatives, brothers, sisters, boyfriends, soldiers, sailors, families. At the Biltmore Hotel. They had a tea dance in the afternoon and when my brother would come in with his friends, we'd go there. We'd bring girlfriends to dance with our brother's boyfriends or our boyfriends would bring in friends and we'd get the girls together. It really didn't make any difference, but years later I found out a lot of these friends were homosexuals. At that time I didn't even know what it meant. They were "in the closet," so to speak. I don't think many of the gays realized they were gay.

During the war there was a lot of homosexuality. Straight people became very friendly with homosexual people, more so the women. I'm not a homosexual, but I had a great many friends who were, like the bus driver, Margaret. She was very tall. And there was one girl from aircraft. She and Margaret were always riding the bus, even when she wasn't working, and I'd say, "Don't you ever get off this bus?" I sensed there was something different about them when I would show a picture of a boyfriend or I would talk about some fellow

I knew who was going into service. You'd exchange pictures in wallets, and you'd see a picture of a WAC or a WAVE.

We met one time at the beach, and there they were together. I said to them, "Hey, you guys act like you're married or something." They handed me a book, all wrapped up in a nice package with a ribbon on it, and they said, "You know you have a lot of friends. We want you to read this book and then if you have any questions, you talk to us and if you don't ever want to talk to us anymore, it's all right too." The name of the book was *The Well of Loneliness*. It introduced me to the fact that there were people who were different from me. It didn't make a damn bit of difference to me. I still liked them; they were still friends.

We accepted people then. People were more respectful of each other, too. They respected each other's privacy, and when you had conversations you weren't noisy [sic]. You talked about the weather, a book, a movie, what are we going to do next week, how many were shot down, who lost a friend or a brother. It was innocent. I think the end of innocence came after the Second World War. By the time the Korean War ended, we were hardened and tough.

I think people just clung together. They were closer. Even in aircraft, the friends you made, even though you didn't really know them very well, you were concerned. When you said good-bye to them, you said, "Well, I'll see you again soon, I hope," and you really meant it. Today you meet someone and you say, "Ill see you later," and you don't even remember their names five minutes later.

Most of the fellows that I knew, by 1943 were gone in three days or a week. I mean they were just gone! The next thing you'd get a letter with just a PO number. "Can't tell you where I am, but will see you when I come back." The song that was very popular then was "I'll Be Seeing You." I think it was symbolic of that time. "I'll Be Seeing You," not when, where, how, or if.

Then I began to see boys coming back. One fellow I'd gone with in 1942, I got off the bus and I'm walking home and I heard: "tap, tap, tap." I turned around and looked and I thought: "Gee, a soldier in uniform with a cane." I turned back again and I said, "My God, it's Dick." Still in uniform. He came home blind. That was my very first shock, seeing him come back blind. He could see just a little, but later became totally blind—at twenty-three years! There were two or three other fellows I had known at the bowling alley who I went with, my age. When I began to see them coming back like this, it really did something to me.

You know, this is the first time I ever talked about this. I've never actually admitted to boyfriends that I worked in aircraft. A lot of the fellows coming home thought we were pretty frivolous—gum popping, silly, flowers in our hair, working and looking for men and roaming the streets looking for soldiers. It's not true. By the time you got out of work, you were so damned tired you didn't want to do anything. In my case, the first thing I wanted was a bath.

By mid-1944, the country had been at war for over three and a half years. The fervent patriotism that had been the driving force in the beginning of the war was beginning to wear thin. People were getting tired, and the strain of long hours of work at noisy jobs was beginning to show. High turnover and absenteeism rates reflected declining morale.

I quit because I'd look around me on the outside and I saw people not working in aircraft living an easy life. Women I had known, some that had worked and quit right away, went in and worked three or four weeks and said, "This is not for me. Forget it. To hell with it." This is touchy. I don't how to bring this up. The morale was not that strong at the end. On our day off, we saw our friends in the neighborhood that were not working in aircraft: "I know this fellow that owns this store and I can get you anything you want"; "I can get it for you wholesale." You heard stories of people buying up the Japanese stores and of hoards of supplies in warehouses. Soap was rationed, butter, Kleenex, toilet paper, toothpaste, cigarettes, clothing, shoes. And you saw these people making a lot of money and not doing anything for the war effort, even bragging: "I kept my son out of it." You thought here are these special, privileged types of people and here I am working and sweating and eating our hearts out for the casualty lists that are coming in.

By 1944 a lot of people were questioning the war. "Why the hell are we in it?" We were attacked by the Japanese and were fighting to defend our honor. But still, this other side had the Cadillacs and the "I can get it for you wholesale." They suddenly owned all the mom-and-pop stores and suddenly owned all the shoe factories. The rumblings began with that—and the discontent.

It raced through the plant, through the bowling alleys, through all the places where the young people got together. We began to break away from the older generation. We said, "Well, they brought the war on." I think when we actually began to see the boys come home in late 1943, 1944—those that had been injured had started coming back—then the rumbles grew into roars, and the young people thought maybe they were being led into this. Maybe if we would stop working so hard, they would end the war. There was also rumors that they were holding Patton back and that they were prolonging the war. That was what got us!!

I got an aversion to making anything that would hurt anybody. But I probably wouldn't have stayed in aircraft, anyway, because my skin disease got worse. It started out like a psoriasis patch and it scaled and I scratched, and I got it on my arms, my neck, my face, everyplace where I was exposed. But I had a change of heart again when I heard that my brother had been injured. I went to work for Hartman making small parts, bench work, which I hated. I stayed there about three months and I said, "This is no good. I can't do this. I've been too active and I've been a racehorse too long." I used to run up and down that plant and it must have been a mile long from one end to another.

But I felt I ought to do something to contribute. Then I reasoned with myself that I was buying war bonds, that's enough, and I'm a member of the USO. I'm doing my share! I would never have stayed as long as I did if I hadn't been motivated by the fact that in my mind war was hell. I could visualize it, but I wanted to black out some of it. I never went to see a war picture and I never wanted to read a newspaper. I never wanted to know what was going on. Maybe the older people did, but the young people didn't want to hear about what was happening in the war; they just wanted to know we were winning.

The workers in aircraft hated it. I don't care whether they worked on the assemby or the training bench, the cockpit or in the wings or the tail; whether they riveted, wired, or were the managers or group leaders; whether they were in the final assembly—I have yet to meet one who really enjoyed it. The final assembly was the best job of all because you got out of the heat and you got out of the noise. The heat and the noise, I don' know how I ever lived through it. And I've kept in touch with two or three of the women that I worked with, and most of them have tremendous hearing problems. Most of them say it came from that noise.

I would never do it again! Never, ever!!! I don't think any other woman would either. They might say they would, but no, I don't think if most women would really be truthful with you, they enjoyed working or would have stayed in it if they hadn't really been motivated by patriotism or actually having a member of the family in the war. Some used it as an excuse to break out into the world. And it was the first decent opportunity Negro women had to get away from domestic work.

When Juanita quit her defense job, she was still only twenty years old. She thrived on the initial fever-pitch activity of the early war years, but she described herself as being lost by war's end. She wistfully recounted that period.

I sort of got mixed up, started drinking and running around and just went from job to job. I couldn't really find my place, wasn't content anywhere. I started being what I should have been—a teenager. After working all those years, I suddenly wanted to live, I wanted to dance, I wanted to go out.

I guess I fooled around a couple of years working odd jobs, and then I got married a couple of months before the war was over. That was a mistake! I had known him about a year and I was really sort of pressured into that marriage. I was drinking a lot and I couldn't handle it. I lost my way. The man I married was seventeen years older than myself. He was part of that "I'll get it for you wholesale"; "You want tires? Got a couple of hundred bucks? I'll get you tires. No problem."

I'm surprised, really amazed that I married him. I was twenty years old and should have known better. But I was weak. Then I got pregnant right away. But before my daughter was born, in 1946, I left him. When I went to the hospital, I called my friend who had since come back from the navy and had gone into the police force. She came with her friend, and they paid my hospital bill and brought me home. They cleaned up the little court where we had been living in Hollywood. Then she had a talk with my husband and told him to kindly, politely, get the hell out and not come back. She said, "Now is this what you want? You'll be taken care of. Carol will take care of the baby. You don't want him here?" I said, "Hell, no, I don't want him here. I want him out." Later, in 1947, I was divorced.

When my daughter was three weeks old, I got a job in a restaurant. I used to take her in a basket and put her in the office while I worked. It wasn't easy. For a while I lived in homes where they took care of the baby while I worked. In those days it was very, very common for two or three mothers and babies to share a home, or some widowed lady had a home and would rent rooms to mothers with children, and then they'd hire a colored maid. There were so many babies then that it was like a business or a profession. People got together, rented a house and rented a housekeeper. I did that for a few years. That's how we made it.

Later, she went to a girls' school. Quite a few mothers in my circumstances, divorced, had their children there. The parents would come and the kids would do little ballets and little plays. The parents that I got to know were like myself, single women or divorced women who were bringing up their own children. We found that we all had the same thing in common. One parent might be asked for a weekend to take care of the other's child. Or we'd switch off watching them.

I thought I knew all about babies, but I started reading Dr. Spock. I don't think I have to say too much more. In other words, I wanted her to have all the schooling, the ballet lessons, the piano lessons, the pretty dresses, the parties. "Don't work; don't empty the trash; don't do anything, just clean your room. Just have a good time!" I don't think she ever lacked for anything in her life. I don't think it was the right way. I think children should be told no. They should learn the value of money, the value of work. But that can't be undone. The past is prologue. But don't think that the postwar babies turned out to be the best lot of all. They themselves are becoming better parents because they are being more strict.

I know most mothers went through the same things. I used to think I was the only one until I talked with other mothers. Kids of her era, growing up particularly in the sixties, they went their own way. They had their ideas: the flower child. "I'm going to go to San Francisco." "Sure, go ahead." "Well, mother, can you send me money?" "What for?" "Well, Ma, I have to live." "Well, you're eighteen, you can get a job. You're old enough, you do anything you like." All children of the sixties were like that.

Juanita's social life during the postwar years continued to revolve around the subculture she had described earlier: a quasi-bohemian, intellectual group on the fringes of Hollywood. She remained a single parent except for a

brief marriage in 1955 to a Mexican-American who
worked at the same restaurant where she was working.
Opposed to the military, he packed his bags when he was
called up for service, went to Mexico, and disappeared.
She maintained contact with him until 1960.

For social life I went to the opera. I never gave that up, and I
never gave up my concerts. I was very interested in poetry and philo-
sophical meetings at that time, so I never really quite gave that up.
Friends? I'd have two nights a week off. What can you do in two
nights a week? Go out to dinner one night and go to friends' homes
the other night, if you're lucky.

My friends were a mixed group: bohemians, beatniks, divorced,
gays, singles. There's only one couple that I know from the forties
who got married, stayed together, had children; lived an absolutely
totally normal life. One couple from all those—what did they call us
then? Bohemians. Later they became beatniks and then hippies. The
only difference between the bohemians of the late thirties and forties,
and the beatniks and the hippies of the fifties and sixties and seventies, and the punk rock of the eighties is that the bohemians had no
television. They had less radio, less money, less cars. They socialized
in block parties. We all lived within a radius of two or three miles of
each other, and we met each other walking to work or waiting at the
bus stop. In those days we knew the whole neighborhood!

We got together and we played music, and we talked about the
artists. We all liked classical music and jazz and, of course, the big
bands. We all liked to dance, so we entertained. We had conversations. We discussed books, poetry, music, jazz artists, musicians, con-
ductors, composers, musical pieces, opera, light opera. Today punk
rock, loud music, and drugs seems to be the topic of conversation.
Very funky.

That was the world we lived in then. There weren't any fantasies
about our world. If you could get a record, it was something that was
treasured because we didn't have the money to go running around.
We had money during the war, but in the lean years following the
war—and there was some lean ones—prices shot up and everything
started escalating. The city got bigger, spread out, and people had to
move. They started tearing down apartment buildings and everyone
was uprooted. Actually television is what really broke up the neigh-

borhood togetherness, the friendship of neighborhoods. So each generation has its own, and yet it's parallel one to the other.

McCarthyism? Banning of some of the writers. Let me see if my memory goes back. Now we are going into the coffeehouse era where we used to go and sip coffee and drink wine and discuss communism, Korea, the Russians, the cold war. We were now getting into our late twenties. Two of our people were communists. We didn't know it at the time, but we had an idea.

Leo had been just like us, and he'd come home from the war and gone back to work in a gas station. Then, all of a sudden, he started sporting new clothes, a new car, and he wasn't working in the gas station anymore. He was going to do something in television. He rented a big house in Silver Lake, and he gave a party and we all went. The front was sort of like a loft. He was an artist before. He'd work, but he would paint in his spare time.

Anyway, when we got there we were all asked to sign a register. There were a lot of people we didn't know. I said, "Who's that, who are these people?" "Well, he's made a lot of new friends since he came back." We were handed out a lot of literature, and then, all of a sudden, the party took on a very political tone and suddenly we realized, "Hey, they're having a rally, a communist rally!" Well, we got out, but we had signed a guest book. Each and every one of us that went began to get communist literature. I don't think any of us approved of communism. Leo, yes. He outgrew us, so he never invited us again.

When Juanita left her first husband and struck out on her own with her daughter in 1946, she became a waitress. It is an occupation that she has pursued for the past forty years and of which she is proud. She is a real pro and was eager to talk about the conditions of her occupation.

I went into waitress work primarily because I had to support myself and my daughter and because it was easy. It was child's play compared to sitting and working with tweezers and straining your eyes. I had ambitions and I had dreams when I was twenty-one, but you just kind of get beaten down over the years. You just say, "Well, this is what I can do." So I have remained a waitress all these years. In between, I've done sales and I've worked in drugstores, cosmetic counters. I've also worked as hostess, I've worked as cashier. In other words, there isn't anything in a restaurant that I haven't done. I've washed dishes, I've gone back and made salads, I can make sandwiches. But primarily and basically I'm a very fine waitress. I'll take a bow for myself.

I didn't start out as a first-class waitress. I started out in a Greek steak and chop house where the meat was in the window and the flies were all over it. I've worked beer joints, too. I haven't always worked in the best, but I have worked in some of the very finest restaurants in Los Angeles: Brown Derby, the Fog Cutter, Century Plaza Hotel. I've worked silver service and I've hashed.

In a good restaurant, even in a bad restaurant, it's a matter of how you serve, your attitude, and how the food looks. Often a cook will put out a plate of food in front of me and I'll rearrange the whole plate. It makes all the difference in the world. I can slam a plate down in front of you and it can be a Chateaubriand for two for thirty-five dollars and I can throw it at you and you'll say, "Hmm." Or I can serve it and cut it and explain and talk to you while I'm doing it, and the way I present the plates to you makes all the difference in the world. You can do the same thing in a coffee shop giving someone a corned beef sandwich, and they'll walk away and say, "Hey, this is a nice place." It's something you have to develop.

I've worked in dinner houses for the last twenty-five years. When you make spinach salads or Caesars or steak Diane or cherries jubilee, it's a presentation, the way the plate looks. It's also timing—knowing when to approach the table, when not to, when to ask about coffee, when to push the other drinks. And it's an art to serving wine. These are the things that I learned.

I like my work. But there are times when there is a lot of stress and a lot of headaches. It gets more so all the time. Some of the changes that are happening now make me feel so angry I want to call the Health Department—the lack of sanitation in the kitchens. But we have to put up a front. We can't let it go past the kitchen door. But when you're working with people that are being exploited—I don't know if I should be saying this, but restaurants today tend to exploit the foreign workers, and they don't have the sanitary feelings about food that we have. It makes me very cautious ordering salad and food in restaurants.

In a restaurant you walk in with what you have in your pocket, and when you leave you have what you have in your pocket. We are paid $3.25 an hour. We pay $2.20 for dinner, which is what they want to give us, not our choice, and we pay $1.65 for lunch. We end up with about $2.90 per hour. We have no pension fund; we do not get paid holidays or time-and-a-half for the sixth day; we do not get sick leave. We get sick and if we have to be off, we're out of luck!

Now union houses are different, but in Los Angeles there are very few union houses left. The union was, at one time, very strong, the Waiter and Waitresses Union. They had a lot of good benefits. In fact, I was one of the very first that they sent out on the picket lines. That was in 1946 or 1947. The union was just gaining a stronghold. The agents came to the restaurants and they would talk with you. One agent would talk to one person; that person would talk to another; then they take a vote. At that time I was willing to join because I had lost out on some good jobs by not being able to get into the union—when I tried to get into Technicolor and film cutting. You had to be union.

But over the years the union has lost until it is so weak now that only a few of the major hotels are union. I think the only reason they are union is that the rest of the hotel employees are union and every delivery that is brought in is by union drivers. So the hotel cannot fight the union, but an individual restaurant can avoid it. The last union job I worked was the Brown Derby ten years ago. Now when you work with waitresses and you say to them, "We ought to be getting paid for Christmas, or we ought to be getting paid time-and-a-half on the sixth day," they say, "Well, you know it's a job and if you say anything they'll just fire you." There's always nine weak links to every strong link in a chain, so I'm passive. I used to stand up and have a voice but now I just drift along. That's bad!

I usually stay on a job for six to ten years, and then I move on, mostly because I need a change. You get set in your habits; burnout. I've walked in one night and feel like I've had a burnout there and I'm leaving. I just give notice and I go. I might not do this so much now because of my age. It's getting harder to get a job.

Like three months ago the kitchen was snowed. They had overbooked and everyone came at one time. The cook had forty orders in front of him and he's still calling in more orders, and I said, "For Christ's sake, get some of these orders out first. Let those wait." My manager came into the kitchen, and she said, "What the hell is going on? If you girls can't do it I'm going to get rid of all of you old girls and get some young ones in here." I said to her, "Do you know that's discrimination? You're not supposed to pick on us because of our age." She didn't say another word. But now, each time she hires a girl, it's a girl in her twenties or thirties. That was three or four months ago and the attitude of every waitress in that place—and some of them have been there for thirty years—has changed.

I think my attitude is that I can still do my work and I still have a lot of compliments. I know from the money I make whether my work is good or not. But you know yourself when you're doing a good job. When I give bad service, I will apologize. But when I give service that is bad because of the kitchen, I go back to the people and I explain to them that we are very busy and and it won't be much longer. These are the little things that make a good waitress. So this is restaurant work, but you accept it. If you're going to stay in it, you have to take it. The only way there would ever be changes would be if there were a union again.

As a woman who has had to work to support herself since the age of thirteen, Juanita is sympathetic to the goals of the women's movement—with qualifications.

Women's lib, I think it's a good thing. To begin with, today most women who marry still have to work. Unless the men are really in the upper echelon, thirty, forty, fifty thousand dollars a year. The ordinary couple get married, the man may be earning eighteen or twenty thousand dollars a year, and the girl, if she's working in a bank, the most she could be making is maybe twelve thousand dollars a year. You almost have to have a two-family income to survive—if you're going to buy a house, have furniture and clothes, and bring up children. Then there's a lot of women who are not married and divorced or pushed aside. Then there's the young girl that's being educated in college, a career. She needs the breaks.

We've just had a tremendous break. Sandra O'Connor. Now this is the best thing that could ever happen. Women can do these jobs. They do have the education now to do them. So for women's lib, yes, it's a good thing, if women do not become too aggressive and too masculine; if they will remember that they are still women and act accordingly and dress accordingly. What I've been seeing in the last year or so in bars, restaurants, even in theaters, and occasionally at the Music Center, are women who are just too aggressive. They have forgotten femininity. They have forgotten that men can open the door for them or that a man can light their cigarettes or that he can greet them without having sex on his mind.

Abortion? God, that a tough one! I've never had an abortion. I've known some women that have had legitimate, clean, sterile hospital abortions. Going back to the forties and fifties, I've known girls who struggled and scratched on my door or a friend's door when they've had a back-alley abortion. They've been very sick cookies. Still, women, if they don't want a child, are going to have an abortion one way or another. The only fair and decent way if a woman is determined to have an abortion is to make it legal, where they have to go to a hospital and be counseled before they do it.

Juanita is still vigorous and active, and intends to continue working despite the increasing difficulties and age discrimination she faces in her occupation. Until her daughter moved out of Los Angeles a few years ago, she spent a great deal of time with her two grandsons, regularly taking care of them. She was very close to them—closer, in fact, than to her daughter, and clearly misses them.

I reflect occasionally on my life. I had to work. I didn't really know the difference. Certain stages of my life, I realized that what I missed out on was school, classes, parties, a childhood. I never had my childhood. Then a marriage that was such a disaster. Since then, I've been to many, many beautiful weddings of people who have been in love and gotten married properly, and I think to myself that I missed out a lot. But, actually, I really didn't know any better.

Now, if I really wanted to just chuck it all, I could go on welfare. I could say to myself, "Now look here, girl, you're going to be fifty-seven in a couple of months. You've worked hard." But I like to work. I need to work. My body loves work. I do get tired. Then I need to be off and I can't. Now that's when I see what I'm missing.

If I were young today and with all the freebies and benefits that people have, I'd go to school and become a musicologist or a classical musician or a composer. I would study music, I'd write music, lyrics. I'd study grammar, English, literature. I'd write stories, poems, prose. I'd take advantage. I'd really make something of myself today. The opportunities are there. I mean if you have something in you and it wants to come out, then go for that! If I could do it today, NOTHING would stop me!

PART IV

Should Your Wife Take a War Job?

The Homemaker Turned War Worker

Among the single women, the picture is one of almost complete employment. But only one of five [of] the <u>married</u> women have yet gone to work. Moreover, the wives constitute the overwhelming majority of the female population, so that they represent the most abundant supply of workers.

Since our ability to keep the production machine running in high gear depends largely on the enlistment of women workers, the public attitude toward this issue—and especially the attitude of wives—is of paramount interest.

Office of War Information, 1943

Recruiting homemakers into war industries meant challenging—or at least temporarily abandoning—the very definitions of womanhood that American culture promoted and that most women seemed to accept. Coming on the heels of the depression, when hostility toward married women working was so intense, the campaign was especially difficult.

The recruitment efforts were finally successful, and married women eventually made up one-third of all defense workers. By emphasizing the temporary nature of women's wartime work the cultural values were kept intact. Yet, in a 1944 survey of women workers, half of the former full-time homemakers said that they wanted to continue working after the war. Many of them did continue; others returned home only to rejoin the work force later; still others permanently returned to exclusively homemaking roles.

Charlcia Neuman, Helen Studer, Beatrice Morales Clifton, and Marie Baker all returned home by war's end, at least temporarily. They were a part of the labor force statistics that showed almost 3 million women leaving the work force. But such statistics tell only part of the story. The changes experienced by women like these four were often played out in the private arena—hidden from a historian's eye.

CHAPTER 7

Charlcia Neuman

Charlcia Neuman, 1982.

*I didn't plan on working. My husband
didn't want me to. Now, that would be
considered terrible, but this was the usual
thing then. I mean taking care of a house
isn't the easiest thing in the world.*

Charlcia Neuman was a self-professed housewife who was
bound and determined to tell the housewife's story. But
getting her story was not easy. She was initially suspicious of me—in fact, downright hostile. Charlcia had
called our project after the appearance of a story in the
Los Angeles Times. She felt that the housewife had been
misrepresented and was convinced that I would not accu-
rately reflect the point of view of women like herself.
When we finally met face to face a year after this initial,
somewhat unpleasant, phone conversation, Charlcia told
me that she was "teed off" because the article had implied that I viewed women like "poor little things" who
had no choice. They *wanted* to return home, she insisted.
And she was living proof.

Despite this testy introduction, Charlcia and I did hit
if off. We spent time talking about my ideas about the
role of women during the war, and she came to understand that my views of women's experience were considerably more complicated than the newspaper story had

implied. After that discussion, Charlcia was ready to tell
her story.

Born in Oregon, Charlcia was raised in southern California, the fourth of five children. She married at nineteen, shortly after graduation from high school, and right
before the crash of 1929. Her only child, a daughter, was
born two years later, and Charlcia's life revolved around
her family and her activities in the Order of Eastern Star.
She took a war job "for the duration" and returned home
after war's end to resume her domestic duties. Always interested in art, Charlcia used her artistic talents and skills
both in her home and for the organizations to which she
belonged, playing the role of decorator for their func-
tions. Charlcia kept up these activities after her husband's death in 1970, and did not curtail them until three
years or so before I interviewed her. By then the arthritis
that she had lived with since age nineteen began to se-
verely limit the work she could do with her hands.

In March 1983, despite suffering from a severe depression, Charlcia attended the special ceremony held at
California State University, Long Beach to celebrate Rosie the Riveters, bringing with her the recognition pin
she earned at Vultee. A year later Charlcia died. Her
daughter informed me of her death and commented again
how proud her mother had been of the part she had
played in the war effort.

Charlcia was thirty-two years old when she got her
job at Vultee Aircraft in 1942. It was the first time she
had been a wage earner. Although Charlcia's husband
would not have tolerated her taking a job during the depression when he was unemployed, patriotic duty during
the war provided the justification for temporarily trans-
cending these traditional values. Charlcia admitted, however, that it was not only patriotic duty that motivated
her, but that economic necessity played a vital role. The
scars of the depression were still fresh. The Neumans
had used up all their savings, and Charlcia's husband's income was still not sufficient to support the family.

What is so interesting about Charlcia's account is that

she obviously went beyond the bounds of what was expected. She was practically the only one in her social circle to take a job in a defense plant. Her friends and acquaintances who went to work during the war took more traditional women's jobs, taking up the slack as the former service workers flocked to the war plants. I can't help but feel that Charlcia was proving something to herself: that she was competent and could do the job. The job at Vultee Aircraft also expanded Charlcia's social horizons enormously. She came into contact with blacks and Mexicans—even a communist.

Charlcia told her story in a crisp fashion, speaking in relatively short simple sentences. She was very serious, determined to complete her mission: to give the "housewife's version." Once this was done, she relaxed and ended the interview on a joking note. She then took me by the hand and led me off to the kitchen to display proudly the complicated mosaic above her range that she had designed and executed.

Although Charlcia and I had worked through our differences, I found myself holding back during the interview, unwilling to disrupt the fragile rapport we had established. Regrettably, I backed off from asking my usual questions about the Equal Rights Amendment and abortion, despite the fact that Charlcia had revealed an openness about women's contemporary roles—and even a heightened consciousness. She seemed to understand that she was a product of her time. The war job had made her realize that she was not trained for anything, and she became determined that her daughter's life would be different.

Before I left her house, Charlcia turned over to me a valued period photograph taken by the company showing Charlcia at her work station during an official military inspection. Charlcia felt it was an important historical document that should be preserved. I was touched by this gesture. It meant that she did, after all, trust me to tell her story.

On both sides of my family, they were pioneers in this country. On my mother's side they were traced back to about the time of the *Mayflower*. I have been told my father's people were here at that time, too. Later, they opened up the Oklahoma Territory and my older uncle homesteaded there.

My maternal grandmother was from Michigan and my grandfather was born in Ohio, but he was in Michigan in 1861. He was a blacksmith and served in the Civil War. And my grandmother's brother was an Indian Scout during the Civil War. He used to tell me stories. I was just a child, but all these things impressed me—he lived in the open so much.

There was someone in every war that the country has had. I had an uncle in the First World War, so that war was a very personal type of thing to me, too, because we received cards and different things about what was going on over there. So I was brought up in a very patriotic family; you know, everything was "we do this for the country." And discussions were made about running the country. My mother, she was on the election boards in California before women were allowed to vote elsewhere.

She became a teacher, and when she took the tests in the area, her average was ninety-eight. So Mama had a brilliant brain, really. She had memory and mathematics, even up until the time she died, when she was eighty-seven years. She taught in the country, where you taught the whole school. She did that until the time she was married at twenty-two.

My father was seven years older. He grew up as a farmer in Kansas and Iowa. I don't know just why he went to Oregon; it was adventure. Daddy was a jack-of-all-trades: he was in a garage and he was a barber and he was a carpenter. He was the more easygoing one and smoothed things over, so your problems seemed to go away. My mother was a very nervous type of person, very quick, very capable. I always felt closer to my father, but, of course, I was the one that was closer to Mama as we were older.

I was born in 1911 in Oregon. Then they came down here to Los Angeles when I was about eighteen months old. My grandmother was down here and my aunts and other parts of the family. I imagine that they felt that things might be better down here; living wasn't so easy in those days. The house we first lived in when we came down here didn't have a bathroom. We had to go outside to a toilet and it was in the chicken pen. The rooster didn't like me, so somebody had to

Charlcia Neuman on left, 1943.

carry me out there. I remember all of that; so a child remembers when they're quite young.

Later, when we moved to Bell, we had an acre of ground and there was always work to be done around the place. We got up to about six goats one time and we had chickens. We had any kind of an animal that we wanted; there was always room for one more. We grew quite a bit of our food, but we still bought meat and milk. Well, there was the goat's milk. After my younger brother was born, he wasn't real well. The goat's milk was real good for him, so that's one reason we had the goats. But each time one was born, one of us would claim that one for a pet.

We didn't have a whole lot, moneywise, but I think we were happier because we didn't. We had plenty of room to play, trees to climb. Our backyard was full of fruit trees. I very often would go take a book and go out in back and climb the tree and eat fruit. That was my breakfast.

I read any kind of adventure stories: Indian stories, dog stories, animal stories. I can't remember when I learned to read, but before I went into the first grade I was able to read the funny paper. My dad read them to us all the time, and probably from reading them to me, I learned to do that.

My dad worked sometimes seven days a week, and there wasn't very much time for our family to do things together. He worked at Stilwell's Garage downtown, and he would fix the cars all up and then he would take them out. Well, when he tried them out, he'd usually come home and pile us all in for a ride. And he had a motorcycle with a sidecar on it. We'd all climb in the sidecar. When he had a few days off, we went to the mountains or desert, camping. I leaned to take care of myself outside.

I was particularly fond of sports of all kinds. We played baseball quite a bit and basketball and then tennis when I was on into high school. We played baseball from the time we were quite small. There was quite a large lot between our house and the next house, and all the kids in the neighborhood were there playing after school. The way I grew up if some couldn't play so well, they were always used anyway. Now, they have structured baseball for children, and they just don't have a chance. I was very active until the time that I got arthritis real bad.

I wasn't an outstanding student, but I got by all right. Math and spelling were my downfall. Geography, because of the books about traveling, I particularly enjoyed. But art work of any kind was what I really cared about. I always thought that somewhere along the line I would keep studying art, but that didn't pan out too good.

I got married when I was eighteen. My husband was a fireman here in Bell and a very close friend of the father of the girl that I was close friends with. We are still very close friends. I met him at their house. He was nine years older than I am. We just planned on getting married and having a family. I didn't plan on working. He didn't want me to. Now, that would be considered terrible. He wouldn't want you to, but this was the usual thing then.

My daughter was born in '31. That was before my husband lost his job. The fact that my husband wasn't working when she was little, we just felt that it wasn't the best thing to have another child. So we were careful. We used a condom. I can't see why it isn't used a little more. That is certainly one of the safest ways and it doesn't hurt either one. It's just because a man maybe would be too selfish to want to use it is what I feel. I can't see a woman using all this dope, when a man could very simply use something that would work. So my husband was very considerate.

Later, when things were better, it just didn't happen. Whether I could have gotten pregnant again or not, I'm not too sure. But my health wasn't really too good to have more children. I've had my share of pain. I developed the arthritis when I was nineteen, but you learn to live with it. For one thing, I had a small child and there was no one else to take care of her.

Charlcia and her husband started their family in the early days of the depression. Initially they had few worries and were even able to save money and to pay for the house Charlcia's father had built for them. Her husband was earning $165 a month as a firefighter.

Finally, he lost his job, which was a political job in a small town in those days. When the City Council changed, then they put out the firemen and the policemen, and then they hired somebody else that they knew better. Losing a job in the middle of the depression was not good. There was no work. Nothing. He was out of work for three years.

I could make five dollars stretch farther than most people. I could sew and did cooking. My father-in-law lived next door, and he had fruit trees in the backyard and he raised chickens and rabbits. He would take and cut up a chicken and put it in my icebox—he didn't think I could do it—ready for me to cook. That would last a while.

We had another friend that had been with the fire department and he lost his job, too, so we'd invite them over if we had chicken. Then they'd get a little bit of money, and they'd invite us to go to the show. There was a theater in Huntington Park, you could go for ten cents. So that was our recreation.

For those three years we lived off the money we had saved. It was very difficult. We just about thought we would have to let the house go. Then they put in the home loans through the government. At first the loan company wouldn't let us get it, so we quit paying and said, "Well, then you'll just have to take it." Then they let us get the home loan on it. So getting that we were able to squeak by a little more, by paying them just a very small amount.

I forget exactly when it was, but then Eddie got a job in a laundry over in Huntington Park. He was paid fifteen dollars a week. It was still difficult, but it was money. We managed. Then he went to work for the school board. That was a political type of thing, too. He went out and worked for some of the board members, and when they were elected, then he applied for a job and was able to get it. He was already working there when the war began. He stayed where he was, though, because other things that made more money—it was always the type of thing that would end at a certain time. Consequently, I'm much better off now. I have a pension that I can live on comfortably.

But the depression wasn't pleasant, and it made a difference in how you lived, maybe always. It made you a little afraid of taking chances, on going into debt on different property. You had the feeling that something might happen and you wouldn't be able to hold it.

Until the war began, Charlcia's life revolved around her family, her neighborhood, and her Eastern Star activities. She and her daughter were very close and the family did everything together, though Charlcia did not participate very much in her daughter's school activities.

Charlcia and her husband often played cards with the next-door neighbors, but most of her friends were members of Eastern Star. It was in that organization that she was able to express some of her artistic abilities. She decorated the tables for their events and on several occasions decorated large halls. She took this work very seriously and enjoyed the challenge, even studying various techniques from books. With the onset of the war, the pace of her daily life changed—at least temporarily.

Pearl Harbor. I remember that very definitely. I was standing at the sink. The man next door, he was a captain in the reserves. I remember opening the window and calling to him and telling him to go in and turn the radio on. I didn't like it, naturally—no one did—they came in with no warning at all and bombed Pearl Harbor. It was a terrible thing.

The patriotic feeling was so strong that anyone would have done anything to help. You never had any of this protest type of thing. There were a great many things that were wrong, especially what they did to the Japanese people that lived here. I knew one family that because the grandmother was Japanese, they had to leave their home. This was terrible. On the other hand, my husband had worked on Terminal Island in the schools there and amongst those people there were Japanese that were spies. Because of that, everybody suffered and it was wrong.

I started defense work in '42. I think a lot of it was because one of my neighbors found out about it, and she wanted me to go with her. I thought, "Well, now, this would take care of the situation." I still was getting along on next to nothing; it was still difficult. And my husband was talking about whether he should quit the school board or not. In those days, they didn't belong to any union, and they were paid a very small amount. As prices were going up it wasn't enough to cover our expenses. So I said, "No, I'll go see what I can do."

My husband didn't like it. He was one of these men that never wanted his wife to work. He was German and was brought up with the idea that the man made the living; the woman didn't do that. But he found that it was a pretty good idea at the time. It was a necessity, because he would have had to do something else. We couldn't live on what he was making, so that's the way it goes.

And my brother, especially my youngest brother, he thought it was terrible. My father, oh, he was very upset. He said, "You can't work amongst people like that." They were people just like me, but they thought it was people that were rough and not the same type I'm used to being with. They just couldn't see me going over and working in a factory and doing that type of work. And they were trying to protect me, I'm sure. Well, there again, I had quite a bit of arthritis and they felt that it would just be a bad thing to get in there.

But I wasn't trained for just any type of work. See, most of the women I knew, they went into stores and into that type of work. It was easier to do. They wouldn't go into the war plants. My oldest sister worked at Lockheed and she was a drill press operator, but the sister right next to me, she was a waitress. When she looked at my wages and what she collected, she said, "No, no part of that." She was making more money by the time she figured her tips.

So, my family thought I was a little off for doing it. But if that's what I wanted to do, that's what I did. And my husband got used to the fact that his wife worked.

I went over and took tests to see about getting a job at Vultee. When I took the test, as far as using the hands and the eye and hand movements, I passed just about the highest. See, anything using my hands—I could take a little hand drill and go up and down these holes as fast as you could move, just go like that, where most people would break a drill. It was a very simple thing. The riveting is the same way. It's just a matter of rhythm. So it was easy to do.

They had a school set up in Downey to show us how to do assembly work and riveting and the reasons for things—what was a good rivet and what wasn't. We went there about two weeks before we started to work. It was mostly women on these jobs. See, so many young men were in the service that it didn't leave very many of them to do these types of jobs; the ones that were kept out of the service could do the more specialized work. They had to have men to make these jigs and to make the forms for the ribs. That was beyond us.

I was started on this jig. The P-38 that Lockheed put out was a twin engine, and we worked on the center part between the two hulls. It was a much heavier rivet that went into this. It was what they call cold riveting; you took them out of the icebox real cold and riveted it. That was harder work.

Well, the jig would be empty, see, so the first job would be to mark your ribs. We took a red pencil and just put a line right down through the center. That was so that when we pushed it into position, then we could be sure we were hitting the center of the rib when we drilled. You'd ruin the whole rib if you've got too much in the curve or something like that. So we fastened the ribs in; then we put the skin on and fastened the Cleco clamps on it. The jig was in place so we could drill it. We marked along the edges so we could trim it, and then we took it off and trimmed the excess piece. We put it back together again and riveted up, and then we'd loosen the whole thing and take it off and put it in a special holder to be inspected for bad rivets. After inspection, it went to the next two girls and they added the next part.

Sometimes I had someone working with me and that made it a little faster, because otherwise I'd have to reach to the back and be sure it's in place. The person in the back would drill and you'd drill in the front, and then they'd be there all ready to rivet. My partner was better at the bucking than I was. She could hold it steadier. I wasn't strong enough. You had to hold that square bar on the other side while the gun was shooting on this side. It was quite a force on it. It was hard to do—but that didn't mean I didn't buck on some things.

> For the traditional homemakers, especially, the defense plant widened their social world. Charlcia had a sense of history and was proud of the fact that she was participating in a turning point in the relationship between the races.

Vultee was the first plant of this type in the area to hire a black girl. She was a very nice person. Wilhelmina was her first name, but I can't remember her last name. Her mother was a schoolteacher and she was from Los Angeles.

The girls that worked together became quite friendly. If someone happened to quit and went in the WACS, we would have a party. I remember this one time, we thought, "No, we're not going to have it at the restaurant; we'll have it in one of our homes and ask Willie to come, too." We didn't want to leave her out. About seven o'clock that night, we got a telegram from Willie saying she was so sorry she couldn't come, but that she appreciated us asking her. She didn't want to break the color line, but those things wouldn't happen anymore today.

But she was among the first blacks in our department. In that three years that I was there, then they began coming from the South. You could really tell the difference. The ones coming from the South were shy. It was very hard for them to mix with people. It was a very hard situation for them, but they were treated nice.

When these black people were beginning to come in pretty steadily, I went over to show them how to do smaller types of assembly work, get them used to working with people and like that. The only difference that I could see was that they were inclined to get very angry at things. Maybe they hadn't understood something and they would get very upset. But they didn't do that to me. There was something about the way I worked with them that they didn't get so upset with me. So that was my job for a while and that was a good experience.

Then there were the Mexican girls. They were treated just like we were. There was no such thing as brown; they were white as far as we were concerned. There again, they were very nice. They couldn't pronounce my name, and they always called me Charli. I remember this one, when I would walk up toward them, she would say, "Now you speak English; you know Charli can't speak Spanish." This one particular group was clustered in that area, but there were others scattered through the plant. It wasn't that they were separating this group; it just happened. I couldn't see that they were being discriminated against in any way. But at that time, the Negroes were just treated very badly. Here again, I've always been different, where things like this was concerned. I could see the wrong.

But the women on my crew were a bit like me. One girl lived in San Pedro. I think her folks were fishermen down there. And another one lived over in Huntington Park, just a plain ordinary family. At thirty-one, thirty-two, I was considered fairly old. There was one woman that I think was forty-eight when they hired her, and she was an old lady! But these girls were mostly younger; they were in their early twenties. I don't think any of them had children.

We kept pretty busy working all the time, and there wasn't much personal talk. We sat down as a group at lunchtime, though. We would just find some spot to sit and eat and talk about different things. We didn't have any close connections, so there wasn't very much that we could talk about. I just knew where they lived.

But the one who was bucking rivets for me, she talked more because she was trying to make me a communist. She was very active with this group downtown and it was a communist group. Of course, I was telling her, "No, I'd never join a communist group." I said, "You wouldn't either if you knew what they were like." There was one other man that worked around there and he was a Republican, too. Of course, this was quite noticeable. We would stand out like sore thumbs because the majority of people that you met in a plant at this time were all Democrats. I never said anything about my affiliations because they were so—almost radical. But this other man was talking about it, and I said, "Sure, you can talk, look how big you are." He was saying to her, too, that if she ever had a chance to go to Russia and live under the conditions there, she would change her mind in a hurry.

I talked to her quite a bit. She owned property up in San Fernando Valley. She felt that things should be divided with other people, that one person shouldn't have everything and somebody else have nothing. Her beliefs, when she was talking, were for socialism, but she couldn't see the difference between socialism and communism.

Despite the enjoyable aspects of the job, the pace was hard and fast and the working conditions, particularly the noise level, were unpleasant. Charlcia described how noticeable this was at lunchtime, when the motors were all turned off. In fact, if anyone broke the relative calm by turning on a motor, the others would all rebel. Industrial accidents were not uncommon

Most of the time when you have an accident, it's your own fault. The first one, I was working when the jig was moving; they had a moving line in one section. I was doing some safety wiring and I wanted to move. I just hopped down off of where I was onto one of those stools and it flipped. I had the blackest fanny for a long time. But nothing broke. I went to the first aid station and a report was made out.

The second one, I was working with this one girl on a section where it was sort of blind for me in the back. I had to put my hand in. She was working along the edge. Well, there's a guard that goes over the spring on the rivet gun so when the gun shoots that can't possibly come out—'cause they come out with quite a force. Well, she couldn't get into what she was trying to shoot, so she took the guard off. I was on the other side, see. I remember that it hit me at quite a blow, right next to the nose. Luckily, it hit the one spot that it could hit and the bone was solid enough that it didn't break it and kept from going on through. I was taken to the infirmary. I thought the fellows would take her apart. They were so upset with her. That was a definite thing that you don't do. Had it hit me in the eye I would have been dead. I think there's a little mark still someplace.

At the time of her accident, Charlcia was working with the heavier rivets and had the higher rating of assembly-man A. She was quick to point that it was assemblyman, not assemblyperson.

We paid off the house then, is what we were doing. We had a horror of being in debt—for anything. The depression left that feeling with us, that we had to get out of debt. We saved. Well, we didn't have time to spend very much then, anyhow, and with the two of us working, it made it easier.

But, of course, it was hard. I worked six days all the time and sometimes seven days—which was terrible. If I didn't have a family that supported me so much, I couldn't have managed it. I had a daughter that was very capable. She did all the shopping. See, by the time I got home from work, the shops were closed. She took the ration books and she figured that all out. The shop owners all knew her, and they'd let her have things that they wouldn't let me have if I did have time to go. She was in junior high school at the time. It helped make her a stronger person, I'm sure.

My husband helped me a lot with the housework; he was always good about helping. He was very strong and could do his work and then help me with some of mine, too. So whoever had time to do that did it. Typically, what I'd do, I'd get up before 6:00 and get things going. I was ready to leave at 7:00 and I was picked up. Then we got off at 4:00 P.M. and came home. I had dinner to fix and what could be done around the place. So it was a full day. If it hadn't been for my family, though, it would have been much harder for me.

Then things began to slow down. We knew the war was about over. For that matter, I think the bomb had been dropped already and we were just kind of waiting. You could see the difference; it wasn't that push and the trying to do more all the time.

I was laid off in September of '45. I just got a slip of paper saying that I wouldn't be needed again. Most of us went at the same time; it was just a matter that there was no more work. There were a few jobs that they kept open, but most of the women were off then—and men, too. It wasn't discriminatory; it was what they happened to have left.

The idea was for the women to go back home. The women understood that. And the men had been promised their jobs when they came back. I was ready to go home. I was tired. I had looked forward to it because there were too many things that I wanted to do with my daughter. I knew that it would be coming and I didn't feel any letdown. The experience was interesting, but I couldn't have kept it up forever. It was too hard.

So, I just had to sort of try to get myself straightened up again and get back in the groove. My daughter became more busy in different things, so there was always something to do then. She belonged to the Civil Air Patrol for a while and she belonged to the Rainbow Girls, the teenage group sponsored by the Masons and Eastern Star. So that kept me busy doing things. And I did a lot of Eastern Star work again that I couldn't do while I was working.

And I had a mother at home that needed different things, and I helped do things for her and my own daughter and my husband. I was kept very busy. And it wasn't a bad word to say you were a housewife, either. You know, it was considered a job that needed to be done, too.

But I always felt that if married women needed to work, then that was their choice. I felt with my own daughter that if she wanted to work, she should be trained to do something where she would be paid good money, not that type of physical work. After I worked, I realized that if I had to work all the time, I would be very limited in what I could do. It's not that I couldn't learn to do something else. I think I would be capable of doing that. But with her, I told her there was no use spending her time and not really studying to do something that would be good. We talked of college as just being a part of what she would be doing. That way she kept through high school with the idea that she would go on to college.

She had one advantage. After the war, the government sent out people to examine students to see what they were most capable of doing, what their qualifications could be and what they would like. She had always thought she wanted to be a scientist. This man talking to her when she took the test, he told her that she was just a natural teacher and that she should follow through with that. So she did and it has proven to be right. She never had any problem with her job. They just offered her jobs wherever she was. Then she kept going into psychology—just taking extra courses—and they kept pushing her into higher classes because she had a natural trend toward that. So that's what she ended up doing. She is married, but she doesn't have children.

> Charlcia thinks she herself would have liked to have become a teacher, although it was difficult for her to conceive of other options for herself in her own day. As she reflected on my question of what she would do differently if she were a young woman today, she seemed almost embarrassed to fantasize about it, and laughed self-consciously. But she was not at all self-conscious about her pride in her wartime work and her mechanical abilities.

The women got out and worked because they wanted to work. And they worked knowing full well that this was for a short time. We hoped the war would be over in a very short time and that we could go back home and do what we wanted to do. So that was what I felt. And my friend that worked in the smaller assembly work, she was the same way. She went to work during the war because there was a need for workers, but she wanted to go back home. So that was the main thing. We knew when we went to work that it was not for all the time.

But it was a very good experience for me because of the challenge of doing something like that, to prove to myself that I could do it. And working with all the different types of people—I'd always been very shy about meeting people. Actually, I was afraid of going out and asking for a job because I didn't think I could do it. So I found out I could do it; it was the type of thing that I could do, that I liked to do. I had a natural knack. There again, the rhythm of riveting is natural. You know if you're good at tools and good in using your hands, your eye and hand coordination is good then. And riveting is a very easy thing for a woman to do.

Of course, my father was a mechanic and I was always around with him. And we didn't have boughten toys. If we wanted anything, we made it. If we wanted a scooter, you took an old pair of skates and you put it on a couple of boards and you made yourself a scooter. If you wanted a dollhouse, you took an old box and put it up on a tree. So I was used to using tools, but it probably made me a little more efficient in using tools. I could always use any kind of tools I wanted to up until about three years ago when my hands began going bad with arthritis. That was one of the worst things because I can hardly cut out a dress now. In the kitchen, when we're through, I'll show you over my stove one type of work I did with tools. I took a class in jewelry making and, oh, just anything. I've done everything from wire sculpture to paper sculpture. Just everything.

But it was very important, yes. I'm very glad I did it. Of course, it was also selfish on my part. I went out of necessity, but also to help. Whether I would have gone just to help, I'm not too sure. You see, it was an effort for me to go. It was not something that was real easy to do. But I'm glad I did it. I'm sure it helped the arthritis. Shook them all loose.

CHAPTER 8

Helen Studer

Helen Studer, ca. 1978.

That was a primary reason to work,
because I had a son that was in the
service. . . . And we needed the money.

Helen Studer was already forty-four years old when she
went to work at Douglas Aircraft in 1942. Like many
women whose sons were in the service, Helen made a direct connection between her work and her son's well-
being. Not many mothers of servicemen were still alive
in 1980 to tell their story. In fact, we were fortunate to
have interviewed Helen when we did, because she died
just a year later in August 1981.

At the time she was interviewed, Helen was not
quite as robust looking as in the 1979 photo of her, but
she seemed to be in good health and was still in good
spirits. By the time I went to her house in the summer of
1981 to review the transcript with her, she was frail and
bedridden. And she was enraged at the humiliation of being helpless and of dying a slow, painful death.

Helen's own children seemed to be taken aback by
the change in her personality—the shift from a sweet,
gentle person to a demanding and sharp one. But Helen's
oral history reveals such an independent and strong spirit
that it is easy to understand her rage at being rendered so
dependent at the end of her life. Although it was not ap-

parent at the time of the interviews, Helen probably knew that she was suffering from a recurrence of cancer. In retrospect, she seems to have been preoccupied about it. Her oral history is filled with references to friends and acquaintances who died of cancer.

What stands out, above all, in Helen's interview is her strength, determination, and self-confidence. Although she already demonstrated these characteristics long before she took her war job, the perfection with which she performed that job was a major source of pride. Ignoring blatant age discrimination, Helen stood her ground and fought for a promotion to an inspection job. She was eager to leave her job at war's end, but it is clear that her three years at Douglas had been very important ones for her. She had carefully preserved her Douglas badge and employees handbook; tools, including her little inspection mirror; and even the black rayon jumpsuit she had specially made in Hollywood.

Helen, like Tina Hill, liked to tell stories—once she overcame her initial nervousness. At one point early in her interview she asked, "Do you want me to tell some silly things?" Whenever she used salty language, she would lower her voice to a whisper. Helen's memory for details was impressive, and on the few occasions when she had lapses—especially in trying to remember names—she became very impatient with herself. It was as if she was constantly watching for signs of age and was annoyed when they would surface.

The "silly" stories that Helen told from her early childhood—usually accompanied by laughter—contrasted sharply with the painful experience of being taken away from her grandfather as a young girl. After seventy years, it was still hard for her to talk about this period in her life, and she frequently interrupted the interview by rummaging through drawers and photo albums.

There were a lot of hard times in Helen's life. Born in Kansas in 1898, she was first raised by her grandfather and eventually adopted by an older couple. After high school, Helen went into nurses' training and then to business school. She worked until her marriage in 1918. Once she set some of the ground rules for their relationship, Helen had a very happy life with her husband, Bill, whom she called "Daddy." Lifelong companions, they raised three children.

Like Juanita Loveless, Helen and her family were hard hit by the depression—beginning with the farm depression of the early 1920s. Her account of living in a tent in a Golden, Colorado, city park and of the droves of people going to California brings to life the enormous disruption experienced by rural midwesterners during the depression years. The Studers later joined the trek across the Great Plains, seeking a better life in the West, where the war jobs were beckoning. Helen intended to help with the family finances, just as she had done—despite her husband's opposition—when she picked up some seasonal packinghouse work in Kansas during the depression.

When the war ended, Helen was forty-seven years old. She was tired and ready to return to full-time homemaking, especially after she and her husband bought their own home. Helen spent her time sewing, crocheting, gardening, and socializing with her circle of friends. She kept all the tools she had used during her Douglas job and regularly used them for home repairs. After almost forty years, she was still proud to ply her mechanical skills.

By the time Helen's oral history transcript was ready for her to review, she was too weak to read it herself. Her eldest daughter read it to her in the final weeks of her life. She enjoyed hearing her story back and was still able to laugh at the stories she had "told on herself."

My mother and father separated when I was too little to even remember, and I lived with my grandfather and step-grandmother. And there were two younger sons at home, my uncles Chris and Glen. My grandfather, he was a gentle man and he was kind to children. I loved him with a vengeance. He had long red whiskers like they have today and I always played in his whiskers. He never sat down that I wasn't in his lap.

We lived on this small plot of ground. We just had a two-room house: a kitchen and eating place and a bedroom filled with beds. And they was four of us children and grandma and grandpa. He raised rows of sweet potatoes and rows of peanuts. Those are the two things I can remember and I wasn't but five years old. When it come time to harvest them, why, we kids and grandmother would go along and pick them out of the dirt. That'd be our winter food. We didn't have any chickens or anything like that, but we lived off of what he raised mostly.

I don't recall when, but he got this team of horses and he had this covered wagon, and he would start out during wheat harvesting. Whatever would be in season, he'd follow it with this team of horses and they'd work the horses, like you'd do tractors today. Grandmother would cook for the harvest hands and us kids. We tagged along and played around while they were working with this team of horses. My grandparents had a tent, but we kids slept in the covered wagon. If it rained, then we'd all have to get in the wagon and grandfather said, "Now, don't touch the top of the wagon." There's four fingers went up to the top of the wagon, and wherever it stopped, there was a drip, drip, drip.

The team of horses, they don't go very fast, plodding along, and we'd walk behind the wagon and the wind would blow. We little kids were supposed to find firewood. We burned what they call cow chips and we'd have to go pick those up. Well, my brother and my youngest uncle, they didn't want a little girl tagging around after 'em, so they'd say, "Oh, sis, here's a nice one." And I'd go to pick it up and it was all soft. Then they'd get a whipping.

From Kansas, we'd go to Pueblo, Colorado. My grandfather had a bee farm up there in some mountain. That would be part of our food. Traveling along in a covered wagon you don't have access to buying food; you carry it with you. He would buy maybe a hundred pounds of flour, bacon, whatever would keep. If we had nothing like that, the boys would go out and shoot prairie chickens. One time they couldn't find anything and they killed a big rattlesnake and they made

Helen Studer with husband, Bill, ca. 1940.

steaks of it. As far as I can remember, it was delightful. When grand-father cleaned the snake, he gave me the rattle to play with. I had that rattle for years.

I don't know how many years that went on, following the har-vest, but we'd make two trips a year. Then, sometimes in there, they were building a railroad through Kansas and they had to clear timber stuff out of there.

Oh, and I had a pet crow. It'd been injured somehow and they gave it to me to play with. He sat on my shoulder, but then he got so he could fly real good. Everywhere I went, this dumb crow flew along: "Caw, caw." The men in camp began missing their watches and they were accusing everybody. Then, all of a sudden, my grandmother says, "The silverware . . ." After I don't know how long a period of time, on a slow day, they were sitting around. My grandfather was smoking his pipe, looking up in the air, and he saw this bird flying. It looked like he had something shiny in his claws. He'd land in the tree and pretty soon he'd come back and he'd get another piece of whatever was shiny. Well, they climbed the tree and I don't know how much they brought down, but it was all the men's watches, all the silverware.

From the absolute delight Helen took in talking about her years with her grandfather, she sunk into despair as she began to discuss her later childhood. Choked with emotion, she paused frequently and asked that the tape recorder be turned off.

I lived with my grandfather until I was at least nine years old. By that time my mother was already dead. What happened is a terrible story. I was playing alongside of the road by the house and my stepmother came by with her fancy horse and buggy, and she told me if I'd get in the buggy, she'd take me for a ride. Well, she didn't only take me for a ride, she stole me away from my grandfather. He tried to get me back, but, of course, the law said my father had prior . . . so I stayed with them. Eventually, they got my brother, too.

How long I was there, I can't remember. Every chance I got, I ran away. I went down to this aunt. She lived not too far from where we lived, and she had a bunch of children of her own. But they'd come down and get me and I'd get a whipping. And then I'd run away again.

Then the law steps in. We had a sheriff from El Dorado, Sheriff Jollif. His wife wasn't very well, but they took me in their home. The law tried to send me to a reform school because I ran away all the time, but the judge and the sheriff said, "A little blond, curly-headed, pink-complexion kid, eight or nine years old—there wasn't any reason to send her to a reform school." So the sheriff kept me. I lived in his home some months and then his wife passed away. So they sent me to State Orphan's Home in Atchison, Kansas.

I never saw my grandfather again. And I never saw him and I never saw my uncle until I came to California in '42. I never heard from any of them, except my brother. When he got out on his own, he hunted me up.

But the orphan home was fantastic. They were very good to me there, and I got to go to school and I got to have decent clothes to wear. There were two colored girls, Cynthia Bly and Lillian. They took care of me like I was their baby.

One thing that happened while I was there was Halley's comet. They would take groups of us, and we'd take this *long* walk out on the road to see Halley's comet. That was unreal. I couldn't figure the world being so big. We couldn't see any farther than the end of our noses.

When I was round ten or eleven, there was this man and woman from Wathena, Kansas. They had never had any children, and they were almost in their fifties. They lived on a little berry farm. He wanted to get a little boy from the home to help him out on the farm, but she didn't like little boys and she wanted a little girl. Well, the instant she saw me, she had to have me. He was awfully good to me, but he wanted me to work out and hoe berries. I couldn't hoe. My side would hurt and I'd cry. I decided I wanted to go back to the home. Well, Grandpa—I always called him Grandpa—promised if I would stay he wouldn't insist that I hoe.

On days that we didn't have to work, rainy days or bad days, Grandpa La Bounty and I would play dominoes and checkers. And I could never beat him; he wouldn't let me beat him. I got very frustrated. And my foster mother didn't believe in a girl sitting around with idle fingers doing nothing and she had me embroider. To start out with, I had to hem tea towels. And I didn't get away with sloppy work! If it didn't look to suit her, I had to take it out and do it over again. I learned to hem fairly decently by the time I was thirteen. Then she tried to teach me to crochet. But she was around fifty or so when I went to live with them; she just didn't know how to teach a child.

In other words, we would cross. This is funny. I was somewhere between twelve and thirteen and it was a rainy day. She finally got so exasperated, she says, "Oh, you're so dumb, you'll never learn nothing." Well, I'm kinda sensitive. I don't like to be called dumb. My stepfather had what they called an old Morris chair, a big armchair with a floral velvet-covered back and cushion. I turned around in that big armchair—turned my back on her—and I sat there the rest of the afternoon fooling with this crocheting. By the time she says, "Let's go fix dinner," I could crochet circles around her. And before the end of the week, I could read every pattern that was out.

I lived with my foster parents until I went into nurses' training when I was about sixteen. But I never was strong, and nurses' training in those years, you had to do a lot of things outside just nursing. You had to clean rooms and you had to shake rugs and all that. The work was too hard and I had nose bleeds. Two different times I was bending over a patient and I spurted blood all over them. So I had to give it up. Then I went to business school in Kansas City, and I graduated as a stenographer. I worked at Wyatt Hardware store for maybe a year or two until I got married.

Helen and her husband faced some very hard times, but she recalled their years in Kansas with great warmth and happiness. Although she was still nervous about the interview process, as she started to reminisce about their early family life, she quickly warmed to the subject. Instead of tears, her account became punctuated with laughter.

I got married in November 1918. The boys were being drafted. My husband was deferred three times because he was a wheat farmer, but he thought he was to be called around November. Then they called it off—the war was over—so we went ahead and made plans to get married.

We lived in Wathena, Kansas. He bought a farm from his uncle. It was 160 acres and it had a house with big pine trees out in front. When the wind would blow, the pine trees'd sing. He was a wheat and corn farmer, and, of course, they raised some animals and stock, but not too much in that line.

During the peak of harvest, I would help. We didn't have private help. Neighbors helped each other in those days. They didn't put any money out. Wherever they were, whose farm they were working on, that was up to the housewife there to prepare the noon meal. I'd go help my neighbor, and they'd come and help me. Later on in years we hired a man.

I tried to make a little home. I had supposed everyone had to wash like my mother washed, with a big boiler on the stove full of water, and you had to bring it to a boil and you put soap and lye in it, and then you'd put your sheets and stuff in there to get them white. But my husband got this old washing machine. It was a hand-cranked thing. And then you'd hang the sheets out on the line and in the winter time they'd freeze stiff as a board. My husband wore long underwear and he'd go out and hang 'em up. You never saw such funny ways of hanging clothes as he'd hang 'em. And there'd be his underwear, just stiff as a board. Some experience, learning how to keep house!

My oldest daughter, Betty, was born there, a year after we were married. We didn't know nothing about birth control in those days; did what come naturally. Fifteen months after she was born, our son was born. He was born on the Keefer place. We sold the farm when Betty was about a year old and rented. I don't know how we managed to pay that; I suppose crop sharing or something. We moved into this big eight-room house, but we just lived in the downstairs.

My third, Shirley, was born in 1928, almost ten years after the first one. I'd had some misses in between, too. My babies were all born at home. I had a baby doctor—a pediatrician I guess you call them—from the big city, St. Joseph, Missouri. The lady that cooked our wedding breakfast was the midwife. She came out and stayed with us about the time the baby was going to be born. Then the doctor came out to the house and you had the baby.

I spent my time just taking care of the kids. It was really quite a chore to raise children. We lived in the country with the first two. We couldn't run to the doctor. You learned how to take care of your illness. Everybody seemed to have home remedies of some kind. They still call me Dr. Studer. They come all around the neighborhood: "Helen'll know what to do."

I learned to do my own sewing, and my babies had the prettiest clothes. I was creative in a way, 'cause I tatted a lot and I crocheted a lot. My first baby, she had tatting all over her clothes. Then, when the little boy came, they had brother-sister suits, in the same colors. When Shirley came along, why, she had all kinds of pretty handmade things, too.

I always enjoyed my children, and they were good children, very good. Like all kids, they'd get into mischief, you know.

It was a ritual. Sunday morning you go to church, either eight or ten o'clock. Then you go home and have dinner, and then you might go visitin' a relative or somebody'd come and visit you. During the week, it was a regular routine. You washed and ironed and you cleaned house and you scrubbed the floor every Saturday—whether it needed it or not.

When we lived out on this Keefer farm and Betty and Greg were little, we played cards one night a week. We'd gather up the neighborhood. We might have had as many as eight, maybe ten couples and we'd play pinochle. We'd always take our children with us, or whoever came to my house; we'd get them onto the bed and then we'd play. I had lots of friends, and then later on in years, we had a bridge club.

We'd have quiltings during the wintertime. We'd have it set up some place, the church or anyplace you could set up the quilt frame that wasn't too cold. There was a room upstairs over the Farmers State Bank in town that they would let us use it and it was heated. We would go up there and we'd quilt. When summer comes along you've got lots to do. I did lots of canning. My husband bought me a pressure cooker, a big one, and I would can asparagus, corn, peas. You had an awful lot to do on the farm.

Then, back in 1920, they had what they call a market crash. My husband had decided to raise hogs that year, 'cause the price of hogs was good and the price of corn and wheat was nothing. Three weeks before they were ready to go to market, the market crashed. We lost everything. All we had left was a little bit of broken furniture, two kids, and an old Model T Ford. So we moved into town, into a house up above my husband's sister that was vacant. We lived there for I don't know how long.

Then we stored what little furniture and stuff we had at my folks' place and we got our old Model T Ford rigged up and we went to Colorado. We stopped in Golden and visited some friends. And this old colored man that took care of these two old girls that was from Wathena told Daddy he could get him a job digging ditches for water pipes.

Golden is a college town, and you couldn't rent a house for love nor money if you had a child. So my husband told his boss that he'd have to give up the job because he couldn't find anyplace to live. His boss said, "Well, would you live in a tent? That's where we're living in now." They had this city ball park, and then the little creek run along the edge and it was quite flat ground in there. He said he had a sixteen-by-sixteen tent that he didn't use very often, and if we wanted we could take that and set it up out there. So we did and we had camp cots we slept on. The ground was hard and you could sweep it just like a hard floor. We stayed there until Labor Day; then it got cold.

We headed for California, but we got as far as the Birthed Pass and we met several cars coming back from California. They said they had the hoof-and-mouth disease out there so bad and that there was no milk for children. And, oh, they gave us these awful stories, so we got scared and headed back for Kansas.

We went on down as far as Canyon City, Colorado. It was right in the heart of apple-picking time, and they were paying fair wages for people to pick apples. So he got a job at this one orchard, and the man told him we could pitch our tent right in the orchard there. He picked apples high on a tree where he could climb, and I picked them from the lower parts. We made fairly good money there. Nothing exciting, but we went back to Kansas with a lot more money than we left with.

After returning to Kansas, the Studers moved into a house on her stepparents' land, and eventually when Helen's husband came into some money after the death of his parents, they picked up the payments. By then Bill Studer had gotten a job with an oil company as a maintenance man. Their financial situation improved, but it was hard on Helen because Bill was away for several weeks at a time, covering the territory of western Kansas and Missouri.

After Shirley was born, that was depression time. While my husband had a job, it didn't pay big, and he had this life insurance policy. It was just awfully hard to make ends meet to keep the policy going. And Wathena, Donothan County, is noted for apples and fruits of any kind: strawberries, blackberries, raspberries. And they had this big apple packinghouse. These apples run over a roller, come down this chute, and as they hit down this chute, why, then you sort out good ones from the bad ones. We started out working twenty-five cents an hour. Then the next year, the depression was worse and my pay dropped down to fifteen cents an hour. The last I worked for ten cents an hour. I never got any use out of that money, except I would take and apply it to the insurance payment so that we could pay off. Times were very hard in those days.

Actually, I went to work at the packinghouse against my husband's wishes. He was away and when he came home and I wasn't home, he didn't like it a little bit. He thought my place was home with the children. He said I didn't have to work. I said, "All the other girls were going: Constance was going down there and Hazel"—oh, about four of us neighbors. And I said, "Their husbands aren't objecting." So he sat there and thought about it, and he said, "Must be all right then." And after he realized that the children were well cared for, he didn't resent it anymore. Grandma Clark took care of them when they come from school till I got home from work in the evening.

My husband and I, we had very few arguments. I always figured marriage was a fifty-fifty proposition. We lived fifty-fifty. He was the head of the household and that, but didn't have control over me or anything like that. We were equal. And he always helped me whenever he was around. And I never had to ask him to do anything. He just automatically did what had to be done. I never picked up dirty clothes after my husband in my life, never. When he took a bath and changed his clothes, he always took them to the washing machine. He cleaned up the bathroom when he was through. When he took off his clothes, he hung them up.

I do remember this one time, though. This girlfriend of mine—we were girls together before we were married—always came over to Wathena and taught music. It was a lovely day and I said, "I'll come and get you." I never gave it a thought. My husband taught me to drive before we were married and I was a fairly good driver. But he did not want me to take the car by myself and go to town. Now why, I don't know, just masculine, I guess.

Anyway, I just run out and got the car and went to town. I never thought to leave him a note. On the way home come up a real hard rainstorm. Ooh! Well, there was just like a ditch on each side of the road and you had to turn sharp into our driveway. It was muddy and I kept slipping and sliding, but I finally got in.

Boy, was my husband mad. He was even nasty to Beulah. She stayed till when we went to church Sunday morning. Then I packed me a little bag and I went home. I told him, "You going to act like that, I don't need to be married." 'Cause I thought married life was a fifty-fifty proposition and I knew how to drive a car. I didn't think I had to ask permission.

Well, I don't know the times he called me for almost two weeks. By that time, I wanted to go home, too, so I went back. But I said, "We'll have an understanding. From now on, my name goes on the bank account the same as yours." 'Cause once he'd asked me to go to town to get some money to get something. Well, I went there and made a fool of myself, 'cause I couldn't get any money. I came home and told him. They sent a piece of paper home and he didn't sign it. I said, "You sign that piece of paper if you want me to come home so that I won't have to be embarrassed in front of the bankers that known me all my lifetime." Then I said, "Another thing, if I want to go to town for some reason, I'm going."

Well, then he got over all of this, see, and from then on there was never a more generous person in the world. He got over his being his own boss. See, he was twenty-nine years old when we were married, and he wasn't used to somebody. But after that little episode, why, that was the end of it.

After a lot of hard times, the Studers eagerly left Kansas to seek opportunity in the West. Helen's account of the war years and her job was frequently accompanied by the display of photographs and her carefully tended mementos.

My husband lost his job for the oil company. They had oil and they had filling stations, but they couldn't keep on that kind of help. He was a maintenance man and cleaned the glass [sic] tanks and anything else that had to be done. So he was out of a job and that was December 7th, 1941—Pearl Harbor.

In the meantime, I was corresponding with this uncle in Long Beach and also with my husband's brother that was in Bremerton, Washington. We were either going to Bremerton or Long Beach, where the war work was. They were building ships in Bremerton and in Long Beach, they were building ships and airplanes. Well, my husband's brother wrote about how bad the weather was there. So much rain, rain, rain. Out here the weather was so much nicer, although they did have earthquakes. So we came to California.

We had a 1940 sedan and we packed that up, loaded it to the

gills. We stored our furniture in the upstairs part of our house and
rented the lower part. We came out here in July of '42. My oldest
daughter, Betty, was working in St. Joseph. She stayed on there at
first, but as time went on she got lonesome and came out here and
got a job in the shipyard. Greg was already in the service. He was
going to Kansas University in Lawrence, Kansas, and was in his third
year. In June, instead of trying to keep up with school, he enlisted in
the air force. We had Shirley with us, and that was a very trauma [sic]
experience, to take her from her friends.

Everybody kept saying, "You're crazy to go to California across
that Arizona desert. It'll burn the tires off your car." Well, we started
out with canvas bags to put ice water in. Do you know where it was
the hottest? Coming across Kansas. When we hit Barstow, we went in
to have some dinner, and my husband said to the waitress, "Where
are we going to hit the desert where it's going to burn the tires off
our car?" She says, "Mister, you are in the heart of the desert right
now. It's 110 degrees right outside." We came to Long Beach, to my
Uncle Glen and stayed maybe a couple, three nights, and then we
found a little place to stay till we could rent an apartment.

It was probably the latter part of July or the first part of August,
we went down to Douglas to see if we could get a job. My husband
preferred I didn't work at Douglas, but on the other hand we needed
the money. We still had some bills back there in Kansas.

He went to work without any training, and I was with a group of
women that we went in training. There must have been forty or fifty
of us. Some trained for one thing, some trained for another. My education was limited, so I didn't try to go in for any office work. I went
into the industrial part of it. I really had no idea what it would be
like. I had never seen anything like that, you know. But it was really
exciting to see how they'd do all these things and fly in the air.

We were most all housewives that were doing this, and I felt that
I had just as much ability as the next one. I hadn't worked too much
out. I worked before I was married as a secretary, and then later
years, I worked at the apple house every fall. But that was the extent
of my working away from home. But I always felt that if you give the
best you have, you can do as well as the next one can. In fact, sometimes I think most of us housewives did better than a lot of the men
who were there, 'cause they'd goof off.

We didn't train in the plant; we trained someplace else. You had
classes and somebody'd be talking and get you familiar with what the
process was going to be. We didn't get right down to basic working

for, oh, probably three weeks or more. Then we went out to the plant.

I was awed, really awed. It is so huge. Well, you can imagine how big it would be to have that big airplane. And all these fluorescent lights. The place was just like daylight. Really, it takes you several hours almost to quit looking. I had never been inside anything like that. And the noise was absolutely terrible. There were times that the noise was just so bad, you'd have to really lay your tools down and walk outside. I wore earplugs a lot of times.

To begin with, you're issued a badge. You can't get in without it. You go through the tunnel, go through the gate, and if you have a lunch box, you have to open it so they can see what you've got in there. Then you go in and report to your particular spot where you're going to work. But the first day, nobody did anything but walk around and look. They gave you a list of what you have to have: a list of what is there that you work with that belongs to the company and then a list of things you have to buy or if you have them at home, bring.

I was going to work on the wing section; I was going to be a riveter or a bucker. The one that drove the rivets had to have the drill and a whole set of different-sized bits, 'cause you never knew what size you were going to use. I didn't do a whole lot of bucking because I wasn't that strong. They furnished you with a rivet gun, but you had to have your own drill, your own hammer, your own flashlight. Small things.

They assigned you your job according to what they thought you could do. My husband's cousin's granddaughter, she went to work out there at the same time. She didn't rivet, either. She got a job with inspection right off the bat. Young and beautiful, see. An old lady don't get anything like that. I was assigned to this wing section on the C-47. There was usually two of you paired together, and you stay with what you were doing, and then they'd have an inspector come along.

The men really resented the women very much, and in the beginning it was a little bit rough. You had to hold your head high and bat your eyes at 'em. You learned to swear like they did. However, I made myself stop because I don't think it's too ladylike. The men that you worked with, after a while, they realized that it was essential that the women worked there, 'cause there wasn't enough men and the women were doing a pretty good job. So the resentment eased. However, I always felt that they thought it wasn't your place to be there.

But some of the characters they had working there was just something else. We had a leadman and that was more or less a disaster. He was a young fellow, about the same age as my son who was overseas in the war—that was a primary reason to work, because I had a son that was in the service. Anyhow, this young fellow, they lived in Santa Ana and they were quite well-to-do people and his father bought him off. Got him a job in the defense plant so he was deferred. Boy, was he useless. He didn't know as much as we girls did. Time and time again, I've gone around the side of the plane, and he'd be sitting there playing mumblety-peg. And we women working our heads off! Just goes to show the politics.

Once in a while, when you buck a rivet and it bucks crooked, you had to take it out. Now that makes a bigger hole, so now you have to have a bigger rivet and that's where somebody comes along with their inspection. If they don't know what they are doing—I have seen some of those inspectors pass up two or three different times. I remember we deliberately left some that, when she got out of there, we knew we were going to replace them. She never even checked 'em. But some rivets were harder to buck than others, and if you don't get that bucking instrument set just right, it'll be crooked.

In my department there were at least four, maybe five of us that had been in the class together. There were some of them who went in training together that worked together, and we stayed together all while I was out there. You pick up good friends. I kept in contact, oh, I don't know how long. I remember there was one lady that was one of the ones that car-pooled. Her name was Iva. I talked to her on the phone one time, oh, I don't know how long ago.

There were black men in the area where I was, but I don't recall seeing any black women. They were there, 'cause I did see them going through the plant, but what they did, I don't know. We had some Mexicans, too. I remember we had this one little Mexican girl. She was kind of heavyset. She'd always bring this hot good stuff to eat. One day she had something, and I said I'd seen those things and wondered what they were. She said, "Well, tomorrow, I'll bring you one." She did and it must have been extra loaded with hot stuff, 'cause I took one bite and I like to—— Whew, I couldn't get my breath. Oh, it just tickled her to death.

The women I worked with was most all housewives. I don't know of anyone that I worked with that wasn't married. The only ones were these young girls that were inspectors and they didn't work; they walked around and looked pretty. This one, she'd walk around there with her mirror and her tight pants, tight tops. But they had a couple of them who were really good inspectors.

Helen, like most women riveters, started out at the basic rate of sixty cents an hour. The weekly check added up to a fair amount of money, including overtime and pay differentials for swing and graveyard shifts. It was more money than many workers had seen before, but wartime shortages and rationing usually limited their spending.

When we first started out, we was making around forty-five dollars a week; that's just a rough guess. Every so often we'd get an automatic raise. And, once in a while, depending on your foreman, different ones would be picked out and get a merit raise. I had a couple of those.

People didn't know what to do with their money when they were making so much. 'Course I came from the ridiculous to the sublime, 'cause we went through a depression in the thirties and we were in debt when we came out here. Between my husband and I, within a year we were out of debt. But I never squandered my money either.

Out in the parking lot at lunchtime or maybe you would have a fifteen-minute break, if there'd be a lineup, whatever that line was you went and got in it. You didn't know what you was going to get. I remember one time we got nylon stockings. But usually it'd be cigarettes. We all wanted to get in line for cigarettes, 'cause cigarettes were hard to get.

There was a little grocery store over near where we were, and the lady that runs the cash register—you know how you'll meet some people and you either clash or you blend somehow? Well, she and I got along beautifully. When I'd go to the grocery store, maybe once a week, whatever they would get in a good supply of, when my grocery sack went over the counter, she'd reach down and have another sack and that'd go over the counter. When I'd get home, I'd have three or four things on my bill that wasn't said out loud. I'd have a carton of cigarettes for myself and a carton for my husband. There might have been a couple of pounds of oleo or there may have been five pounds of sugar. I never knew what I was going to have. But the people that didn't work didn't get this privilege.

I worked nights because I had this daughter and I could be home when she'd come in. I'd get home probably between 7:30 and 8:00 in the morning, in time to do a few things around and then I'd go to bed. I was so tired and I'd sleep fifteen minutes and I'd wake up and think I'd slept for hours. I didn't sleep well in the daytime. But you just do your normal things that you have to do to keep your home up. I'd have washings to do, have ironing to do, cooking to do. You let a lot of other things slide.

Mostly we'd go to church Sunday morning and relax the rest of the time. Take a ride. We had gas rationing in those days, but being that we both worked, we had gas. We used to go to Redondo Beach. They had a place where you could buy smoked fish, and I'd take along some crackers and beer and we'd sit there and eat smoked fish and watch the birds and watch the ocean for a couple of hours. You couldn't go very far, 'cause you didn't have that much gas. Other than that, I don't really remember if we did much of anything. We had company come in now and then for a little dinner; not too often, he was too tired.

Like many graveyard-shift workers, Helen was not able to get enough sleep during the daytime. After about a year and a half, by which time her daughter was already fifteen years old, Helen switched to the day shift. Shortly afterward, she began to have problems with her right elbow.

I got so I just couldn't handle a drill. I really wanted to quit, but they won't let you quit, so I asked for a different job. They wanted to know what qualifications I had for something different. I wanted to be an inspector 'cause I knew the job from A to Z. But the inspectors were beautiful young girls. You hardly ever saw somebody that was older. And me, I didn't have any . . . I wasn't built like they were. Well, they said they didn't have an opening for an inspector, but they had a different job for me. Well, they handed me a broom. I said, "If I can't use this arm to do the work on that, I can't sweep with this arm."

I still wanted to quit, but they wouldn't let me, so I went home and I stayed. We didn't have telephones in those days, but my uncle still worked out there. They would get ahold of him to tell me to come in, that they wanted to talk to me. Well, I had a chip on my shoulder, 'cause I wasn't going to sweep the floor. I told him I'm not coming in. Finally my uncle told them he wasn't carrying any more messages back and forth. Well, they wanted him to deliver this one more: for me to come in; that they really thought they had something I could do. Well, I went in with my arm all bandaged up. I talked with this one man, and he would not come up with me to have a job of inspections. They'd give me something else. So I went home again.

Then they sent somebody to the house, so I went in. I didn't see the same man. When I walked in, of course, I had my Irish up, and he said, "Sit down, Mrs. Studer." I said, "Thank you, I'll stand." He said, "Oh, please, take this chip off your shoulder and let's talk reasonable." Well, he talked nice, so I sat down and talked. But I said, "I'm going to tell you before you start. You're not offering me any other job. I know what I can do and if you can't come up with a job of inspection, let's don't even talk about it." So he asked me this and he asked me that. Well, I give him a straight answer everytime, and he finally figured out I could do it. So they gave me a job of inspection.

I was on the job of inspection for a year and a half till I fell—by no fault of my own. I was inspecting on the platform when the bell rang for lunch, so you just let your things down right where you are. And once that piece is turned over for inspection the leadman or nobody has a right to touch it. When I came back from lunch I went up in there, and I had my little inspection mirror. I stepped up and just as I put my arms up, the platform gave way and I went down ten, twelve feet and landed on my feet. That darn near killed me. The leadman come arunning, "Oh, I thought I put that down right." Admitted right off. Come to find out what they did. One of the workman said he remembered there was something they didn't do, and before I got to it, it should be fixed. So that's why they took the platform out. And when they put it back they didn't put it back solid, see.

Well, I was pretty ill for quite a while, and the doctor said I couldn't go to work. Oh, I started flowing. I wasn't able to go back to work for a while, and they weren't going to pay me my wages or whatever it was called, so I got a lawyer. That's dumb! Douglas had lawyers. You're like a fly trying to swallow an elephant. So I didn't get anywhere with them. However, the judge did allow me six hundred or seven hundred dollars. It didn't amount to much, though. And my health was ruined 'cause I still lay the injury to my cancer operation in '51.

The Douglas plant in Long Beach had been organized in 1942 by the United Auto Workers. They might have assisted Helen in her fight to get disability, but she never joined the union and never sought their help. Like many of the housewives who took defense jobs, Helen did not think of herself as a permanent worker and did not see the need for a union.

I went back to work after I was able to. I probably worked for, oh, several weeks after the war was over. My son had been in the Hebrides Islands, and I remember that he was home on furlough. They came around and gave a list of everybody that was being laid off. But also there was a clause or something that said if anybody preferred to stay on that they would talk with them about it. So I had an opportunity to stay on if I would have wanted, but I didn't want to. A lot of them did. This one lady I know, she just retired about twelve years ago.

I was glad it was over. I wasn't working 'cause I wanted to. I was working 'cause I thought it was necessary. I thought, I'm going to stay home and be a housewife. My husband never wanted me to work in the first place.

But I felt I had accomplished quite a feat. I never was called on the floor for any work I'd done. I just learned the skill of doing what I was doing to where I figured I was just almost like perfection. This other girl and I worked together and we always bragged on ourselves. Nobody else would. You have to be pleased with yourself and know you've done a good job.

Around the home, you don't have anything to rivet, but I know all these things because it was the line of work that I was doing. I'd drill a hole in something if I can't pound a nail; drill a hole little so I can get the nail in. Oh, yes. This is my little saw. If a rivet or something just wasn't right and you had to saw a piece of metal or something, you had a little metal saw. And I used that, I couldn't tell you the times I used that. Still do. And just the other day I was out here using my drill.

I was happy to stay home and be a housewife. I still am. It was delightful to not be working. Things had got kind of shoved back and I was able to catch up then a little bit with that. And I sewed a lot for my girls and for myself. I made the mistake one time years and years before that making my husband a sports shirt, and I made the sleeves long enough. He always had trouble. If he got the collar big enough, the sleeves were too short. Well, anyhow, after that his good dress shirts, the boughten ones, laid in the drawer and he'd wear the one. So I made his shirts for years then. I enjoyed keeping up my home.

Then, about three years after the war was over, we bought a house. We had a little piece of property back in Kansas and I always wanted to buy something out here. He wouldn't stand for it. He said that he didn't want property in two places. Well, we sold the place back there, and I was afraid the money would get away so I stashed it in my name only so that nobody could check on it but me. Not that he would without my consent.

I kept telling him that I wanted a home. It was terrible living in an apartment. I just felt completely lost, like I was out in a desert somewhere; nothing to hold on to. We lived in the same apartment down on Mountainview from 1942 to 1948 and all I had to show was a little handful of pink rent slips. So when we got that money from selling our property back there, I said, "We're going to invest it in a home." He finally gave in. Well, he didn't want just a house with a little spot of ground. He was a farmer: he wanted ground around him where he could go out and spit and fart if he wanted to.

We bought this place in March of 1948 for $9,400. It's got two lots. Today it's worth a good $100,000. And I'm going to sit here.

My husband always maintained the yard and kept the trees trimmed. He loved to do that. He had his duties to do and I had mine. No argument one way or the other about it. Heavier things in the house to do, he'd always help me. If he needed help, he'd holler and I'd go out and help him a while. He had his roses and I had my other kind of flower.

Now you're coming to the arguments. Outside of a rosebush he couldn't tell a flower from a weed. And he'd be out there working in his roses and I'd have some flowers planted in there, and I'd go out there and they're all hoed down. I couldn't tell you the flowers he chopped down and then we'd get in an argument of it. When people tell me they've lived all their life and never had an argument, I wonder what's the matter with them.

We never argued about money because that's all we had and we had to make it do. He never was demanding of special clothes or anything, except his work clothes. It didn't make any difference what I did with the money. Of course, I'm not extravagant, but I do love to buy yarn and crochet and knit. He didn't care. I thought a man would raise the roof if you had all that yarn around, but not him. He was very even about it.

But there was one thing. He'd pout. He had a terrible case of pouting. He got over it as the years went on, but I learned to pout 'cause he did. If he wanted to pout, I'd pout with him. Then all of a sudden, it's all over with and you're back on easy street again. Nowadays, the young people that get in these kinds of arguments go get a divorce. We never thought of such a thing. You ironed it out over a period of time.

After the war was over and we weren't working, I had a couple or three different friends that we visited back and forth. One, I don't know whether she's still living or not, she lived over in El Monte. We'd go to their place for Sunday dinner and they'd come to our place for Sunday dinner for years. And I still have contact with two from Douglas. One, she lives right over here; she was in my work group. And then there was several others that, oh, we'd meet occasionally at the store or something.

And I played bridge. I got in with a group of girls that needed a substitute. That started probably in the latter part of 1942 and lasted up until about three years ago. There was twelve of us. Out of that group I couldn't tell you how many had passed away, 'cause we were down to one table. And then one of the girls had a terrible cancer operation and we've never played bridge since. That was just a church group.

I met a number of ladies through the church that we were very, very close friends. When I make a good friend, we're forever together. Like this Evelyn who worked for me so long. I met her at the bank the first month we moved out here, and we've been just real close friends ever since. She's the one that has cancer of the lung now very bad.

After recovering from cancer surgery in 1951, Helen resumed her active life. Then, in 1963, at the age of sixty-five, she began having health problems. Her husband had just recently retired, and they could not afford the regular vitamin shots she required. In characteristic fashion,

Helen arranged a work exchange with her doctor. At the time of the interview, she was no longer doing the paperwork she once did, but she continued to bottle pills.

After Helen was widowed, she gradually built a new life for herself, which included a Saturday night ritual of attending church with friends and "splurging at McDonald's for dinner." Up until her death, she maintained close ties with several women in the neighborhood and with her children.

My husband passed away the second of November in 1972. That was most undescribable—'cause he always was fairly active around. He never ran around any. A lot of times in the evenings, when I crocheted and whatever, he sat and watched television and smoked cigars. And he'd go to sleep. Pretty soon he'd wake up and he'd say, "Well, I sure haven't been any company to you tonight." And I said, "But I know where you are."

For a number of years after he died, it was awfully hard. That was before I got sense enough to learn that you could have company by having another widow in your same boots. You could get together and do something. Of course, I went to church activities as much as possible, but it got so we'd hardly go out at night unless there is a group of us.

Anyhow, after I fell and broke my back in 1976 or 1977, this friend, Evelyn Rosch, she came right over, and she's been with me ever since, until this deal come up with her for cancer. We had our evening meals together. She stayed in her home at night, but she would come here early in the afternoon and do yard work or housework or whatever. And I paid her. For a long time, she did the cooking, besides all the other work, until I finally was able to get up and around enough, and I decided I had to try to do something. It would be around 4:00 P.M. and I'd think, "Well, she had stuff sitting there to fix for dinner, I could do that." So I got to partly fixing the meals until, finally, I did most all the cooking and still do.

I don't have Evelyn anymore. But now this little neighbor down the street, she works and she's all alone. So she puts so much in the kitty each month and I do the cooking. I buy the groceries and stuff unless she decides to do something. That way we're not alone. We eat our evening meal together. Before that, I'd stand up there at the sink and eat a sandwich. Sometimes I'd make me a bowl of soup, or I might take my bowl of soup and my sandwich and go in and turn the television on and visit with Walter Cronkite. I would get sick spells, mostly 'cause I wasn't eating right. Now we eat right.

I see my son, Greg, more than I see the girls. He has seven units of apartments not too far from here, and he has to come down once a week to take care of things there. He works in Los Angeles at Prudential Life Insurance, a very responsible job. He is thinking of retiring after the first of the year when he'll be sixty. He's got hobbies and things, and I think it's a good idea if he wants to.

My younger daughter, Shirley, she's been working part time in the wintertime just to get out of the house, more or less—get away from twelve or fourteen loads of washing a day. She has four children, ten to twenty-one. And then the oldest one, Betty, lives in Baton Rouge, Louisiana. She had five sons and her husband is an engineer. All the boys except the youngest one, they've all graduated from Louisiana State University. I was down there last winter, and now they've sent me a round-trip ticket to come this winter. So I'll be down there about a month this year.

I have a very lovely three kids. They're just wonderful to me. I wouldn't want to live with any of them, as long as I can live here by myself.

Although Helen was strong willed and independent all her life, she revealed the same ambivalence about the contemporary women's movement that many of the women of her generation did—especially the women who, like herself, defined themselves as housewives.

I had a wonderful husband. He never pinned me down for anything. Well, in the very beginning, he didn't know how to cook or anything, but it didn't take him long to learn. But after that, after he got his eyes open, you couldn't have asked for a more wonderful person. But it took him about, oh, I'd say, right at a year of married life until he decided that there was another one besides him. Then, of course, as time went on, he turned to me for everything. It was more that, I would say, than that I turned to him.

So, never having experienced a lot of things those women that are doing a lot of this have, I don't agree with them. Well, I believe in part of what they're doing, but I think they're going at it wrong. For instance, I know there is a vast discrepancy in how they're paid for the quality of work they do. I know that. That, I think, should be changed. I don't think that should take an act of Congress to change it. There should never have been such a thing ever brought to mind about equal rights. It should have just been equal that way all along.

But there are certain things that men do and there's things that women do. God put us on earth for a certain thing. A man can't have a baby; he might could make it, but he can't have it. So what's going on? What's equal there? For instance, I have lots of work to be done around this place. I know how to do it and I know how it should be done, but I don't have the strength to do it, where a man does. If God had wanted us to have been a man, he would have made us a man. So there's lots of pros and cons.

But I feel sorry for women that have children that have to go out to work in order to keep their homes going. I really feel terrible about that, 'cause I think, in my estimation, a woman's place is in the home while the children are small. I was always there when mine came in from school and I think that means a lot to children.

There's a lot of things I don't agree with and there's some things I do agree with. But I guess the only way they're going to get them is like Carrie Nation with her hatchet—and get it, if that's the only way we can. Now, I thoroughly think if there is a woman capable of being president of the United States, she should be president of the United States. The fact of the matter is, I think they'd make a better president. If we run our homes like the government runs the government, wouldn't this be an awful world?

CHAPTER 9

Beatrice Morales Clifton

Beatrice Morales Clifton, 1986.

The changes started when I first started working. They started a little bit, and from then on it kept on going. Because after I quit the first time at Lockheed, I wasn't satisfied. I started looking for ways of getting out and going to work. See, and before I had never had that thought of going out.

Bea Morales Clifton is such an exuberant woman, she could be described as bubbly. Her words come rushing forth in a speech pattern that reveals her Mexican ancestry. Bea marvels at herself—at all that she has accomplished, at how much she has changed. Indeed, it was very difficult for me to imagine this confident, sociable woman as the timid, frightened homemaker who burst into tears the first few days on the job at Lockheed Aircraft some forty-odd years ago. Although Bea was not an embellisher, her habit of repeating phrases and her dramatic reenactment of dialogue made the story of her transformation convincing. For Bea, the entry into the defense job was the first step in this transformation.

Bea never fully conformed to the expectations for women of her era. For example, she married at fifteen, but when that marriage proved to be a disaster, after the

birth of her second child, she left her husband. Nevertheless, on the eve of the war, Bea was "just a mother of
four," a woman whose world had been largely circumscribed by men. She had never gone anywhere alone,
without a man, until the day she boarded the bus for her
new job at Lockheed. Although Bea surprised herself
when she defied her second husband and took the job,
her earlier determination to decide on her own future
showed that a spark was present. All that was needed to
ignite it was cultural permission—and the propaganda
mills that were busily convincing married women to take
defense jobs provided just that.

That first move, that crack in the door, expanded
Bea's horizons enormously. As a Mexican woman—that is
how women of Bea's generation refer to themselves—she
had lived in a tight ethnic community, her social activities revolving around the family and friends of her husband. At work, she rubbed shoulders with men and with
women of different ethnic groups. She made her own
friends, even though she did not see them outside the
job. They were white women—as she calls Anglos—as
well as Mexican. Later, after her return to Lockheed in
the early 1950s and after the death of her second husband, Bea married two more times—Anglo men whom
she met at work.

Bea Morales Clifton has come a long way from the
protected household in which she grew up in San Bernardino. Much younger than her three siblings, Bea was
raised practically as an only child and was admittedly
spoiled—perhaps strong willed is a more apt description.
Spurned by a high school boyfriend, at fifteen she married a man twelve years her senior and moved with him
to Los Angeles. By the time she left him at age eighteen
or nineteen, she was already the mother of two. Julio Morales, whom she married a few years later in 1935, was a
good husband, but very traditional. He objected to his
wife, by then a mother of four, taking a defense job. Although Bea initially defied him, she returned home when

one of her children became sick. Not satisfied with the old way of life, however, Bea tried several other jobs after the war, and in 1951 she returned to Lockheed Aircraft, staying until her retirement in 1978.

Today Bea lives in a house at the northern edge of the San Fernando Valley, an area of wide-open spaces that is still semirural. In fact, the sounds of goats, ducks, and chickens emanate from the large fenced backyard. A boat and camper parked in the yard testify to Bea's continued interest in the activities to which her third husband intoduced her. After four marriages, Bea is not soured on men. She shares her home with Manuel. Bea's two sons have been dead for many years (the older one was killed in an auto accident in the 1950s and the younger died in the late 1960s after open-heart surgery), but Bea is close to her daughters.

Although Bea and I immediately took to each other, I found it somewhat difficult to interview her. The first time we met, she was tightly wound like a spring. It was as if she had been waiting a long time to tell her story. The words came rushing forth, and I could barely ask a question. She spoke nonstop for almost two hours. At our second meeting, I mistakenly commented that there were some questions that I hadn't had a chance to ask. Bea seemed to take this offhand remark as a chastisement and initially held back. But her natural exuberance prevailed, and she was off and running. My head was spinning, barely able to keep up with her. When we seemed to come to a natural end and I had asked my last question, Bea commented, "I think I've blabbed everything that I know of." She then took me out to her backyard to watch her feed the goats and ducks.

Even though Bea thought she had "blabbed everything she knew," there were certainly a lot of things about Bea that *I* didn't know. I knew that she embroidered—the table we sat at while we recorded her oral history was covered with a hand-embroidered cloth; I knew about her animals; I knew that she doodled and that, had she been born in another period, she might easily have become a draftswoman. But, much to my chagrin, I discovered that Bea was also a ceramicist only after she was interviewed for a short television news segment on women defense workers. I was humbled by that discovery and was reminded, once again, that the oral historian's glimpse into someone's life is only partial.

Beatrice Morales (Clifton), ca. 1943.

My father's family was born in Mexico. They were from Durango. And my mother used to mention Paral and all them places in Mexico, so I guess that was the area, Chihuahua, that my grandmother and grandfather were from. My parents married in Mexico. My dad was a factory worker. He used to weave material for the textile mills. Supposedly he was a very good worker. The companies were always asking him to work for them. My mother was one of those workers, too, and that's how I think that they met. They had three children in Mexico, two girls and a boy. Later, on the change of life, I came.

They came here in 1912 or '13, right around the time of the Revolution. My mother used to say that it was so hectic. They would come around and say, "Who lives?"—Madero or whatever. If they didn't answer the right word, they'd shoot them. She was afraid that they would take my father into the army, 'cause there—it's not like over here—they make you. So that's how they more or less escaped.

My dad came to Texas and he started working for a rancher, an American man that had cattle. The ranch was in Marfa, Texas. We had a little house and the ranch owner, they had their house. The lady used to take one of my sisters and she'd have her do little chores around her house. My dad was very happy, but my mother kept on nagging him about getting over to California. She had brothers that were over here. My dad always used to say that if my mother had liked it, he would have stayed there and my brother would have been a good cowboy.

I remember we lived in 659 Harris Street when we came to San Bernardino. I was a little girl. It was a small house, two bedrooms. My mother didn't have gas until later; she used to have a wooden stove. It had a toilet, but no bath. My dad made a little shed, close to the house, with a shower. It was cold water. He took a tin can of sardines or something and he poked holes and soldered it.

There was a big tree in the back. This house used to belong to some old people, and they used to say that the tree had been planted by their daughter when she was little. My mother used to put her stove under the tree in the summertime. And my dad had a workbench. He was always busy doing little things. He always had a garden for my mother—corn and squash—and he used to plant a row of sugarcane for me. So I think that I was a little bit spoiled.

There was a little girl, Trini Gillien; we used to play. And then across the street, there was some colored people, Laura and Birdie, and I used to play with them, too. There was some colored boys up towards the other corner—their father was a fisherman—but I seldom played with boys. I'd play house and dolls and stuff like that. My dad had a little shack. It was supposed to be a woodshed, but I took it over and he fixed it up for me. I had my dolls and everything in there. I used to play a lot by myself.

Since neither Bea's mother nor her father learned to speak English, Spanish was spoken in the Morales home. Bea's two sisters, however, who were at least fifteen years older than she, and her brother, who was almost ten years her senior, all spoke English. As a result, Bea had little trouble with the language when she started school. Unlike Margie Salazar McSweyn and many young Mexican-American women of the period, she was not closely supervised.

After my second sister got married, then my oldest sister died and then my brother got married. So they used to do things for me. My father with the little check that he used to get, I don't know how they managed. Wages were low, but things were cheap, too. So they could afford to give me little luxuries. Maybe a new little dress once in a while.

My brother would ask me—on weekends I'd go visit him—"You got money for the show?" I'd say, "No." I never admitted I had money. So he'd give me a quarter and that was a big deal. Then I had an uncle, a cousin [of] my father. I used to go visit him, too. Every Saturday I used to go and make the rounds. He'd ask me if I have money to go to the show. "No." So he'd give me a quarter, so I'd get maybe a couple of dollars for the week. And I used to go to school, and I'd have chocolate bars and everything else, which some of the kids couldn't afford.

I didn't have no particular friends, just the girls we saw at school. I didn't have anybody coming to my house. When I went to the movie, I'd meet some other girl that I knew and we'd meet the boys in there. I was pretty young when I had a boyfriend, Alfonso Ortiz. He was about seventeen and I was maybe thirteen. We went together for about two or three years. I went to school and he was working as a janitor in the school. Afterwards, he got little jobs. I wanted to get married, and he couldn't get married because he was making only twelve dollars. He had more sense than I had. But I was determined that I wanted to get married. We got into an argument, and this time I goofed. I went and got married with the first man that came along.

He came around selling tonics. The night that he came back, my mother wasn't there. I was standing outside, and he said he would like to see me sometime. That's how it all began. Right away I went and got married. I knew him just a month or two.

His name was Luis Escobosa, a Basco; real light complected. He was twenty-seven years old when he signed the marriage license. I was fifteen. I was supposedly to have a big wedding, but his family started taking me to those cheap little bargain stores to buy me stuff. I was spoiled and I didn't like that, so I told him, "The heck with it. Let's go get married just like that." So we took off and went to San Francisco and got married.

The next year, I got pregnant. That's the first thing that comes at that time. You know it isn't like today that you can plan things like that. At that time, at least me, I didn't know anything.

There were hints of both sadness and anger in Bea's voice as she spoke about this period in her life. She didn't want to linger on the topic and instead moved the discussion along very rapidly, providing only a bare-bones description of her short-lived marriage to Luis Escobosa.

I hardly was ever with my husband because he was a salesman. He was always out of town. When my son was born, he saw him three months later, 'cause he was up in Arizona. And he was one of those guys that had a woman in every port. But I didn't know about that. He would be gone for very long stretches, and he'd leave me with his mother, stepfather, and three sisters in Los Angeles, without any money. There I was stranded. I got to be real bitter.

He'd come and go, come and go. Then I got pregnant again with my daughter. I was constantly fighting with him because of money. At the same time that I was pregnant with my daughter, he had a woman—another sixteen- or fifteen-year-old girl. He had taken her from Riverside to Mexicali and was living out there in Mexicali with her. She was pregnant, too. I was desperate, so I got his clothes and took them into the kitchen, and I was searching to see if he had money and I found this letter from the girl to her mother.

My husband's mother hush-hushed everything; she was going to take care of everything. I told her, "You take care of everything all the time. What the heck." Then he told me, "Well, why don't you divorce me? You know how I am. I'll pacify her. I'll go on with her, and then I'll come back to you." I told him, "Oh, you're a scum. I hope they put you in jail." So things were not good.

Then when I was in the hospital having my baby, the social worker came around. I didn't want to go back to them, so the county fixed it up so that I could have a little house when I got out of the hospital. They gave me clothes for my little boy and clothes for my little baby.

So I went to live in my little house. But I didn't know anybody there. The only thing was that the landlady was very nice, and I used to talk to her. That was all. She was a white lady. My life, it was kind of alone all the time. I used to get up early and walk to Los Angeles and come back.

My husband kept coming around. I said, "No, I don't want no part of you." We kept arguing and fighting. That lasted for about a year or so, and finally I said, "This is it, no more." So I quit him. Then my folks came to live with me. Later, I divorced him. I didn't know how I was going to manage. When I was separated, I was trying to get jobs, but they just had these jobs like bartending.

So then this man came up, this friend that knew us from way back. He would come around and take my mother to see my sister at the TB sanitarium. Sometimes I'd come along with them. That's how it started. Then he told me that he wanted to marry me. I said yes because I figured that I had to have some support for my kids. I figured he was a good man and he had a job. During the depression, he always worked. I wasn't crazy in love or none of that stuff, but I liked him. He was older, maybe thirty years old, and a bachelor. So I got married with him in '34 or '35.

Bea was twenty years old when she started married life with Julio Morales. Julio did janitorial work in theaters in the Pasadena area. Within a couple of years, Bea and Julio had a daughter, Julie, and a son, Genaro. Bea's life revolved around her immediate family and an extended circle of friends.

Bea and Julio lived with their four children and Bea's parents in a large house in Pasadena. Bea's two children from her previous marriage didn't know their biological father. When they were older, Bea told them about him and allowed them to choose their own surname. They considered Julio their father and adopted his name.

Julio was a good provider. We'd buy groceries and whatever it was supposed to be. But with the children, he never interfered. He would tell me alone, "You're being too hard with them." But we got along perfect. He never beat up on my children or anything like that. I was the one that tightened the rein. I used to be real strict. I was the type of person that went to visit people and I would take my four little ones. But they would sit down. If they started moving, I'd say, "Gerry" or "Mary" and they knew what I meant, so they sat right back and the stayed put. Everytime we went out, before we left, I said, "Go to the bathroom, drink water, do everything that you've got to do now because you're going to behave." We'd go to the movie house and the same thing. Not that I'm bragging or anything, but they were pretty good kids.

We used to come to Los Angeles to see Julio's mother, see my sister. There was a little area there that all the family lived together in East Los Angeles, near Evergreen. We used to sometimes go out on parties and I always had parties in my house: birthday parties or Christmas parties or Thanksgiving parties. I had a lot of friends by that time. Julio had a friend that he had known for years and he brought these other people, and we got real close and they would bring other people.

After Pearl Harbor, we moved to 214 Pasadena Avenue. They took a lot of Japanese away, and they left a lot of houses. But I had a lot of trouble because they wouldn't rent to me because I was a Mexican. They'd tell it to my face. That used to make me feel kind of bitter. One time, one of them told me, "Why don't you say you're Italian? You could pass." But finally I got this house, that was a pretty good size. There was blacks and there was white, Mexicans, and I guess over there on Pasadena Avenue there must have been quite a few Japanese people. All these people owned their house, but I didn't own mine.

I'd never thought about working. My brother at that time had separated from his wife, and he had an adopted girl. His wife remarried and the stepfather didn't like the girl. We considered that girl like ours because my mother had gotten her when I was a kid. She used to take care of children from the Welfare, and she got that baby when she was six months old. She gave it to my brother because he didn't have no children. He brought that girl to me and says, "I'll have her stay with you and I'll give you some money every week." She was sixteen or fifteen and she wanted a job.

They had these offices everywhere in Pasadena, of aircraft. I went in there to try and get her something, but they said, "We've got aircraft work right now for everybody, except she's too young." He says, "Why don't you get it?" I said, "Me?" He said, "Yeah, why don't you get the job?" I said, "Well, I don't know." But the more I kept thinking about it, the more I said, "That's a good idea." So I took the forms and when I got home and told my husband, oh! he hit the roof. He was one of those men that didn't believe in the wife ever working; they want to be the supporter. I said, "Well, I've made up my mind. I'm going to go to work regardless of whether you like it or not." I was determined.

My family and everybody was surprised—his family. I said, "Well, yeah, I'm going to work." "And how does Julio feel?" "He doesn't want me to, but I'm going anyway." When he saw that, he just kept quiet; he didn't say no more. My mother didn't say nothing because I always told her, "Mother, you live your life and I live mine." We had that understanding. When I decided to go to work, I told her, "I'm going to go to work and maybe you can take care of the children." She said, "Yeah."

The intensity of emotions Bea felt on that day some forty years ago when she first walked through the doors of Lockheed was communicated through her demeanor as well as her words. She crouched in mock meekness and whispered hesitatingly, feigning fear.

I filled out the papers and everything and I got the job. Why I took Lockheed, I don't know, but I just liked that name. Then they asked me, "Do you want to go to Burbank, to Los Angeles?" I said, "I don't know where Burbank is." I didn't know my way around. The only way that I got up to Los Angeles was with Julio driving me there. I said, "Well, Los Angeles. The streetcar passes by Fair Oaks, close to where I live, and that drops me off in front."

To me, everything was new. They were doing the P-38s at that time. I was at Plant 2, on Seventh and Santa Fe. It was on the fifth floor. I went up there and saw the place, and I said, "Gee——." See, so many parts and things that you've never seen. Me, I'd never seen anything in my whole life. It was exciting and scary at the same time.

They put me way up in the back, putting little plate nuts and drilling holes. They put me with some guy—he was kind of a stinker, real mean. A lot of them guys at the time resented women coming into jobs, and they let you know about it. He says, "Well, have you ever done any work like this?" I said, "No." I was feeling just horrible. Horrible. Because I never worked with men, to be with men alone other than my husband. So then he says "You know what you've got in your hand? That's a rivet gun." I said, "Oh." What could I answer? I was terrified. So then time went on and I made a mistake. I messed up something, made a ding. He got so irritable with me, he says, "You're not worth the money Lockheed pays you."

He couldn't have hurt me more if he would have slapped me. When he said that, I dropped the gun and I went running downstairs to the restroom, with tears coming down. This girl from Texas saw me and she followed me. She was real good. She was one of these "toughies"; dressed up and walked like she was kind of tough. She asked me what was wrong. I told her what I had done and I was crying. She says, "Don't worry." She started cussing him. We came back up and she told them all off.

I was very scared because, like I say, I had never been away like that and I had never been among a lot of men. Actually, I had never been out on my own. Whenever I had gone anyplace, it was with my husband. It was all building up inside of me, so when that guy told me that I wasn't worth the money Lockheed paid me, it just came out in tears.

At the end of that first day, I was so tired. I was riding the streetcar and I had to stand all the way from Los Angeles clear to Pasadena. When I got home, the kids just said, "Oh, Mom is here." My husband, he didn't have very much to say, 'cause he didn't approve from the beginning. As time went on, his attitude changed a little, but I don't think he ever really, really got used to the idea of me working. But he was a very reserved man. He wasn't the type of guy that you'd sit down and you'd chatter on. Like me, I'm a chatterbox. You had to pull the words out of him.

As Bea described her initiation to her sixty-five-cents-an-hour assembly job, her tone of voice slowly changed. The hesitancy that had reflected her sense of awe and fear as she faced this new experience was replaced with a more forceful delivery that displayed her increased confidence and pride.

They had a union, but it wasn't very strong then. It wasn't like it is now. But I joined. I joined everything that they told me. Buck of the Month, everything. And they gave me a list of the stuff that I would be needing. At that time they used to sell you your tools and your toolboxes through Lockheed. So I bought a box. I bought the clothing at Sears. It was just a pair of pants and a blouse. To tell you the truth, I felt kind of funny wearing pants. Then at the same time, I said, "Oh, what the heck." And those shoes! I wasn't used to low shoes. Even in the house, I always wore high heels. That's how I started.

As time went on, I started getting a little bit better. I just made up my mind that I was going to do it. I learned my job so well that then they put me to the next operation. At the very first, I just began putting little plate nuts and stuff like that. Then afterwards I learned how to drill the skins and burr them. Later, as I got going, I learned to rivet and buck. I got to the point where I was very good.

I had a Mexican girl, Irene Herrera, and she was as good a bucker as I was a riveter. She would be facing me and we'd just go right on through. We'd go one side and then we'd get up to the corner and I'd hand her the gun or the bucking bar or whatever and then we'd come back. Her and I, we used to have a lot of fun. They would want maybe six or five elevators a day. I'd say, "let's get with it." We worked pretty hard all day until about 2:00. Then we would slack down.

I had a lot of friends there. We all spoke to each other. Most of them smoked, and we'd sit in the smoking areas out there in the aisle. Then, some of the girls—on the next corner there was a drugstore that served lunches. There was a white lady, she used to go, and Irene would go. We'd talk about our families and stuff like that.

Irene stayed on that same operation. I don't know why I got a chance to learn all the other jobs, but I learned the whole operation until I got up to the front, the last step. They used to put this little flap with a wire, with a hinge. I had to have that flap just right so that it would swing easy without no rubbing anywhere. I used to go with a little hammer and a screwdriver and knock those little deals down so that it would be just right. That guy that I used to work with helped me, teached me how to do it, and I could do it just like him.

New people would come in, and they would say, "You teach them the job. You know all the jobs." Sometimes it would make me mad. I'd tell them, "What the heck, you get paid for it. You show them the job." But I would still show them.

Then, like that leadperson, they'd say, "Look at her now. You should have seen her a year ago when she first came in. You'd go boo and she'd start crying. Now she can't keep her mouth shut." I figured this is the only way you're going to survive, so I'm going to do it.

I was just a mother of four kids, that's all. But I felt proud of myself and felt good being that I had never done anything like that. I felt good that I could do something, and being that it was war, I felt that I was doing my part.

I went from 65 cents to $1.05. That was top pay. It felt good and, besides, it was my own money. I could do whatever I wanted with it because my husband, whatever he was giving to the house, he kept on paying it. I used to buy clothes for the kids; buy little things that they needed. I had a bank account and I had a little saving at home where I could get ahold of the money right away if I needed it. Julio never asked about it. He knew how much I made; I showed him. If there was something that had to be paid and I had the money and he didn't, well, I used some of my money. But he never said, "Well, you have to pay because you're earning money." My money, I did what I wanted.

I started feeling a little more independent. Just a little, not too much, because I was still not on my own that I could do this and do that. I didn't until after. Then I got really independent.

Although Julio had originally opposed her going to work, he and the children pitched in to do the household chores, along with Bea's mother, who also provided child care during Bea's work hours. Still, Bea, like most working mothers, was ultimately responsible for keeping her household running smoothly and caring for her children.

Like so many homemakers, Bea was able to deviate from her traditional role because her work was viewed within the context of patriotic duty. Few of these working mothers, however, were ready to openly challenge conventional values. When there was a family crisis, they were likely to quit their job in order to take charge at home. As a result, the absenteeism and turnover rates were high among such women.

I got home and my mother told me, she says, "Gerry is very sick. He's got a lot of fever and it won't go down." I never thought of having a family doctor, so I had to call the police station and they sent me this doctor that was real nice. He started giving him shots and that's what brought him out. It was pneumonia and he was very sick for quite a long time.

My husband, right away, he jumped: "You see, the kids are like this because you're not here." My mother was there, but he blamed everything on me. We got into a little bit of an argument on account of that, and then I said, "Okay, I'll quit." I didn't want to, but I said my boy comes first. Afterwards, I realized I could have gone on a leave of absence. But I wasn't too familiar with all that, so I just panicked and quit.

When I quit, I just took over the same as I was before—taking care of my kids. Well, it was kind of quiet and I wasn't too satisfied. That's why I started looking to go to work. I had already tasted that going-out business and I wasn't too satisfied. I stayed home about a year or so, and then I took a little job at Joyce; they used to make shoes. It was walking distance from where I lived. I would get the packages of leather already cut and mark the shoes with a marking machine and put them in pairs and put them on the belt so the stitchers could sew them.

I worked there about a year. Then my husband told me, "Well, if you're going to be working, why don't you work with me?" There was this man that got sick—he was a janitor—so they gave me his theater. My husband would help me. He would get the biggest mopping and the windows. I would do mostly the auditorium—sweep it and vacuum. We would do his job and my job together. They were giving me a hassle. It was union and they didn't want me to join the union. I would be working on a permit with the union, and I said, "Well, if I can work on a permit, why can't I work as a member?" I finally said, "Look, go jump in the lake." So I quit.

I was already thinking of Lockheed. I wasn't satisfied. I felt myself alone and I said, "Oh, I can't do this; I can't stay here." In 1950 I wrote to Lockheed asking them if they had a job for me because I knew that they were still taking people. They wrote and told me that they weren't taking any women, but that they would the following year. The next year, the minute I received that telegram, I headed for Lockheed.

I went to the office all ready. This was in Burbank. They give you a list of rides and stuff and that's how I started—riding with people from Pasadena. I think they started me at $1.65, or something like that. Riveting. We were working on the side panels of the T-33.

It wasn't like it was before because I already knew a little of it, so it wasn't as hard. I was working two months when they told me, being that I was new I had to either go on nights or I'd be laid off. So I told them, "I'll go on nights!"

Then, you see, if you knew blueprints, it would help in your job. I figured sooner or later I might need this. This friend of mine—she lived around where I lived in Pasadena and she was a black lady—she was going to Frank Wiggins School, and she told me, "How about it, do you want to go?" We were working nights, so we'd go to school in the morning and we'd get out of there about 1:00 or 1:30, and we'd go have lunch and then we'd go to work.

When Bea returned to work in 1951, her two youngest children were old enough to look after themselves. Still, her schedule was hectic. Julio had become sickly, suffering from heart trouble, and Bea had to help him with his job cleaning the theaters. In early 1953, he died.

It affected me pretty bad because I was left alone. Geno was already in the seminary. I just had Julie with me. She was fifteen, and then after he died she got married and I was left alone. I didn't know just what the heck I was going to do. I moved to the Valley to be closer to my job.

So then, when I was left alone I married my leadman, Frank Jones. I don't like to do alone. When I married Frank, I told him "I've always wanted to buy a house." We could have done it because I was making that little money and things were not that expensive, but Julio wouldn't hear of it. So Frank said, "Well, we'll buy a house." I had a little bit of money that I had from Julio when he died; they give you lump sum from the Social Security. So we put that and then he put some more and then we borrowed. That's how we got the house.

When I married Jones, things changed completely, from day to night. The first thing he did was show me how to drive a car. He said, "You have to learn because you need to have a car to get yourself to work and places." Then he took me to a lot of places. He showed me how to do fishing; he showed me how to go camping—stuff that I had never done in my life. All that stuff that I love now, he taught me how to do all that. My oldest daughter, she says, "Well, that's one thing that we can thank Frank for, because he got you out of that— that you didn't know anything."

All the things we did, we did them just him and I. We went camping, we went to Vegas, we went everywhere. We got along very well. But he resented my kids. At the time that I fell for him and married him—because I fell in love with him and I was crazy about him—I didn't realize it. My kids never did anything with him. They weren't here. Geno lived with me just for a while, not very long. He got out of the seminary. They told him that being that he had heart trouble, they didn't want to take that responsibility. So he came here and went to high school in San Fernando, and then when he was nineteen, he graduated and he got married.

Frank and me, we got along perfect, but then all of a sudden something got into him. When he started tasting supervision at Lockheed, he thought he was too great and that I was nothing. He started working vacations of the supervisors and stuff like that until, finally, as years went on, he ended up in a position of supervision. But he always thought, I guess, that I wasn't good enough for him. I never dreamt that he was like that until afterwards. I guess I was so crazy about him that I overlooked all that in the beginning. We were married about fourteen years. When this happened, that he wanted out, it tore me up very bad, because I was so crazy about him. I thought I was going to die. I lost weight. I went to 118 pounds. Then I started drinking. Finally I said, "No, this cannot go on." So I snapped out of it.

Then I had another leadman, [John] Clifton. He was real nice to me, and I used to tell him my problems. He had never been married. So he told me that he'd like to marry me. I said okay. Frank was coming around, coming around. He wanted me to go back to him. I knew that I would probably eventually weaken and go back to him, and I didn't want that. So I think that I married on the rebound. That's one bad thing that I did. John was a nice guy. I cannot say anything bad about John. He was very thoughtful and very kind with me. But his family didn't quite agree. His sisters, I think that they're a little bit prejudice. I don't think that they like Mexican people. We couldn't make it, so we finally split up.

Bea continued to work at Lockheed and moved up the occupational scale. The competency she demonstrated when she worked during the war continued to serve her well. She enjoyed her work, and her foresight in taking the blueprint classes when she first returned to Lockheed eventually paid off.

I first started with riveting, and then there, in that department, they started putting me towards "final," where you get to inspection. Then, afterwards, they changed me to another department where I worked in small parts. When they started building the 104, they said they wanted me to try the 104. The man in the office there told me, "I see here that you took blueprint, advanced and beginners. I want you to try it." I said, "I took blueprint, yeah, but I've never worked with blueprints because there's no blueprints around here." He says, "It's true, but I want you to try it."

So then I went into the line. They had the airplane already built and we would put parts on it. I used to spread my blueprints, and I'd tell the inspector, "Look, here's that part there and this is right there and this is right there." That's how I started working with my blueprints. I think it was in the sixties or something like that when they started building the 104.

I worked on the 104 for a long time; then they stopped building it and they put me in the paint shop. I said, "Why do you put me in the paint shop? Send me someplace." He said, "No, because we're going to be building a few 104s and we want to have you right there where we can get ahold of you." They changed my classification, and I did not even know it until one day I was talking to a foreman. He told me, "Well, we had to do some changes to keep you here because other people would find out and wonder." I didn't have the classification to be up there, but they wanted me. If the company wants you, they'd do anything.

I was supposed to identify parts. They'd bring out trays full of little parts, big parts, different parts, and I'd identify them and then package and sell them to the inspector. The inspector would come and check them and see if they were good, and then they'd put their stamp—and that is that they're "sold."

Afterwards, they opened Department 24 and took me off of the paint shop and brought me there. I was told to set up my area. I got blueprints of all the jobs that were going to be coming in. I opened my blueprints and I'd check the list of what parts were going to be needed and I ordered them. I had pans on the walls, full of all the screws that were going to be taken for that job. This order needs so many screws, so many rivets, so many of this. I would put it into the job, and when the guy got it in blueprint, all he had to do was just open his blueprint and start working.

I was there for maybe a year until they got going; then they made me a leadperson. I had maybe forty-five or fifty people, about half and half men and women. That was in the early seventies and I did that until I retired.

In this last job that I had, I was very conscious [sic] of my job. I always tried to get my work out. I could not see orders laying around. They would have these "flag orders": there was an airplane on the ground waiting for parts. Well, that's the first operation I would take. I would try to find my parts, even if I had to go steal them from downstairs in the parts control. If I needed a certain length of a screw that I didn't have or anything like that, I'd call them up and I said, "Hey, I'm in trouble. I need so many of this, so many of that. Look them up in the plans and see if you can find them for me." And they would get them for me. I'd do likewise, you know. I would help them because they would help me.

The last year as lead, I used to go in sometimes on Saturdays. My foreman would give me a list of orders that were lost, and he had to make a report on that. He could depend on me. I'd find those orders, whether they were lost or what. I'd have an answer on his list everytime. I used to really take pride in my job which, sometimes, it don't pay because they don't appreciate what you do. They think that you do things like that because you're dumb. But that's just the way I was. Now, I hear that that area where I was, orders are all over scattered. Nobody gives a darn for anything. I used to fill the mercuries—they had like a platform with wheels and a handle—with orders and I'd push them. Now, I went up there one Christmas and three or four women were pushing one!

But I've got no beef against the company; they treated me all right. Outside, you can get a good-paying job if you're trained for something high. But Lockheed, I've always said that Lockheed is the highest paid place for women to make the money, women that don't have experience of anything. Where other places do you find a woman that makes eight or nine dollars just for riveting and stuff like that? You find women that make probably more, but they have to be trained to have a better position.

Bea retired in 1978. The camper and boat parked in her backyard are a clue to some of her postretirement activities. Bea also stays busy taking care of her barnyard animals, embroidering, and making ceramic vases and sculptures. She also spends time with her two daughters, her only relatives still living.

I always said that I was going to retire when I'd be sixty-two. I said, "I want to be able to do things when I get out of here. Not get out of here all crippled up or old and everything else." A lot of people there, they'll be there until they kick them out, and then they get out and in about a year or two they die.

It feels good to be retired. I don't have to get up early in the morning, rain or shine, and punch in a clock. Though, sometimes, it's a little bit lonely. But if it gets where the walls are closing in on me, I get in my car and go up to town and go have a sandwich or a hot dog or something like that and walk around town, and then I come back home.

I don't like being alone. That's why I got Manuel here. I'm not crazy about Manuel. I like him, but like I say, the only person that I ever felt in love, that really hurt me, was Frank Jones. But with Manuel, he's company. We go out places; we go fishing; and we go sometimes to parties and stuff like that.

I'd like to find me a rich—well, not rich, but at least they'd have a little money—little old man that would be retired. He would be like me, and I can go places with him. See, Manuel ties me down. He's quite a little ways from retirement; he's only fifty. I can't very well leave the house and go places. I feel that I should be here when he comes—give him his food and stuff like that. But it's not right. He's holding me down.

But every chance that I have, I go up to Monterey and see my daughter. I fly over there and I take my little dog with me. I spend a week or two weeks and then I come back. I'd drive, but my daughter gets all out of shape. Sometimes when my other daughter, Julie, has time, we drive up there. But she works in a nursery and she only has maybe one or two days off.

One of the daughter-in-laws is pretty close, too, the mother of these kids of my son. She remarried after he died and her husband treats me as if I was his mother. He comes around—"Grandma" this and "Grandma" that. So we go out with them sometimes or we go camping with them. Manuel gets along very well with him. The other daughter-in-law, I don't see her very often. I don't see my grandkids very often, either.

Both my daughters, I was just hoping that they would have a happy life, that they'd find them a good man, which my oldest daughter didn't. She's alone right now. She's been alone for several years. But Julie married this Mexican boy after her father died and she's still with him. She's got seven children.

I would have liked for both of them to have gotten a good education, but they didn't want to. Now I imagine that they're sorry they didn't. Like Mary Lou's daughter, she's fifteen years old. She says, "Grandma, I want to get a good education. I want to be a doctor, but," she says, "Grandma, I just love to cook and I want to be a cook, too." I said, "Well, be a cook then. Take that up. Cooks make a lot of money." She's very ambitious on doing something. She says, "I don't want to be like mother, working the way she does." She does housework to support herself because she's got no other means.

In closing, I asked Bea her feelings about the women's movement and if she were a young woman starting out today what she would do. She laughingly replied that she'd probably do it all over again—except maybe not get married at fifteen. Like so many working-class women of her generation, one of Bea's major regrets is her lack of education. Bea now says she would have liked to have been something like a draftsman [sic], recalling how she used to draw blueprints in her childhood.

I wouldn't want to lose my identity as a woman. I wouldn't want a man to treat me like a man, to say, "You go dig ditches. Because I dig them, you go dig them, too." There are a lot of things that a woman can do—and good—but to lose your identity completely, I just can't see that.

My life, it was changed from day to night. I'm not the person that I started when I first married Julio. The changes started when I first started working. They started a little bit, and from then on it kept on going. Because after I quit the first time at Lockheed, I wasn't satisfied. I started looking for ways of getting out and going to work. See, and before, I had never had that thought of going out.

CHAPTER 10

Marie Baker

Marie Wright Baker, 1986.

*I needed a job because I was going to be
very independent. I wasn't going to ask
for any alimony or anything. I was just
going to take care of myself.*

Those simple, decisive words of Marie Baker, spoken in
retrospect, mask how insecure she really was when she
left her husband and took a war job. The thirty-year-old
mother of a ten-year-old daughter, Marie had not worked
outside the home since high school, nor had she ever
been on her own. But the wartime jobs in Los Angeles
provided an opportunity for her to make her move. It did
more than that. As she tells it, she was transformed from
a Caspar Milquetoast into a self-confident woman proud
of the physical competence she displayed as an aircraft
worker.

A lively, curious woman who looks almost fifteen
years younger than her seventy-odd years, Marie is now
very comfortable with herself and her world. Seated in
the upstairs den of her suburban home, Marie was
pleased to be telling her story. Not only is she proud of
her own individual accomplishments, but she has a sense
of the importance of her story for understanding women's
history—an idea fostered by her younger daughter, who
has been studying and teaching women's history. The

wartime photographs and memorabilia Marie had saved—including her achievement pins from North American and a ration card—testified to how important this period was for her. This was confirmed by her excitement as she talked about those years, frequently punctuating her account with laughter.

The third of eight children, Marie faced economic hardship as she was growing up in San Francisco. She had few plans or goals for herself. An incurable romantic, she fell in love with her first husband when she was in her early teens. They married when she was nineteen and settled in the desert area of the Antelope Valley, about sixty miles outside of Los Angeles. Marie busied herself in the usual round of domestic activity and was a "typical housewife" until she left her husband and went to work at North American Aircraft in 1942.

By the end of the war, Marie had met her second husband, and they were married shortly before the war's end. She quit her job to join her husband, who had been given a teaching assignment in San Bernardino. Essentially, Marie settled back into domesticity, especially after she and her husband returned to Los Angeles and she started a second family. To help buy a family home, she returned to work at North American in the early 1950s. Although she enjoyed the job, her work interfered with family life and she quit, eventually pursuing a longtime ambition to become a beautician, a trade she still practices today. In fact, Marie's clientele carefully followed the progress of her wartime saga and were delighted when a brief television news clip with Marie was photographed in the shop.

Marie symbolizes for me the underside of women's history. On the surface, she seems to have made all the "right" choices and lived out her life as a woman of her generation was supposed to do. She did her bit for the war, but gladly returned to domesticity. In later years, she chose a traditional woman's occuapation, beautician. Her life revolved around her family, and she prided herself on her domestic skills, sharing the products of these with others. Yet, beneath the surface, Marie is a woman who came into her own. Deciding to leave her first husband was the first step. And once she went to work at North American she gained increased control over her life. Although the options available to women were contained within narrow cultural boundaries, Marie maneuvered within those boundaries and made active choices. She is aware of that fact and that is why her oral history was so important to her.

My father's mother was a very clever artist, taught piano, and gave painting lessons. She lived mostly in San Francisco and was there during the earthquake. So was my father. My grandmother had a shop, and, of course, it was destroyed, so my grandmother, my father, and his brother lived in Golden Gate Park—which was a sand dune at that time—for three weeks, I think, in a tent. Then she moved to Vallejo.

That was fun because there used to be a ferry that went from San Francisco to Vallejo, and it took an hour and forty-five minutes and it went past Alcatraz. And my grandmother's porch—she could wave to us as the boat was coming in. That was a big thrill. That was really most of our vacation, going to grandmother's in the summertime. We took turns because there were eight of us. She taught us how to sew and she had a little place in the country she took us when we got to Vallejo. She was a real grandmother. We used to fight to sit next to her at the dinner table when she came to see us.

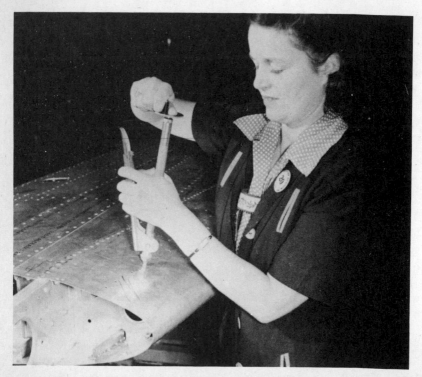

Marie Wright (Baker), North American Aviation, 1943.

My mother, she didn't have any skills, but she made a very good mother. I'm still close to her. She met my dad at the depot, when she came out here after her father died. She asked my dad where she could find a room, something like that, and that's how she got acquainted with him. They got married not too long after that. She was sixteen, and he was nine years older. She was a supermom. She raised eight children and she miscarried twins at six months and I think she had a couple of miscarriages other than that. I'm the third to the oldest, third pea in the pod. I'm the one that was always dependable. I was just old enough that I was sorta' taking care of the rest of the kids.

My father, he was terribly spoiled by his mother. He wasn't trained to do anything, which was sad. He was twenty-five when they were married, and he would go to his mother if he wanted anything. So he just had to do whatever he could find. He was a furniture mover for a while and a foreman at Pacific Coast Syrup Company. During the war, he was a guard at Mare Island Navy Yard.

When I was old enough to realize it, he worked at the Scottish Rite Auditorium. Today you'd call it a custodian. He had charge of the stage. It was a huge building. At that time, other than the Civic Auditorium in San Francisco, it was the only place for different groups to have their affairs, so there was always something going on there. Mother has three autograph books of famous people who came there. Oh, they're priceless! Will Rogers and Wiley Post. We saw a lot of different things. It was educational for us. Lectures. One was Dr. Estes. He was a raw food and health person and he would sell courses. I worked in the box office taking their money. When they had a dance, my mother worked in the hatcheck room and my brothers were hired to move the chairs. So we all got in on it.

We were poor. Proud, but poor. We wouldn't accept any welfare. That was a disgrace in those days. As soon as we got old enough we had little jobs that we did for pay. I'd run errands for a lady and I got 10 cents for doing it. That bought two loaves of bread in those days. My brothers had paper routes.

The lady that I ran these errands for, she was a seamstress. I would go down to the tailor shop and pick up a vest that was all cut out in a roll and bring it back and she'd make it. "Felling a vest" is what they called it. She'd get $2.50 a vest, which was a lot of money. When they were finished, I had to take them back to the tailor shop. She'd just fold them gently in the suitcase. Oh, I hated carrying that! I used to think people'd think I was a bootlegger carrying this big suitcase. Isn't that crazy?

We didn't do anything as a family. I have pictures of us going to the park when we were younger, especially on May Day. Oh, I took dancing lessons paid for by a friend of the family, and I would be in the Golden Gate Park dancing around the Maypole. Mother made me costumes. That was fun, but I don't remember going as a group anyplace with my family.

We were practically raised in a church that was just at the end of the block, Trinity Center. And I belonged to the Bluebirds and the Campfire Girls. They had a gym with a basketball court and my brothers were always there. We went to daily vacation Bible school in the summertime and it was our second home.

But I was very timid in school. I had a terrific inferiority complex. I was kept back in the second grade 'cause I couldn't read and my brother caught up with me. He was sixteen months younger. Of course, that didn't help my ego. But I graduated on the honor roll in junior high.

Then I went to high school—down the tube! I wasn't crazy about school, and I didn't go to the high school in our neighborhood, Mission High. Even at that time it was considered tough. I was taking a commercial course, so they allowed me to go downtown to the High School of Commerce. I was taking shorthand and I don't know what. But I wasn't planning! I didn't have anything in mind. Blah. I was too busy helping mother take care of the kids and the family, so I just didn't think about it. Probably was thinking about marriage more than anything else. When I was younger I thought about nursing, but not for very long. I guess I just didn't have any ambitions.

Like most young working-class women of the period, Marie would have probably gone to work after her graduation from high school while she awaited marriage. Instead, as a result of contracting acute bronchitis, she was forced to stay home. She described that lull of one year, until she married at nineteen, as "just not doing anything." In talking about her first marriage, Marie's voice was tinged with a tone of sad resignation.

My husband's brother was married to my sister. I went up to the mountains, up near Yosemite Valley, and lived with his family so I could be a companion to his sister, who was my age. I lived up there a year and just loved it.

My sister's brother-in-law was working in a lumber camp and he came home to see his mother. So I saw him when I was thirteen and thought he was really something. Of course, he didn't see me. Then, the next time I saw him, he came to San Francisco to visit his brother and sister. I was sixteen and he didn't see me. Then he came back when I was eighteen and he noticed me. "Would you like to come back up to the mountains, see my mother?" So I went up with him, and we were up there two weeks at his mother's. That's when he proposed, and we were married the next month. I was crazy about him.

He was working in Lancaster for Shell Oil Company, driving one of those big tankers that delivers gas to service stations and farms. I came down on the train from San Francisco and he met me at the depot.

I was pretty green when I was married, extremely so. The first year we had a daughter. My husband didn't really want any children—'course he loved her after she got here—so then he asked me to find out from the doctor some way to keep from having any more. Ah, what do you call it? Isn't that funny, I used it for a hundred years—the diaphragm, the fitted diaphragm.

We lived in Lancaster for three years, and then he was transferred to Mojave. Ever been through Mojave? It's nothing. I was just taking care of the house and taking care of my daughter and taking care of the husband. And going to PTA and the Ladies' Aid at the church. You made your own entertainment when you live in the desert. There's nothing up there. And then, the school put in a swimming pool and I took Red Cross swimming lessons there. Things like that. You'd go to somebody's house and you'd sew or do something. It was a very quiet, uninteresting life.

My husband was a very quiet person. We had friends we played cards with, and there's a group of young people we started when we lived in Lancaster. We called it the Lucky Seven Club. It was seven couples. We'd go on wienie bakes and scavenger hunts, and we'd always end up eating. It was a potluck kind of thing and it was a lot of fun.

Then what happened was that my husband started going out with this girl who was my best friend. That went on for five years! We'd be at different affairs, maybe even standing against the sink in the kitchen or something, and they'd be holding hands. That almost killed me. That was a terrible period in my life. I would never want to go through that again. But I look at it this way. Look what I've got now: a loving husband and two more beautiful children. So things work out, don't they? You think you're going to die at the time, but you don't.

But for five years I was miserable. I got so skinny. I couldn't eat. I was very much in love with him and didn't want to lose him. When I accused him, he said, "I love you, but I like her, too." Isn't that awful? I finally realized that it was going to go on forever. In fact, she left her husband thinking he would leave me, but he didn't, so then she went back to her husband and she had another child. But I lost respect for him—which is sad. If you don't respect somebody, you can't love him. He wanted me to stay, but he was still seeing her and I wouldn't do it. He's married to her now.

When Marie discovered that her husband had taken out a loan without her knowledge, she got a job at a local restaurant for a couple of months. Then the pull of war jobs in Los Angeles finally helped her strike out on her own. As she talked about this decision, her voice gained authority and strength and revealed the excitement she felt as she became a part of the war effort and discovered her own competency. In a short time she jumped from the sixty cents starting pay to a dollar an hour.

I needed a job because I was going to be very independent. I wasn't going to ask for any alimony or anything. I was just going to take care of myself. There was no jobs in Mojave in the desert; you had to come down here.

Women, everyone, was going to work at that time. We were really patriotic in those days. 'Course, we were in a real war. We were being attacked; you know, Pearl Harbor and all. I think the people came together better than they did during Vietnam. 'Course, Vietnam was such a mess; I mean, it was a real tragedy. But during World War II, everybody got real patriotic and got in there and worked. Grandmothers, mothers, daughters, everybody. I was real patriotic and I wanted to help. I was going to work right out in the factory. I wasn't going in for an office job. No, no, I didn't want that.

So I came down and had an interview and went to work at North

American. I had a friend and I had a room at her house in L.A. My daughter stayed in Mojave with my sister until I could have her down here.

I started after just a day or two. I was very nervous. I had the impression that women were tough that worked in factories, and I was scared to death, hoping nobody would hit me. That was silly. But it didn't seem like nice people worked in factories. I don't know where I got that idea. So I was nervous about going. Because I had been so sheltered. I was a Caspar Milquetoast, I really was.

Anyway, I just went straight into the plant. You get your badge and someone takes you up to your department, introduces you to the supervision, sets you down to this little table where you're going to sit for all these hours. It was such a huge place and we were upstairs, not near any planes, of course, because it was just this little section where you did all the buffing of the tubes. But it was exciting. In spite of being nervous, it was exciting. Here I was, being a war worker.

The first day I worked at a machine that had like sandpaper on it. When the tubes are cut, they're rough and not smoothed off at the ends. So this is a wheel that goes around and you'd hold the tube up to it to try to smoothe it off. Morons could have done it, sitting there just buffing the tubing.

I was so excited about a job that I didn't really care. But when I got a chance to go into another department, I was delighted. I was hoping that I would be transferred because it was boring, but you didn't think much about that because you were so busy being so patriotic and doing something for your country.

They put me in the empennage department, which is the tail section of the plane, the B-25 bomber. We put the de-icer boot on the vertical and the horizontal stabilizers of the bomber. The men had been doing that and they weren't quite as neat as the women. So we were doing a better job. They just showed us what to do and we did it; it was quite a few little operations. They'd bring in the stabilizers, the horizontal ones, and we had to get a template to put on there— that was like a pattern—and fasten it on. Then we took a drill and drilled holes. When that was taken off, we got a notcher and we'd notch the holes. And then we'd get the boot—made of rubber—and we'd powder it, and then we'd place it on this horizontal stabilizer and use pins to hold it in. Then we'd take out each pin and put a screw in to hold it. Then we'd turn it over and do the other side. And it had to be real smooth. The purpose of the de-icer boot, the planes were going to the countries where ice would form, and from the cock-pit they could press a button or something and it would make it expand and the ice would break and fall off because it was rubber.

This girl that came with me from the tube-bending department, she and I got real good at it. Seems like we had it mastered real fast. I think we were the first two in there, and then they kept bringing more girls in and we showed them. The men were thrilled to pieces to get away from that job because they didn't like it. They'd rather be putting the plane together than just standing there putting the boots on.

They were bringing in more girls to do this—because the bombers were really going out fast—and they needed a leadgirl. So they made me a leadgirl. I did have some special training because I had some paperwork to do. At that time Mr. Kindelberger was the president of North American, and his secretary, Bobby Waddell, gave a class on office procedures. It was given through the University of Southern California, and we went right on company time during the day into one of the offices. I think it was once a week for six weeks.

I went in April and this was about August. By that time, there was eighteen girls working in there and eight of them were Negro girls. There were men, too, because the rudders and all that went on right there in the department. After we finished the boots on the stabilizers, then the men put them on the tail sections of the plane. But I just supervised the women.

There was a leadman, a foreman, and an assistant foreman over me, but I had to see if the girls were working and get supplies to do the work and see if they got along. There was a girl from the South. I guess she had never been around Negroes and she didn't want to work near them. I told her I had four brothers out in the Pacific and they were all fighting at the same time, and why couldn't she stand in there and work next to someone no matter who they were? Kind of made me a little angry. Then another girl, she didn't like the perfume one of the girls was wearing. She'd put up a big fuss about that! So minor! But otherwise, they got along pretty good. They finally got over their little funny ways.

I had no problems with the black women. I got along fine with them. The only problem was when two of them got into a fight. The men in the department, the supervision, they're the ones that broke it up. It was a silly fight to begin with. I was terribly upset when I had to go in and be a witness. The union lawyer started throwing questions at me. I was so nervous! They put words in your mouth.

By the time I got out of there, I went straight to the little girls' room and had a good cry. It just really shook me up, terribly. But because I was the leadgirl, I had to tell. I didn't like that part of it at all!

After settling into her job and new life, Marie was able to have her eleven-year-old daughter come live with her. She was concerned about leaving her alone after going to work in the morning, and so she arranged for her own mother to come down and live with her—a common solution to the child-care problem faced by wartime working mothers. The three of them lived in Los Angeles in a little one-bedroom house for about a year, until they were evicted by the new owner.

Well, North American had to find me a house because I was a war worker—which they did. A brand new two-bedroom apartment here in Redondo Beach for $46.50 a month. And my girlfriend, Gwen Thomas, lived in the single apartment downstairs, and we lived in the big one upstairs. She had two children and her husband was in the navy and, of course, gone all the time. My mother was to take care of the two children.

We moved in the seventeenth of December and for some reason or another all the lights weren't on in the house. We didn't have our stove yet, so we used an electric percolator to heat soup that first night and it was raining cats and dogs and there were no men around to help us move. That's a job, to move all by yourself. Gwen and I walked down to the pier and bought some fish or hamburgers. It was really raining, so we were kind of discouraged, but at least we had a nice house to live in.

My mother did the cooking and the housekeeping and looked after Barbara. So it was wonderful having her with me. She stayed with me until after I got married the second time. Coming home, mother always had dinner ready for us, and we'd just sit around and listen— we didn't have television, just radio. Sometimes we'd go to the show, or on Saturdays, we'd go into L.A. once in a while, look around. That's about it. And then we had company a lot because my brothers would sometimes come. And there was other friends who were in the service and would drop in once in a while unexpectedly.

Let's see, I started working in April and by about August, September, I was dating. By that time I was divorced. I started going to USO dances and things like that. I was young. I wasn't sour and I had hoped to get married again someday. So that was easy. They'd tell us in the plant where to go, and they'd pick us up in a big army truck and take us out to where Harbor General Hospital is now, barrack-type buildings, and they had dances there.

Despite her earlier trepidations and her lack of self-confidence, Marie proved herself on the job. After serving as a leadgirl for about a year, she was again promoted.

Later on, when they quit putting the de-icer boot on the bomber because it was going to a hot country and they didn't need it, then they gave me a choice. I could work on the line, which was putting things together, or I could be the general foreman's clerk. Naturally, I took that. I could stay clean, I could stay dressed. I could do the paperwork which I had been doing anyway, keeping track of each worker. I was right there in the same area. It was just elevated two steps, to like a little box thing. The general foreman sat up there and the foreman, and I had a little desk there looking down into the department.

When a new-start came in, I'd go to the front office and pick them up and bring them back and introduce them to the supervision and show them where to get the tools. And when someone terminated, I'd take them out. And then I got supplies for the department, even for the men. I'd keep a record on each employee and when they were entitled to a raise, I'd type it up for the general foreman. Things like that. I liked it. And I had a shop pass. I could roam around a little if I didn't have anything to do. By that time, I had a sister, two brothers, and a sister-in-law working in the plant.

I thought I would continue as long as I could. I hoped that I would. We didn't think they'd be making that many planes after the war and wouldn't need that many workers, but I'd been there so long and I was pretty sure that they still needed a clerk out in the plant. So I figured that I'd probably still have a job. If I hadn't married, I think I'd still be there. In fact, I did stay for a while until my husband came back. He was an officer in the Merchant Marine. We were married [in] April '45, and he left and he was gone until August.

It was real strange how I met my husband. My timekeeper in the tube-bending department, he was an older man. I guess he thought I was a pretty nice girl, and he knew a real nice young man that he wanted me to meet. And he says, "He's over in Ireland right now, but if I give you his address, will you write to him?" I said, "Oh, sure, what's the difference?" I was writing to several soldiers by then and one more didn't make any difference. So I wrote him a letter and he answered. He has a terrific sense of humor and he wrote a terrific letter and I was impressed with the letter.

He came back then and joined the Merchant Marines. He went in as an officer and they sent him to New York, Sheepshead's Bay, and he learned the pharmacy bit there. He could give shots and dish out medicine on the ship. Then they sent him to Catalina and he finished his training there.

One evening, the doorbell rang and there he stood. Two weeks later, we were married. That was fast, wasn't it? People can't believe that. We have been married thirty-five years, so I guess it's going to take. But he liked what he saw and so did I.

We were married on Saturday, and on Monday he got on the ship and went to San Francisco and I got on a bus and went to San Francisco. We had a week in San Francisco while the ship was anchored up. We stayed at the St. Francis Hotel. That was our honeymoon, really. Then he left. I came back and went back to work at North American and he went to South America. He was gone three months and came back the first of August.

He was all ready to teach when the war started, but didn't have a chance to. When he came back, he applied at different schools and he was accepted at San Bernardino. I had to terminate—I hated to do it, but I had to. So we left my mother and my daughter in my house here and we went to San Bernardino and he worked there for a semester.

So at the end of the war, I wasn't thinking about working again. I was just thinking of being a wife and maybe a mother, future mother. I wanted another child, but I was happy to be a housewife.

Even though Marie wasn't thinking about working when she and her husband moved to San Bernardino, she quickly became bored sitting at home in their tiny court apartment. She took a job in a department store and worked there until they moved back to the Los Angeles area the following February. By the time they returned, Marie was pregnant. Her daughter, Kathy, was born in July 1946 and a second child from this marriage was born three years later. Marie settled back into a domestic life.

Then, like so many married women in the 1950s, Marie joined the ranks of working mothers in order to help raise the family standard of living. In Los Angeles, as a result of the Korean conflict, the aircraft industry was once again expanding after the initial postwar lull in production. Women like Marie, who had worked during the war, were welcomed back and they soon became almost one-fourth of the aircraft workers.

I was washing diapers, washing clothes, keeping a house and cooking, sewing, taking care of the children. That's a full-time day, taking care of young children. But we had a good social life in the evenings and on weekends. We had lots of friends. In the summertime, picnics and barbecues in the backyard, things like that.

Oh, I forgot to tell you. My husband wanted his master's degree, so when Kathy was about a year and a half old, I went up to Mojave—my sister was living there at the time and she took care of Kathy—and I went to work in the same restaurant that I'd worked years before and he went to USC and got his master's. It was just for the summer months, not long. Summer in that hot place—but it was air-conditioned. I wasn't especially thrilled about it. I was only doing it to make a few pennies because he was going to school.

Then, we were trying to buy a house, and with his salary not being adequate to do that, I said I'd go back to work. I liked working at North American and I was pretty sure I could get a job because I had a good record. I was hired like that. I went back as an inspector. It was a different-type job altogether. I didn't know anything about inspection, but they taught me. Sent me to blueprint school right there in the plant, one day a week for six weeks. Taught me how to read a blueprint so I'd know what I was doing. I enjoyed it very much. I liked being an inspector.

My daughter had moved across the street from us at the time—by then she was married—and she offered to take care of the children in the daytime while I worked until their dad came back. So I had a built-in baby-sitter. And I would have dinner prepared and my husband would feed the children. That's when he realized what a lot of work it was taking care of them. It was a good lesson.

I was working nights and I would be going down the front stairs when my husband would be coming home from school. After two years of that, he said, "This is no way to live"—because we didn't see that much of each other—"Why don't you quit?" So I did. We were both happy that I stopped. I liked the work, and it would have been nice if it would have been daytime. As it worked out, it was for the best because I always wanted to be a beautician, and so it was an opportunity.

When I left North American, I took my daughter down to have her hair cut one day. She was about four or five. I said to the operator, "I've always wanted to be a beautician." She said, "Why don't you go to beauty school?" "Oh," I said, "I'm too old." I was already a grandmother. She said, "You're never too old to be a beautician as long as your legs hold out." And she told me what school to go to, Harbor Beauty College in San Pedro.

I came home and told my husband what she said. He said, "Well, why don't you? Even if you never go out and work, you've always wanted to do it. I'll take you over there Monday and you can see about it." I thought, "I'll go over, but I probably won't be smart enough to do it." I went over and I still had that idea in the back of my mind that I'd just tell them I couldn't do it. But it only took one day and I knew I was hooked.

I just grabbed the opportunity. I think it was $75 for the course, 1,600 hours. I didn't have to buy any supplies; all I had to have was my white uniform and a theory book. I started in '53 and I went for six months. Then my husband was granted a sabbatical leave, and we went to Ireland for six months so that interrupted my beauty course. Then I went back to school in February of '54 and finished. I still have the examination report. I got 89 percent, which isn't bad, but my teacher was disappointed. She said I should have gotten in the high 90s. I think it was because I was nervous.

I started my first job as a beautician in September '54—and I've been doing it ever since. I cut back about four years ago. I'd been working four days a week and I cut it down to two, which suits me fine. Keep my hand in it, gets me out of the house. I have customers that I've had since I started; they're getting kind of old now, but I still have them. It's kinda sad because you see a lot of people pass away.

Working as a beautician in her small community, Marie was able to cultivate her own social world. She is proud of her accomplishments and is extremely proud of her three children. Looking back, she has some regrets about not having had more children. In recent years, her husband's health has curtailed some of their social life, and Marie's own recent illness has slowed her down a bit, too.

Barbara got married when she was just seventeen. After a couple of years, friends of ours who owned this house across the street were leaving, so they rented it to Barbara—the house. It was real nice having her that close. I heard her tell people she raised two families. That tickles me. She took care of them in the daytime, she did, so I guess she figures that she raised them.

My second daughter, Kathy, has been married for ten years. She lives in northern California, so we don't get to see her as much as we'd like to. It took her twelve years to get through college, but she finally made it. And Terry, we sent him to dental technician school for two years. He's not doing that now, but he can always go back to it. So we did a pretty good job on them, on the children. And now I have grandchildren. But my youngest daughter has been married ten years and she doesn't want any children, and Terry isn't married. He bought a home in Santa Ana and works in Newport Beach. It's been about five years since he left.

It's kind of lonely around here. We still go on just about the same. Our social life isn't too great because of my husband's problem. After he became a laryngectomy, his voice became soft. And if we're in a crowd of more than six people, you can't hear him. That was just too embarrassing. I was told by the wife of another laryngectomy that your social life would change, and it did.

I joined the Women's club here in Redondo Beach and I go to that. Gets me out once in a while. And I've joined the White Shrine, too—that's like the Eastern Star—but I don't go to that like I should. But I just do the usual wifely duties, cleaning house and cooking and sewing. I've made a quilt, beautiful quilt. In the evening while I'm watching TV I'm always making something, needlepoint or something. We don't go out much. We spend most of our time sitting in the living room watching the boob tube.

Now, my plan is just to get over this illness with the pancreas.

Just to stay healthy, get caught up in some of the things around here I've been wanting to do. I like to travel, but I don't think my husband would be too interested in that now. Two years ago, I took my oldest daughter and we went to Hawaii for a week. I'd like to go back. I'd like to go on a Caribbean cruise and on that trip up to Alaska on a ship.

Although Marie now views her life matter-of-factly, when she thinks back to the war years, she still marvels at how much she was affected by that experience.

It was a happy time, really, even though it was wartime. The people that worked there were nice people and the relationship among the workers, all the workers, was great. We felt like we were doing our best. It wasn't easy, especially when we were working ten hours a day. That's a long day. And in the winter it was dark when we went to work and it was dark when we came home, but we were healthy.

You know, looking back, I never thought all these things would happen to me when I was just a little housewife up in Mojave; never dreamed that I'd ever be doing all the things I've done. You know, there I was just going from day to day, sometimes thinking, "This is boring."

Yeah, going to work during the war changed me—made me grow up a little and realize I could do things. Look what I've done since. It's quite a change.

PART V

How Can I Help You?
The Women's Counselors

The factory or shipyard is not located in a vacuum, nor do the affairs of its workers begin and end with the 8-hour shift. There are many ways in which outside influences aid the worker on the job or lead to discontent, absenteeism, turn-over and other production saboteurs. The lack of adequate housing, recreation, transportation and child care facilities is among outside influences that affect women workers the most.

The Women Counselor in War Industries: An Effective System, *Women's Bureau Special Bullentin No. 16, February 1944*

Even before the United States' entry into the war, preparations were made by both the government and private industry for the introduction of women into war industries. For example, in the summer of 1941, Douglas Aircraft surveyed jobs to determine which were the most suitable for women, and male supervisors were interviewed to assess their readiness to incorporate women into production work crews.[1] Later, when women workers became *essential* to the conduct of the war, increased attention was paid to their special needs. The concern centered on the need to maximize worker efficiency, including ways to reduce absenteeism and turnover.

Community services, like child care, were funded under the Lanham Act and became part of the civilian arsenal.[2] It was estimated that each child-care center in Los angeles serving forty mothers made possible eight thousand productive "man-hours" monthly.[3] In California, as elsewhere, the needs were never fully met and the number of facilities opened could serve only about 10 percent of the working mothers with young children. Most depended on family members to watch their children.

Child care, housing, transportation, laundry facilities, and limited shopping hours were viewed as more than individual problems—they required a collective response. Even as personal a problem as menstrual cramps was given special attention. At North American Aircraft a Physical Education Section was established under the Medical Department, and women were taught a special exercise to reduce cramps. As a result, absences owing to menstrual cramps were reduced by 80 percent.[4]

One of the most all-encompassing programs for working women was the introduction of women's counselors into the large defense plants. The counselors' role was to smooth the way for women in the plant and to make referrals to community services. Despite the fact that the Women's Bureau had long advocated the development of such a program, as with so many of the wartime programs, events overtook their methodical introduction.[5] From Susan Laughlin's description of her job as a counselor, it is obvious that she practically created the program out of whole cloth. And like so many of the services created for women workers during the war, it was dismantled at war's end.

CHAPTER 11

Susan Laughlin

Susan Laughlin, ca. 1980.

*There's no question about it, it was a
necessary and an effective program. We
said at the end of the war that in five
years we probably learned and did and
progressed what normally would take at
least twenty years to do.*

Susan Laughlin was recruited by the Lockheed Personnel
Division in 1942 to develop the women's counselor program there. Although she had no previous training or experience in personnel work, as a clerical worker in the
Medical division, Susan had proved herself to be a warm
and sympathetic listener. With few guidelines, she forged
ahead and eventually coordinated a program that grew to
include seventy counselors.

Susan called me after reading about the Rosie the
Riveter Revisited project in the *Los Angeles Times*. A
poised, self-confident, and handsome woman, she welcomed me to her small pleasant home in Laguna Beach.
The proprietor of a gift shop, Susan carved out an afternoon from her busy schedule in order to talk about her
wartime experience and to review her records and scrap-
book with me. As Susan talked about her job, it was clear
how much she had enjoyed being in the middle of the
action, being able to use all her skills to extend herself in
so many directions. She was proud to have been a part of

such a necessary and innovative program—to have been on the leading edge.

I was surprised to learn that this was one of the first occasions that Susan had talked to anybody about her job as a counselor during the war. In order to keep the peace in her household and to placate her husband, she had downplayed her role. Despite Susan's businesslike attitude toward the interview and her reluctance to talk about personal affairs, I sensed a lingering resentment toward the accommodation she had made.

The few glimpses into Susan's personal life revealed that as a wife and mother she faced many of the same conflicts and pressures as the wives of blue-collar workers whom she was counseling. Perhaps it was her ability to identify with the production workers that made her so effective.

Some of the problems Susan dealt with were a result of the newness of the situation—of the recent introduction of women into production jobs in heavy industry. But many of the problems she resolved are universal to working women, and many of the solutions she devised over forty years ago would still serve us well today.

Susan Laughlin, ca. 1942.

I had worked before I was married and up until my first child came. Then I was at home. My husband's position was eaten up. He was in sales with a large road equipment company, and all that they could produce was taken by the war, and there was just no position for a salesman. So he was out of work and was having difficulty getting anything. So I thought, "Well, I will try."

I went to Lockheed in July of '42 as the lowest paid clerk, fifty-one cents an hour. I was placed in the medical unit. Everybody had to have a physical before they actually were hired, so I did see everyone who came, men and women. I was thirty and older than most of the people going to work, and I made up my mind I would speak to each person and let them know that I recognized them as a person. I would frequently call them by name, and I would say something personal: "Your hair is nice" or "I like your blouse." So those people kept coming back and saying, "What'll I do?" "Do you know what I should do about this?" It would be company related or it could be "Do you have any idea where I can get a baby-sitter?"

The company began to be aware that this was something that perhaps they should listen to. So they moved me around the corner into a department where the job was not quite as crucial, so I had more time to talk to these people.

There was a man by the name of Jenkins who was the personnel manager, and he talked to a number of women who apparently had been applying for this kind of a job. He called me in and talked to me at great length about what I was doing and how I felt about it. I didn't have anything in my mind at all, except just to do whatever I could. One lady, a psychologist who had written a book with her husband, came out to apply for that position. Mr. Jenkins called me in, too, and he liked my answers better than hers. I remember he stopped and said, "Do you have any children?" She said, "No." And he said, "Well, that's what I find is a problem. Many psychologists write books on children and yet they have not really experienced it."

It was right after that that he assigned me to this job. He said, "I want you to go into the factory and counsel." I did not know what I wanted to do, and the men did not want any part of me; they didn't want my help. So I decided I had to contact every supervisor: "Well, this is what I'm supposed to do. If I can help you, fine; if I can't, fine. I don't want to bug you, but I am here and if there's anything you need, you can call me."

I remember one of the men who wanted nothing to do with me, about the second week that I was on the job, called and said, "Would you please come down here?" A girl had come in in a bare midriff, and all the men were hitting themselves with hammers. Then, he realized that I could be of some help. So I talked to the girl.

They used us more when we ceased to be a threat. What we'd try to do is say to the man, "This is the problem in your department, and how do you think we should handle it?" Or "She seems to need a little more instruction." Then he would say, "Well, I'll take care of it," and he was grateful to know that it was a problem. If you let them solve it, then there wasn't much of a problem.

When I first went into the factory, they thought I was going to be a threat to their authority. When they discovered that that was the farthest thing from my mind, they felt comfortable with me. Like one man said, "You're not a woman, you're just a worker."

The need for individual counseling about clothing was somewhat relieved when safety procedures, including dress requirements, were formally developed. But there were many other problems to foresee as preparations were being made for the massive influx of women.

They told me to check the restrooms in the plant and see if they were adequate. My husband kidded me. I didn't like that very much and I didn't want to do that very much. But, well, if they want them counted, I'll count them! I came back and wrote a sort of disgusted memo: "We have so many and we have so many women, and we have this and that, and we need this and this." It wasn't my nature to be that way, but I was angry. I gave it to the supervisor of that department, and about a week later it came back from Mr. Gross, the president: "Order everything she says."

Then they wanted me to do every job in production. I think they figured that if I could do it, anybody could do it. And so they tried the different weights of the rivet gun, and all the rest of it. If I could hold it and do it, then they felt comfortable putting a woman on it. Some days I would be down there on a job a full day. I would have like to have stayed longer on each job. Then I would have had a better idea of the job and how tired you got. But I knew what they were doing and what they had to cope with to do it.

In the beginning, I remember one time I was so upset I was going to quit. They were building airplanes in the open and it was pouring rain. The girls' hands would get so cold that they would have to come in the restrooms to warm them. I was so angry. I went down to Mr. Chappellet, the vice president of Lockheed. You didn't darken those executive halls very often, but Elsie Muller, his secretary, said, "Well, go right in." I wasn't quite prepared for that. But I told him that I had intended to give my resignation that day, but before I left I wanted him to know a few things.

At that time I was working for John Fowle, who really thought that all the women belonged in the kitchen. He liked me and we got along all right, but he didn't like women working. He didn't want to do one thing that would help and that just could not go on. I told Mr. Chappellet that and I told him about these women working out there. I went on and on. When I finished, he said, "Well, Susan, I hope you don't quit. I will tell you what we're doing." They had the plans and they were trying. But here were the airplanes; here were the people working on the airplanes; here was the rain coming down; here was the structure coming up.

The kind of gerrymandered process that was used to quickly accommodate production needs was evident in all aspects of the work. Susan's job remained somewhat amorphous and she "winged it" alone for several months. By November 20, 1942, however, the *Lockheed Star* re-

ported that her operation was in full swing. By then there
were nine other counselors, including several from Vega,
a sister plant that merged with Lockheed.

Just as soon as they had enough women working at one of the
other plants, I would go there to see if they were set up, if the facilities were adequate. I would talk to the supervisors and see how much
help they needed. Then, as soon as they had enough women that
they needed the help of a counselor, we would get somebody up
there. Sometimes we would even work with the matrons. They would
become conscious of problems through the restrooms. People would
go in and maybe they would be in tears or something. The matron
might ask the counselor to come to the restroom, and you'd go and
talk to her or take her back to your office. Or if she was sick, you got
the nurse.

I know that I had to work all three shifts occasionally. I would
appear on the midnight shift and on the swing shift. We found that
an awful lot of women whose husbands were gone liked that swing
shift because the hours when they would most miss their husbands,
they were occupied. That was very interesting to me. We recommended it finally to girls who were pretty unstrung.

When the merger with Vega came, I was in charge of them, too.
And they had a whole different philosophy. It was more like a fellow
worker approach, rather than like somebody from a personnel department. For instance, they wore slacks and our counselors mainly wore
dresses. They thought they were more effective if they dressed like
the workers. Our approach was a little different. Also, I don't think
that they were quite as much involved with agencies until it was
pulled together.

By the time the other counselors came in, I had a dandy book
accumulated of everything that we could call on. I got that book by
calling on people. Everytime somebody came to me and asked me for
help, I would try to find the help and I'd write it in my book. Then,
if anybody else came for that kind of help, I would have some place
to start.

I remember Ivy Grace with the Salvation Army was fantastic. She
would do anything for us. If we sent somebody to her, she always
said, "We give soup, soap, and salvation in the order that it comes."
So we counted on that. If somebody really needed help, they would

take care of them. We were developing that kind of relationship so they wouldn't get the runaround. We also talked to merchants to keep the stores open late so people could shop if they worked all day. Or they couldn't get their washing done. The time wasn't right. We did all the things that are done today but which were not done in those days. We talked to the school board, social welfare, YWCA, various organizations.

The counselor's role was clear: keep the women on the job. Easing communications between the male supervisors and the female crew members and locating community resources were relatively straightforward tasks. Integrating the new black workers into the plant, policing, talking to women about personal hygiene and personal problems were more difficult. Reviewing the weekly report sheets that the counselors used, Susan was able to detail some of the problems with which the counselors dealt.

If a person was absent over a certain number of days, then it really looked like a problem. I remember down at Plant 7 I think it was, this one girl only would work Monday, Tuesday, and Wednesday. She would never work Thursday, Friday, and Saturday. And they couldn't figure out why. And so I went down and talked to her. I think that was before there was a counselor assigned down there. She said, "Well, I had made all the money I wanted that week." She had been used to working day work, where she got just so much and she would only work so many days. So she just did the same thing in the plant, not realizing that she had to carry a full-time job.

And some people just didn't eat well. They would just have colds all the time and would not be well. The nurse would let us know or we would get that through an attendance report. We would start to inquire why they were out. We'd ask them what they were eating. You'd find women cooking for their children and not wanting to eat. So we gave lectures on that and had people in to talk about nutrition, vitamins.

Occasionally, we would have somebody who would come in and discuss family problems. We had people ask how to handle your husband, how to handle your money. Do you put it in one account or keep your own? Those kind of questions. Not so much because a problem existed, but more planning so that a problem would not occur. I had a built-in answer, because I had it myself. As with many of the problems, they were my problems. That's why I could empathize with them. When you say, "This is what *I* tried to do," people will listen to you.

I was there when the first Negro was hired at Lockheed. We didn't know what to expect. And we got it! A lot of people objected. And I said, "Well, that person has had the same physical examination that you had and he has a right to the same restroom." Some of the workers were requesting that they be assigned to a different restroom. I said, "No way, why should they be?"

One of the counselors suggested that we speak to Negroes and whites separately, explaining how to get along with each other and what the function of the counselor was. My feeling was that this talk should be given to all the groups of workers, not separating blacks and whites. It wasn't necessary. The only concern that I had was at first when the Negroes came in because we had to assimilate them. But going down there, after that, I don't recall a problem. We just didn't accept a problem. And once you met it immediately without any problem, they pretty well accepted it, like when the women came in.

I learned things I didn't even know happened in the world. Like one time I had to go into a restroom. The FBI had word of a certain woman who was recruiting for the camps, for the girls to go up and sleep with the men. I had to catch her at it. And I did. And I had to catch a couple of lesbians that were at work, and things I didn't even know about, really. And then another time, the FBI came in and they wanted me to talk to this girl who had married, I think, ten men and was just collecting their allotment checks. You name it, I did it.

Although she had had no special training for the job that she was doing, Susan did very well—she had a natural aptitude for counseling. She insisted that common sense and sensitivity were the most important qualifications for the job.

I can remember this one woman. She was telling the supervisor how to do things. I said, "Well, you just listen to me now and I'll tell your story back to you." I did this many times, 'cause she's the only one who can do anything about it. When I would repeat the story back, I would come to the point where they knew what they would have to do. So, really, I didn't do anything. Another woman, an engineer—she was one of the first women engineers—her supervisor called and asked me if I would talk to her. She swore so much that the men complained. I asked her to come in. She was so smart, she could work rings around the men. I just asked her, "Why?" And she said, "Well, that's the only way I can get their attention. If I say we ought to do it this way, they don't hear me, and if I say, 'God damn,' then they pay attention." She had a point. But I said, "Well, you're going to have to find a better way."

The trick was that sometimes they didn't want their supervisor to know they had a problem, that they were trying to get help. That was why it was good to keep it sort of unofficial. I thought that was a very important quality of the job, because they felt if anyone knew they had a problem they might not keep their job. But if they came to me, I'd just give them the information and they could take it from there.

There were abortions, there was just everything—you name it. And they came to us because they thought we wouldn't discuss it, and we tried to keep that trust pretty sacred. I had a woman call me, if you would believe it, about ten years ago. That's thirty years after. She said, "Are you the Susan Laughlin that used to work at Lockheed?" And I said, "Yes." And she said, "Well, I found this name in the book, and I just wanted to thank you for what you had done for me."

She told me this big long tale. The Christmas party was a big thing then in many offices. She had gone to the party, had gotten drunk, and had become pregnant—didn't know who did it. We referred her to some medical people. We were never allowed to give a single referral, but we could give several and then whatever they selected was their problem. That woman got an abortion—and it was before you did that. I think it saved her marriage and she was thanking me for that. She was so grateful that there was somebody.

But, you know, this kind of counseling is the kind you go to a hairdresser and you crab all your problems, because you know they don't know anybody that you know and it doesn't matter. It was just somebody to talk to, and then if they needed any help, you could give it to them. It's something that everybody needs, and always has, and always has found somewhere. But this was in an accelerated period—offering it right where it was needed.

All we dealt with was the problem. We didn't attempt to analyze it, find out why it happened. All we wanted was that worker on the job. Whatever it took to keep them there, we were going to do. And we did. There's no question about it, it was a necessary and an effective program. We said at the end of the war that in five years we probably learned and did and progressed what normally would take at least twenty years to do.

In the spirit of wartime cooperation, the counselors, like professionals from the other aircraft plants, met together as part of the Aircraft Production council. Susan was the chair of the counselors' group and set the agenda for the meetings. Information was regularly shared, and the counselors visited one anothers' plants and programs. In addition to her duties in the plant, Susan became the Lockheed representative on various community boards and agencies concerned with women's issues.

I was also working with the head of Public Relations, speaking to groups. They would ask Lockheed for a woman to come and speak about the women. There was a lot of animosity in the community against women who went to work. They thought these women should be home taking care of their children. I was trying to talk about the kind of problems that women had by going to work and how the fact that she was working didn't necessarily mean that she was neglecting her child.

I didn't neglect my children. I worked hard not to. I extended my life so that each child had their hour in court everyday. And they were well fed. I cooked all night. I had someone there after school until I got home. And then, as we developed the Child Care Centers, my children went there. They were not allowed to leave the playground, and there was enough activity provided for them that they enjoyed it.

I've done all kinds of things so that my home was disrupted as little as possible. I felt that many, many women did that, and I felt just because the audience were mothers didn't necessarily mean they were good mothers. Maybe they weren't working, but maybe they were playing bridge and they weren't paying as much attention as a working mother. So I tried to give that kind of counterconversation.

At the beginning, neighbors were watching children and there were children that were neglected. I'm not saying there weren't. And I didn't intend to tell them that. But I did say what was being done about it, why the Child Care Centers were good. It was good for the children. I sent my own children and to this day they remember it.

I felt that when I finished an evening of conversation those people understood what we were talking about and were no longer hostile. They felt that there was a need, a point, and it was one that they hadn't thought about.

I wasn't functioning to recruit. I was functioning for understanding. And for air travel and for the whole concept of aircraft. Women had to be sold the whole ball of wax.

And I was in many of the different organizations: Women's Division of Chamber, the Metropolitan Welfare Council, the Business and professional Women's Clubs, the Industrial Counselors' Family Relations Institute, YWCA, THE National Vocational Guidance Association, personnel women's groups—they still have an organization. All of these I attended regularly. My voice was Lockheed's on those organizations.

Despite the value of the Women's Counselor program, it was clearly viewed as a temporary measure—like the women defense workers themselves. Because of her own interest, however, Susan stayed involved and participated in postwar planning for women.

It was a general understanding that everyone was going to go home. They were just waiting for their release. And they were released in bunches. Even for the counselors, who thoroughly enjoyed what they were doing and were going to continue to do something, there was no problem. They didn't expect anything else. It was an understood fact.

The counselors weren't the first bunch because we thought maybe they would be needed to help the people who were going out.

We were anticipating adjustments to their husbands; adjustments to not working and not having that paycheck, and to the husband not getting a job right away. Those kinds of problems that we thought might come up. We thought we could see what the problem was and find the answer in the community to help them. So the counselors hung on a little while. The counseling program was phased out at the end of '45.

But after the war, after they were wanting the women to go home, I was on the Metropolitan Board of YWCA and we gave a seminar. It was terrific. We offered the services of all of our women counselors to counsel them in what to do, where to go now. We weren't offering a placement service, we were just offering whatever they wanted to discuss and try to find referrals for them. If they wanted part-time work, then we would try to make contacts again to meet that need. Our seminar was successful, but I could not honestly say that the counseling program was. We probably didn't do it for more than three months. There weren't enough people who were seeking it to warrant our volunteering our time.

>   Susan faced the same conflicts as many other married
>   women in the postwar years. Her husband had always
>   been displeased about her working—even during the
>   wartime crisis—and her career choices were influenced by
>   his attitudes.

My husband didn't want me to work when he was able to keep me at home. Of course, during the war, there wasn't any question about it because everybody was needed. But he didn't like me to talk about my work. If we went out and anybody asked me about it, he would prefer to answer. I think he felt that it was his failure that made it necessary and he didn't like to be reminded of it.

After the war, when the counseling program was phased out, I stayed on for a while at Lockheed, and John Canady wanted me to move into Public Relations and continue to keep the community contact. But my husband wanted me to quit. I went and talked to Mr. Chappellet. I think I figured in my letter of resignation that I belonged to twenty-two organizations for Lockheed. I had meetings up to here. He wanted me to work a half a day a week—continue the contacts and do only that and only report out to the plant a half a day.

I should have done that. But my husband wanted me free. I was gone a lot of evenings because a lot of those meetings were in the evening, and he didn't want that. I could understand that. So I just said no.

But then I went back to work in 1951. My husband, again, was out of a job. I waited longer that time, thinking he might find something. I thought about going back to Lockheed, and I went out and talked to Mr. Chappellet, who had offered me a part-time job at the time I resigned. He sent me to the personnel manager, who referred me to one position that was open. The department head said he would hire me, but he honestly did not want to because he felt that I would not be on the job too long; he felt that other openings would come along that were more suited to my talents. So I thought maybe I wasn't supposed to do that, and I didn't try anymore at Lockheed.

I went to work for an employment agency for a few years, and from there, I went to work for the Collier Chemical company as assistant director of personnel. I worked for them about five years. Then they got their third personnel man. He was a "statistical man" and I was a "people man," so I said that there wasn't any point in continuing. he resented anyone coming to see me. I left there and I went to work for Capital Research and worked there as office manager until I retired.

But even when I went to work for them, my husband was making all kinds of noises. He thought it was a nine-to-five job and would complain if I didn't get home until 6:00 or 6:30. I frequently would have to see my boss or another executive, and they would not be available until after 5:00. I finally explained this to my husband and said I would quit if he insisted, but that it would be difficult for me to find another job that was as suited to my ability as this one. After this conversation, he seemed to understand better and did not object any more.

I wouldn't take anything for the years I had at Lockheed. I was terribly impressed with the stamina and intelligence and the common sense of the majority of women. I think women are fantastic. We just expedited things so that they could stay on the job. And so much of it has been carried on. A lot of it began right then. Because it had to.

PART VI

Conclusion

CHAPTER 12

What Did It All Mean?

Well, men, it looks like Hitler, Hirohito
and Company at last are in for a peck of
trouble. They've got the women of this
country all riled up. And as anybody
knows, when the gals play marbles, it's
really for keeps.

Douglas Airview, *February 1942*

The writer of these condescending lines announcing the entry of women into production jobs at Douglas Aircraft probably had little comprehension of the magnitude of that event. Yet, within a few months of the U.S. declaration of war, these early entrants to the aircraft industry in Los Angeles represented over half of the women aircraft workers in the country. By mid-1943, at the peak of women's employment in aircraft, the Los Angeles women aircraft workers continued to make up over one-third of the nationwide total.[1]

Women's entry into defense jobs signaled a major breakthrough in their employment patterns. Those jobs, concentrated in heavy industry, were both better paying and laden with symbolic value—they were men's jobs. Moreover, many women were drawn into employment who normally would not have been. The debate among historians about the significance of the wartime experience for women partially revolves around the question of how permanent the wartime employment changes were. William Chafe has argued that the war represents a watershed in women's history, whereas Karen Anderson, D'Ann Campbell, and Susan Hartmann have suggested that continuity rather than change characterized women's lives after the war.[2]

The oral histories presented here offer an opportunity to cast the question differently. Rather than debating the *degree* of change resulting from the wartime experiences, the life stories of these former aircraft workers encourage, instead, a study of the *process* of change.

A criticism often leveled against the use of oral history to interpret events is that oral history narrators are "special" people. Obviously, they are the survivors in a society. But more than that, they are usually the "winners," not the "losers"—the people who, according to conventional standards, succeeded. As a result, they think enough of themselves to allow their stories to be recorded. Although this kind of bias is not as apparent in other forms of historical documentation, they have other shortcomings. Aggregate statistical data can measure overall behavior or characteristics and can also be used to compare these at two different points in time. But since little is known about the individuals who comprise the aggregate, it is not possible to explore the variations among them. Furthermore, to study the *process* of change, it is necessary to follow individuals through time, not merely to look at them at a beginning point and an end point. Oral history allows for this longitudinal approach.

When I first began trying to make sense of the total body of forty-five oral histories we had recorded, I thought I saw a distinct pattern emerging.[3] The wartime work experience had meant different things to women, depending on how old they were and at what stage they were in their life cycle. For the longtime workers, the jobs had been important in a basic material sense; and for many of the full-time homemakers they had dramatically affected their self-esteem. In that first reading, however, I dismissed the experience as being a relatively unimportant interlude for the young single workers: I didn't look much beyond the fact that the young single workers had usually rejected the alternative, more lucrative jobs in the aircraft industry in favor of traditional women's roles. In other words, I depended too heavily on an assessment of change that was based on women's participation in the labor force. But that is only one indicator of change. A careful reading of the oral histories points to less tangible effects and also reveals the private face of change.

The World of Work

In his "National Defense blues," Huddy Ledbetter ("Leadbelly") gloated over the fate that had befallen the women who had gotten too big for their britches:

I had a little woman
Working on that National Defense
That woman got to the place, alas
She did not have no sense. . . .
Every payday come, her check was big as mine. . . .
Now the defense is gone
Listen to my song
Since that defense is gone
That woman done lose her home.

It is true that most women working in national defense did lose their jobs. For instance, in Los Angeles, only 14 percent of the women wartime aircraft workers still held their jobs in June of 1946—just slightly over one-fourth the number who had earlier indicated a desire to continue their aircraft employment.[4] Instead, most of them were either working at other jobs or had left the labor force.[5] Leadbelly was only partially right, however. As Tina Hill's and Marye Stumph's stories show, many women were able to buy their first homes—and hold onto them.

Even if they were generally unable to retain their jobs in aircraft in the immediate postwar years, women workers did maintain some of the inroads they had made into heavy industry.[6] These advances were by no means spectacular and were further diminished by the new sexual division of labor that had emerged, wherein women were assigned to different jobs than men—and paid less.[7] Yet women did receive better wages in these durable manufacturing jobs than in traditional women's work, and the work they performed challenged prevailing definitions of womanhood.

Perhaps because they started from an even lower position, black women were able to benefit more.[8] Before the war, the majority of black working women were relegated to the white woman's kitchen. In Los Angeles, for instance, in 1940, two-thirds of employed black women worked as domestics. By 1950, this proportion dropped to 40 percent and was accompanied by an increase of black women in durable manufacturing.[9]

The labor force statistics give us the bare bones—a hint that there was at least a modicum of change in the opportunities for working-class women.* The oral histories give us insight into women's atti-

---

*Some of the changes, like the increased proportion of married women in the work force, represented an acceleration of trends that were obvious even before the war. Others, like the entry of women into nontraditional jobs, might either have not otherwise happened or have happened only much later.

tudes and feelings about work, the personal "whys" and "why nots" of changed employment patterns.

The most obvious employment gains were often made by women who were fighters or by those who were ready to make changes, like Tina Hill and Bea Morales Clifton. Tina did not have to fight on her own, however. The black community had mobilized during the war and, with the help of the United Auto Workers union, had been able to maintain a foothold for both men and women.[10] Bea, even if she was ready to do so, didn't have to fight. Instead, she was able to take advantage of the later industrial expansion stimulated by the Korean conflict.[11]

Unfortunately, not all the women who wished to stay were fighters nor were there organizations to help working-class women fight, except for the unions, most of which have blemished records on this score.[12] As a result, the majority of women aircraft workers who remained in the work force left their aircraft jobs and returned to traditional women's work.

Registered in these statistics are both women who were forced out and others who made the choice voluntarily. There were those like Marye Stumph, who would have liked to have kept their aircraft jobs—and even had a fair amount of seniority—but were not willing to challenge the cultural expectation that women were there only for the duration. They accepted the layoff and sought other work. On the other hand, others had little desire to stay, feeling that the jobs were not "women's work." Like Margie Salazar McSweyn, they were pleased to prove that they could temporarily do the work, but preferred traditional women's occupations.

Not all women, however, who went into service and clerical occupations did so because they were governed by ideas of what was "men's work" and what was "women's work." There were often no other viable alternatives. A single mother of a young child, like Juanita Loveless, could not find many jobs besides waitressing that provided the flexibility in scheduling she needed. Perhaps the lives of women like Juanita would have been different had services established during the war, like child care, been institutionalized.[13] Certainly without support for working mothers, many women were forced to make choices within a very limited range.

Even if most women were not yet ready to challenge the status quo, the benefits reaped by those who were should not be discounted. It is, after all, through the steps made by path breakers that opportunities are expanded. Others waited, expressing themselves more quietly, in the private arena. Today, in the contemporary climate of expanded roles for women, they can more openly express their support for these changes—as evidenced by the overwhelming support for women's rights among most of the forty-five women whose oral histories were recorded.

The Boundaries of Women's Social World

The social world of most working-class women has been more circumscribed, historically, than men's. Women's lives were played out in their own relatively homogeneous communities. Even wage-earning women had only limited contact with other races. Except for black women, who worked *for* white women, there were few jobs where the races worked together.

As the racial barriers in the defense industries were forced down, black women in particular eagerly sought jobs. In Los Angeles, the racial composition of the different aircraft plants varied, depending on company policy, on the strength of the union's antidiscrimination position, and on the geographic location of the plant. North American Aircraft, for instance, was located at the edge of the black community and was represented by a CIO union with a strong antidiscrimination clause. It had the highest proportion of black workers among the aircraft plants—8 percent. On the other hand, Lockheed Aircraft, whose main plant was located in the white community of Burbank, was represented by an AFL union with a white-only membership clause. Thus, despite an active recruitment policy by management, slightly less than 5 percent of all Lockheed employees were black. In contrast, at Lockheed's downtown subassembly plant, over half of the workers were people of color. Although no separate records were kept on workers of Mexican ancestry, there is some evidence that they, too, were concentrated in certain plants, particularly in the subassembly plants closer to the east-side Mexican communities. For instance, both Margie McSweyn and Bea Clifton worked at the downtown subassembly plant.

There is ample evidence in the files of the Fair Employment Practices Commission and in the oral histories presented here, that black women were often assigned different and more difficult jobs. It is also clear that old prejudices and stereotypes continued to rear their head, as when Juanita Loveless, a white Texan, refused to train black workers because they were "slow." The women's counselors, like Susan Laughlin, were often called upon to deal with these problems.

Nevertheless, in many of the accounts, there are signs of relatively open interaction among Afro-American, Anglo, and Mexican workers (Asian and Native American workers were a rarity). Mexican and Anglo women went to lunch together, as Bea Clifton recounted; and Margie McSweyn talked about going to a party thrown by an Anglo co-worker. It was also the first time that both Margie and Bea related to Anglo men. The relationships between black and white women were usually restricted to the plant, and Charlcia Neuman and her co-workers were unusual in their attempt to include a black crew member in a party.

Despite the limited nature of the social contacts between the races, a significant breakthrough had been made. The social worlds of these working-class women had been expanded, and many of the women acknowledged the significance of this intangible by-product of their wartime work experience.

For the younger women, the boundaries of social propriety were extended as well. The war plants served as the hub of social life for the young workers. Each of the large Los Angeles aircraft plants had recreation clubs and many had recreation centers. Activities like horseback riding, bowling, and swimming were regularly scheduled, even after the midnight shift. At North American, the Special recreation Office offered a dating service. The plants also arranged for their women workers to entertain servicemen. That is how Marie Baker resumed her social life after her divorce.

Even if young women did not directly participate in these scheduled activities, the atmosphere created by them and the freer interaction promoted between men and women expanded the boundaries of their worlds. Despite the eight-year age difference between Margie McSweyn and Betty Boggs, both had been relatively sheltered. But within the context of unity and trust engendered by patriotism, it became easier for women like them to spread their wings. From Juanita Lovelesss's account it is obvious that the developing youth culture touched more than just those working in the war plants, but for many, like Betty Boggs, it was clearly their point of contact.

The war hastened the process whereby the United States became a more complex and less homogeneous society. By being pulled into war industries, women were active participants in that process.

The Private World of Women's Consciousness

Men suspected that women would be changed by their wartime work experience, and their reactions ranged from cautious welcomes to vituperative attacks (see chapter 1). Feminists of the period often exhorted women to change, warning that otherwise they would become subjugated like the women of Nazi Germany.[14] Even as moderate and "feminine" a publication as *Woman's Home Companion* sounded the trumpets for change:

> In free nations, I can, with man, help build a better world,
> Or I can shirk the responsibility and assume again the status
> of an inferior creature. The one way is hard and burdensome
> for I must think and act in my own right. The other way is
> easy. I have known it for centuries.[15]

Working-class women who took war jobs might not have read the middle-class magazine where these words were printed, but in their own ways, and by their own actions, it is clear that they subscribed to these ideas. One of the striking themes in the oral histories is the desire of the women to test themselves, stretch themselves, prove themselves. This note was most commonly struck by women new to the work force, but it was not just a matter of being introduced to the world of work. Someone like Margie McSweyn, for example, who had eagerly abandoned production work wanted first to prove to herself she could do it. That done, she and many wage-earning women were often ready to return to "women's work."

Many women with whom we spoke proudly proclaimed how they had "held their own with men." In retrospect, this is probably what laid the groundwork for the transformation of someone like Bea Morales Clifton from a woman who timidly defined herself as "just a mother of four" to a self-confident participant in the wider world. Even Betty Boggs, who was forced to abandon her dream of becoming an aeronautical engineer, was still bolstered by the idea of women being able to do something different. Most of the women were profoundly affected by the chance to prove their competence in the male world—except for Tina Hill, Marye Stumph, and Juanita Loveless who were primarily concerned about improving their material conditions.

In fact, recurrent in the responses of the majority of the two hundred women with whom we talked was this message: the unintended effect of their wartime work experience was a transformation in their concept of themselves as women. This change was not translated into a direct challenge of the status quo. At the time, it was probably not even recognized by most of the women, but it did affect their status in their own eyes—and in their homes.

For the first time, many of these former war workers spoke up and challenged the male prerogative to make the big decisions. The money they had earned and saved lent them moral authority, but it was the confidence they had developed that enabled them to exert that authority. Studies of changing power relationships in the family in the 1950s have suggested that working-class wives who had worked in the past participated more in these kinds of decisions.[16] D'Ann Campbell has surmised that this expanded role was derived more from women's increased exposure to the wider world outside the home than from their work experience.[17] It is hard to separate these issues or to assess their relative weight, but the oral histories do reveal that the work process itself engendered feelings and attitudes in the women that had a lasting effect.

Sometimes the experience was translated directly to the next generation. Charlcia Neuman, for instance, fully accepted the traditional definition of the wife's role. She would never have taken a job had the war not temporarily legitimized a woman like herself going to work for the duration. That brief experience, by her own account, caused her to think about better preparing her daughter for the world of work.

The effect on their daughters of the mothers' changed consciousness is also hard to assess. Eight of the forty-three production workers whose full life histories were recorded had daughters who were between the ages of five and thirteen during the war years. All these mothers had high expectations of their daughters and tried to guide them into getting an education and toward being more independent. This was unusual for working-class mothers in the 1940s, when working-class men, spurred on by the GI bill, were only just beginning to aspire to a college education.

Despite their mothers' aspirations for them, the daughters often married young and initially did not have goals that broke with tradition. Subsequently, many of them did carve out an independent course for themselves—at just about the time when women of their generation were supposed to be in the grips of the feminine mystique. From what can be learned about the daughters in their mothers' interviews, they seem to have broken with tradition more frequently than did the women who were already young adults during the war years.[18]

Margie McSweyn, Juanita Loveless, and Betty Boggs were a part of that young adult cohort: single women aged seventeen to twenty-five during the war. Like the older, married women, many of these younger women were also pleased with their ability to hold their own with men, but the work experience itself seems to have been less important to them. Rather than representing a discontinuity in their lives, it was taken in stride as a natural part of their development.

Most of this cohort married by war's end or shortly after and took up full-time homemaking, at least temporarily. Just as it had been for their mothers, their family role was of primary importance; but unlike their mothers' generation, their relationships with their husbands were relatively more egalitarian.[19] Furthermore, the majority of them expanded the definition of their family role to include participation in the public world of wage-earning work outside the home. (Among the two hundred women interviewed by phone, sixty were single and between the ages of seventeen and twenty-five when they took their war jobs. Among those in this group who later married, over half ultimately combined their domestic role with wage-earning work.)

In their different ways, Betty Boggs and Margie McSweyn are typical of this transitional generation: a generation that differed from the previous one and that charted a course that was adopted with even greater regularity by the next one.[20] The wartime job had left an imprint on young women like Boggs and McSweyn, but they were essentially in step with the rest of their generation and were probably affected more by general social currents than by their specific wartime experience.[21]

Of what broader significance, then, was the changed consciousness of women that resulted from their wartime experience? For one thing, it contributed to the tide of rising expectations of women. That tide, ultimately, led to the birth and growth of a social movement for women in the 1960s, just as the rising tide of expectations among blacks fueled the civil rights movement. Furthermore, we must remember that the generation of older, married women who were so deeply affected was that of the mothers of those who built the current women's movement. Even if the mothers' experience had little *direct* effect on their own daughters, it may have helped foster the development of a working-class feminist consciousness among young women.

Social Change and the "Feminine Mystique"

After four years of war, which had followed on the heels of the Great Depression, the country started gearing up for a return to "normalcy." Articles about accommodating the needs of the returning servicemen were common, and the women's magazines filled their pages with advertising and stories that promoted a renewed domesticity.[22] In this idealization of family life, male and female roles were once again polarized. D'Ann Campbell has argued that this need to return to normalcy helps explain why the wartime potential for change in women's lives was unrealized.[23]

The magazine prescriptions for domestic bliss continued well into the 1950s and 1960s. By then, television was also delivering its own brand of the same message. "Father Knows Best" became the postwar counterpart of "One Man's Family." Suburban home ownership, coupled with a soaring birthrate seemed to lend credence to the reality of this image of stability and a happy return to the status quo. Then, in the early 1960s, with *The Feminine Mystique*, Betty Friedan exposed the myth.

Friedan did nothing to dispel the idea that women were firmly held in the grip of these cultural ideals. In fact, her argument was just the opposite. She took the messages of the popular media to be not only prescriptions for but also reflections of women's behavior. After all, educated middle-class women like herself were suffering from "the problem that had no name" because they had bought into these ideals. Students of women's history understand that the prescriptive messages of popular culture do not necessarily measure behavior. Yet we are still seduced into using these messages as a clue to actual behavior. Furthermore, in a variation of the trickle-down theory, these white middle-class ideals are assumed to be equally valid in describing the behavior of the working class and of all women of color.

The cultural ideals projected in the mass media and other forms of prescriptive literature are important to our understanding of society, but I think we can learn more by viewing them as possible *reactions* to behavior rather than *reflections* of it. If people were behaving according to the cultural ideals, why was it necessary to continue to promote them so stridently? On the other hand, if behavior was running counter to the ideals, then the unrelenting harangues might be viewed as last-ditch efforts to make women fall into line. In other words, perhaps the postwar messages can better be understood as a measure of the amount of change that was occurring in the society—as an attempt to stem the tide of that change.

Indeed, despite the consistency with which the message of the feminine mystique was initially delivered, by the mid-1950s popular magazines were beginning to catch up with reality. In 1956, special issues of both *Look* and *Life* were devoted to the changing American woman. In an editorial introduction, *Look* went so far as to suggest that women were groping their way "toward a new true center: neither Victorian nor rampantly feminist." In an ironic twist that highlights the changing values, Lucille Ball, the brassy, dippy housewife of "I Love Lucy," fought a public battle to continue to work while she was pregnant.

Many of these media acknowledgments of change were a direct result of the increased number and proportion of women in the work force, especially married women. But changes in values and behavior do not occur rapidly and are not easily attributed to an immediate cause. The increased proportion of married women in the work force was the result of a gradual process. It was already in evidence before the war, was accelerated as a result of the war, and was further fueled in the 1950s by the desire to maintain improved standards of living in the face of inflation. That is what brought mothers like Margie McSweyn back into the work force.

The ideology of the feminine mystique was promulgated, certainly, and many white middle-class college-educated women subscribed to it, at least temporarily. But there were also women who had changed and were in the process of changing in the postwar years, including both the former war workers and their daughters. By using the concept of the feminine mystique to describe women's lives in the period between the war and the rebirth of feminism in the 1960s, we see only stasis. We are blinded to the slow incremental process of change, and, as a result, we underestimate the role that women's wartime experience played in that process.

Social change is difficult to measure. Two points in time are examined and a judgment of continuity or change is made based on the similarity or difference between these points. When we look at women's lives in the immediate postwar decade, we can see many ways in which they were remarkably similar to what they had been like in the years immediately preceding the war. The majority of women continued to define themselves primarily as wives and mothers. If they were wage earners, they were usually still restricted to lower paying feminized occupations. Yet these oral histories have revealed the often private and subtle ways in which individual women were changed by their wartime experience.

These individual changes were not merely ephemeral. For it is the changes that individuals experience that both push for and support social transformation. The connection is not always immediate or clear. There is usually a lag, with ideas preceding practice. For example, despite a growing belief in egalitarian marriage over the past forty years, household responsibilities only now are beginning to be equalized.[24]

The potential for social transformtion was created by the wartime need for women workers. For a brief period, images of women were revised, employment opportunities were expanded, and public policy was enacted that created new services for women. These were necessary, but not sufficient conditions. Social values also had to change, including women's definitions of themselves. Women's wartime experience played a vital role in that process of redefinition—the reverberations of which are still being felt today.

Notes

Chapter 1

1. See especially Glen Elder, Jr., *Children of the Great Depression: Social Change and Life Experience* (Chicago: University of Chicago Press, 1974); Winifred D. Wandersee, *Women's Work and Family Values, 1920–1940* (Cambridge: Harvard University Press, 1981); and Susan Ware, *Holding Their Own: American Women in the 1930s* (Boston: Twayne, 1982).

2. As quoted in Jim Harmon, *Great Radio Heroes* (Garden City, N.Y.: Doubleday, 1967), p. 193.

3. Helen Kaufman, "Appeal of Specific Daytime Serials," in Paul Lazarsfeld and Frank Stanton, ed., *Radio Research, 1942–1943*, (1944; reprint, New York: Arno Press, 1979).

4. Herta Hertzog, "What Do We Really Know about Daytime Serial Listeners?" in Lazarsfeld and Stanton, *Radio Research*, p. 25.

5. Quoted by Rudolf Arnheim, "The World of the Daytime Serial," in Lazarsfeld and Stanton, *Radio Research*.

6. Harmon, *Radio Heroes*, p. 173; and Arnheim, "World," p. 51.

7. Irving Settel, *A Pictorial History of Radio* (New York: Bonanza Books, 1960), p. 90.

8. John Gray Peatman, "Radio and Popular Music," in Lazarsfeld and Stanton, *Radio Research*, pp. 345, 371.

9. Robert S. Lynd and Helen Merell Lynd, *Middletown in Transition* (New York: Harcourt Brace, 1937), p. 170.

10. Suzanne Ellery Greene, *Books for Pleasure: Popular Fiction 1914–1945* (Bowling, Green, Ohio: Bowling Green University Popular Press, 1974), p. 87–89.

11. George Gerbner, "The Social Role of the Confession Magazine," *Social Forces* 6:37.

12. Marian J. Morton, "My Dear, I Don't Give a Damn": Scarlett O'Hara and the Great Depression," *Frontiers: A Journal of Women's Studies* 5 (1981):55.

13. Molly Haskell, *From Reverence to Rape: The Treatment of Women in the Movies* (Baltimore: Penguin Books, 1973), p. 51.

14. See Wandersee, *Women's Work*.

15. See Lynd and Lynd, *Middletown*, pp. 27–29.

16. Wandersee, *Women's Work*, p. 26.

17. Sixty-seven percent of the population favored such laws for wives whose husbands earned more than $1,600 per year. Although this support dropped to 56 percent if the husband's earnings were less than $1,000, these sentiments still show extreme hostility to married women working, even when there was obvious economic need (Hadley Cantril, *Public Opinion, 1935–1946* [Princeton: Princeton University Press, 1951], pp. 1044–75, cited in Maxine Margolis, *Mothers and Such: Views of American Women and Why They Changed* [Berkeley: University of California Press, 1984], p. 211).

18. Jessie Bernard, *Women and the Public Interest* (Chicago: Aldine, 1971), p. 149.

19. Margolis, *Mothers and Such*, p. 61.

20. Lynd and Lynd, *Middletown*, p. 146.

21. *Women Workers in Ten War Production Areas and Their Postwar Employment Plans*, Bulletin of the Women's Bureau, no. 209 (Washington, D.C.: U.S. Government Printing Office, 1946), p. 39; also D'Ann Campbell, "Wives, Workers and

Womanhood: America during World War II" (Ph.D. diss., University of North Carolina, Chapel Hill, 1979), p. 222; D'Ann Campbell, *Women at War with America: Private Lives in a Patriotic Era* (Cambridge: Harvard University Press, 1984), pp. 108–13.

22. Gallup Poll, cited in Susan Hartman, *The Home Front and Beyond: American Women in the 1940s* (Boston: Twayne, 1982), p. 82.

23. Surveys Division, Office of War Information, *The Public Looks at Manpower Problems*, Memorandum no. 43, January 5, 1943.

24. Leila J. Rupp, *Mobilizing Women for War: German and American Propaganda, 1939–1945* (Princeton, Princeton University Press, 1978).

25. Ibid.; Maureen Honey, *Creating Rosie the Riveter: Class, Gender and Propaganda during World War II* (Amherst: University of Massachusetts Press, 1984).

26. One-fifth of *all* working women had children under fourteen at home, as did one-third of married, divorced, and widowed workers. The best data available for women working in the defense industries are contained in a survey of aircraft workers in Los Angeles, which revealed that 37 percent of them had young children at home (Aircraft War Production Council, "The Relationship of Adequate Child-Care Facilities to Aircraft Production in the Los Angeles Area," June 1943; Files, Los Angeles Board of Education).

27. For an excellent discussion of the growing independence of young women, see Karen Anderson, *Wartime Women: Sex Roles, Family Relations and the Status of Women during World War II* (Westport, Conn.: Greenwood Press, 1981).

28. *Saturday Evening Post*, February 20, 1943.

29. Willard Waller, "The Coming War on Women," *This Week Magazine, San Francisco Chronicle*, February 18, 1945.

30. This study was conducted by the Women's Bureau of the Department of Labor and was published as Bulletin no. 209.

31. Honey, *Creating Rosie the Riveter*.

32. These figures are for all married women workers, not just those in defense industries. A survey of defense workers conducted by the Los Angeles Chamber of Commerce found that 64 percent of the former homemakers working in defense industries wanted to return home. See *American Savings and Loan News*, May 1944, p. 212.

33. These will be discussed in the Conclusion. The most detailed analysis of the postwar employment shifts can be found in Campbell, *Women at War with America*, and William Chafe, *The American Woman: Her Changing Social, Economic and Political Roles, 1920–1970* (New York: Oxford University Press, 1972).

34. UCLA Department of Industrial Relations, *Employment and Earnings in the California Aircraft Industry, 1940–1953* (Los Angeles, 1954).

Part V, Introduction

1. Louise Snyder, "Preliminary Report on Study of Employment of Women in Aircraft Manufacturing Operations," Education Department, Douglas Aircraft Corporation, August 25, 1941. From personal file of Louise Snyder Fitzgerald. Copy on deposit in Archives, California State University, Long Beach.

2. Under the Lanham Act, funds were available for community facilities for war-impacted areas. In most areas, the funds for child care were funneled through and the programs were administered by the local board of education.

3. Aircraft War Production Council, "The Relationship of Adequate Child-Care Facilities to Aircraft Production in the Los Angeles Area," June 1943. Files, Los Angeles Board of Education.

4. Letter from Estelle Gilman to Mary Anderson, Women's Bureau, June 12, 1944. National Archives, Record Group 86, Box 1564.

5. The Women's Bureau, an agency of the Department of Labor was founded in 1920 as a result of the efforts of women social reformers. In the period from 1920 to 1950, it served as a major advocate for working women, especially for working-class women.

Chapter 12

1. "Wartime Exansion of California Airframe Industry," *Monthly Labor Review*, October 1945, p. 724.

2. For the "watershed" interpretation, see especially William Chafe, *The American Woman: Her Changing Social, Economic and Political Roles, 1920–1970* (New York: Oxford University Press, 1972). For other views, see Karen Anderson, *Wartime Women: Sex Roles, Family Relations and the Status of Women during World War II* (Westport, Conn.: Greenwood Press, 1981); D'Ann Campbell, *Women at War with America: Private Lives in a Patriotic Era* (Cambridge: Harvard University Press, 1984); Susan Hartman, *The Home Front and Beyond: American Women in the 1940s* (Boston: Twayne, 1982).

3. Sherna Berger Gluck, "Interlude or Change: Women and the World War II Work Experience," *International Journal of Oral History* 3 (1982):92–113.

4. In a survey taken in late 1943 by the Los Angeles Chamber of Commerce, 51 percent of all women workers in Los Angeles County indicated a desire to stay with their present employer (reported in *American Savings and Loan News* May 1944).

5. Of the former Los Angeles aircraft workers surveyed, 14 percent were still working in aircraft; 25 percent were working at other jobs; 17 percent were unemployed—in contrast to the 9 percent unemployment rate of male aircraft workers; and 43 percent were no longer looking for work ("Postwar Adjustment of Aircraft Workers," *Monthly Labor Review*, November 1946, p. 707).

6. For Los Angeles, the proportion of women in durable manufacturing jumped from 4 percent in 1940 to 25 percent in 1950. For California, as a whole, the figures were less spectacular: -from 10 percent to 16 percent. Nationally, the increase was a little less than 4 percent, from 22.1 percent to 26.3 percent. For Los Angeles and California, see *16th Census of the United States: 1940: Reports on Population*, vol. 3, part 2, table 13, p. 248 and table 17, p. 302; and *Census of Population: 1950*, vol. 2, part 5, table 74, p. 5–306 and table 77, p. 5–352. For U.S. figures, see Bulletin of the Women's Bureau, no. 253, *Changes in Women's Occupations, 1940–1950* (Washington, D.C.: U.S. Department of Labor, 1954), p. 92.

7. For an excellent analysis of the new sexual division of labor in at least one war industry, see Ruth Milkman, "Redefining 'Women's Work': The Sexual Division of Labor in the Auto Industry during World War II," *Feminist Studies* 8 (1982); 337–72.

8. In "Last Hired, First Fired: Black Women Workers during World War II," *Journal of American History* 69 (1982):82–97, Karen Anderson emphasized the

losses from their wartime highs. The evidence, however, suggests net gains, especially in considering the reduction of black women employed as domestics.

9. Nationally, the proportion of black women who worked as domestics dropped from 60 percent to 40 percent. See Women's Bureau Bulletin. The prewar presence of black women in durable manufacturing in Los Angeles was so low as to be almost immeasurable. From that base, they came to make up 3 percent of the women in durable manufacturing *(Census of Population)* 1950).

10. The pages of the *California Eagle* documented the close cooperation among the Negro Victory Committee, the CIO Central Committee, and the UAW local. These working relationships were further elaborated in an interview with the Reverend Clayton Russell of the Negro Victory Committee conducted by Sherna Gluck and Jan Fischer in 1980. Interview is on deposit at the Archives, California State University, Long Beach.

11. According to the Lockheed statistics of their active work force, the proportion of women hourly workers hovered below 20 percent until April 1951, when it began a slow steady climb. Although no comparable records are available from the other aircraft companies, interviews with women who worked as leads at Douglas Aircraft suggest that about 25 percent of the production workers were women during this time period.

12. Many unions, for example, maintained separate seniority lists for men and women, so that women were not recalled in real order of seniority. Others colluded in reclassifying the work that women did, thereby making them ineligible for newly reopened jobs. For a discussion of the United Auto Workers, in particular, see Nancy Gabin," 'They Have Placed a Penalty on Womanhood': The Protest Actions of Women Auto Workers in Detroit-area UAW Locals, 1945–1947" *Feminist Studies* 8 (1982):373–98; and Lynn Goldfarb et al., *Separated and Unequal; Discrimination against Women Workers after World War II, The UAW, 1944–1954* (Washington, D.C.: URPE Education Project, n.d.). For a more general discussion, see Campbell, *Women at War with America.*

13. Funding for the wartime child-care facilities was curtailed and many of them closed down after the war. In several states, however, greatly reduced programs were maintained and locally funded. Although there were never adequate facilities or funding, even during the war, there is some evidence of underutilization of the centers. Several excellent studies explore both the shaky commitment of the government to providing services for women and the public response to these services. See especially Alan Clive, "Women Workers in World War II: Michigan As a Test Case," *Labor History* (Winter 1978),44–72; Howard Dratch, "The Politics of Child Care in the 1940's," *Science and Society* 38 (1974):167–204; and Eleanor Straub, "United States Government Policy Toward Civilian Women during World War II," *Prologue* 5 (1973):240–54.

14. See especially Susan B. Anthony II, *Out of the Kitchen into the War: Woman's Winning Role in the Nation's Drama* (New York: Stephen Daye, 1943) p. 14.

15. *Woman's Home Companion,* February 1943.

16. Numerous sociological studies of the effect of wives' employment on family power relationships were conducted during the 1950s, usually with the use of questionnaires. Although the findings from these various studies are sometimes contradictory, on the whole there is some evidence that wives employed outside the home increased their authority in decision making. The effect of past employment is documented particularly in Donald M. Wolfe, "Power and

Authority in the Family," in Robert F. Winch, ed., *Selected Studies in Marriage and the Family* (New York: Holt, 1962, pp 582–600). For a good review of the literature, see Robert O. Blood, Jr. "The Husband-Wife Relationship," in Francis Ivan Nye and Lois Wlapis Hoffman, eds., *The Employed Mother in America* (Chicago: Rand McNally, 1963), pp. 290–95; and more recently Campbell, *Women at War with America*, pp. 228–30.

17. Campbell, *Women at War with America*, pp. 229–30.

18. In various surveys of the period, the women who were young adults during the war consistently responded that they preferred a full-time homemaking role to being single or combining work and family life (Ibid., p. 225).

19. Caplow et al. found growing egalitarianism in the family, beginning with the generation that married during the depression years and entered early parenthood between the war years and the early 1950s (Theodore Caplow et al., *Middletown Families: Fifty Years of Change and Continuity* [Minneapolis: University of Minnesota Press, 1982], pp. 313). Because they were studying generations that were determined by the date of the original Middletown study, the generation that married in the immediate postwar period is totally ignored. In their study, of the three generations, the one entering parenthood during the early war years was, undoubtedly, more egalitarian than the previous generation. However, if we were to look at more discrete cohorts, I believe that the major shift toward greater egalitarianism came in the immediate postwar years. The 1950s' studies of family relationships corroborate this later date.

20. The concept of transitional generation is discussed by Caplow et al., *Middletown Families*, pp. 281–84. Because of the particular boundaries of their three generations, their transitional generation was earlier than the group discussed here. See n19.

21. In analyzing survey data from the 1970s, Campbell found that the war generation exhibited a permanent equilitarian shift (*Women at War with America*, pp. 228–29).

22. An excellent examination of this literature can be found in Susan Hartmann, "Prescriptions for Penelope: Literature on Women's Obligations to Returning World War II Veterans," *Women's Studies* 5 (1978 223–39. Maureen Honey's study of women's magazines during the war also traces the changing messages at war's end (*Creating Rosie the Riveter: Class, Gender and Propaganda during World War II* [Amherst: University of Massachusetts Press, 1984]).

23. Campbell, *Women at War with America*, p. 4.

24. Joseph Pleck, "Men's Family Work: Three Perspectives and Some New Data," *Family Coordinator* 28 (1979):481–88.

Appendix
Research Note

Interviewee Selection

Although individual oral histories collected at random from interesting individuals can offer important insights into past events and ways of life, they do not allow us to generalize with confidence. To go beyond the individual experience, it is necessary to more systematically draw a sample of potential narrators, to select a sample of people who can reflect the general group being studied, the target population—in this case, World War II women defense workers. One means of achieving this goal is quota sampling. The important characteristics and their distribution in the target population are established and quotas are set accordingly. In the end, the sample population should reflect the aggregate characteristics of the target population.

The greatest problem in this kind of design is determining what personal characteristics should be used and in locating the baseline data to establish the quotas. Fortunately for our purposes here, during the war the female labor force was studied repeatedly, and defense workers were often singled out for examination. Using this data, quotas were accordingly set within the following categories: prewar work status, age, marital status, migrant status, and postwar plans.

The names of war workers were gathered from a variety of sources, including articles in the *Los Angeles Times* as well as local community, company, and union newspapers; notices in newsletters of community organizations; notices at senior citizen centers; and word of mouth. The resulting list included 212 former aircraft workers who still lived in the southern California area. Most of the women were contacted and telephone interviews averaging thirty-five minutes were conducted. (Obviously, temporary migrants were excluded. Polls taken at war's end, however, showed that most migrant workers in Los Angeles County planned on staying.)

Using the information obtained in these phone interviews, we separated the two hundred women into three subgroups as defined by their status on the eve of the war: wage earners, full-time homemakers, and students or young entrants to the labor force. Selections were then made from each group based on age, marital status, migrant status, and postwar plans. The sample was intended to reflect the aggregate characteristics of women war workers, except that Afro-American and Mexican-American women were deliberately overrepresented. They were such a small proportion of the war workers that their presence would have been meaningless if wartime numbers were used to determine their sample size. Fifty women were initially selected; great care was taken to select at least some women who were not self-referred. Owing to funding cutbacks, not all the interviews could be completed. The final sample included forty three production workers and two women's counselors.

Certain distinct patterns did emerge from the oral histories and the nine production workers and one counselor whose stories were selected for inclusion represent these general findings.

Interviewing and Editing

Life history interviews averaging six hours in length were conducted with the forty-three production workers and two counselors. Some interviews were as short as three hours; others were longer than ten. The interviews usually were conducted in three sittings divided into the prewar, war, and postwar years. Cindy Cleary, Jan Fischer, and I each conducted about a third of the interviews, though I supervised and reviewed each one and was fully conversant with its contents throughout the process. The oral history material used here was drawn from interviews conducted by all three of us.

The original interviews were transcribed verbatim and were edited first by the interviewer and then by me, and were reviewed by the women themselves. In editing, care was taken to preserve each individual's speaking style and syntax. False starts and repetitions were removed—unless they revealed something about the interviewee or represented her speech pattern. Words or phrases were added only when necessary for clarity.

The materials published here, then, are the words of the women as approved by them, though each passage is not necessarily sequential or complete. I chose passages from transcripts that averaged 125 pages each and that originally included the interviewer's questions. Although I tried to preserve the narrator's thought process, passages relating to the same topic were often drawn together from different places in the interview. The accounts presented here have been shaped by me and, therefore, are not pure oral histories.

Index

Meridian

(0452)

THE MAKING OF AMERICAN HISTORY

☐ **LOOKING FAR WEST: The Search for the American West in History, Myth, and Literature. Edited by Frank Bergon and Zeese Papanikolas.** Here is an extraordinary collection of writings about the American West as both a historical reality and a realm of the imagination. Here in song and story, myth and firsthand report is an anthology that gives full expression to the West in all its complex meanings. (007585—$5.95)

☐ **LEE AND GRANT by Gene Smith.** One was the great personification of the Southern beau ideal; the other was a graceless, small-town Midwesterner. Both reached their summits of glory in a war that filled them with horror and each had to build a new life in the war's aftermath. In this book—as in life—they illumine and define each other's greatness, and give human meaning to the conflict that the struggle between them decided. (007739—$10.95)

☐ **FACING WEST: The Metaphysics of Indian-Hating and Empire-Building by Richard Drinnon.** Following the course of American expansion westward historian Richard Drinnon examines the eerie similarities of attitude and action on the part of three centuries of representative Americans. The vision of the American past that emerges is as disturbing as it is meticulously portrayed. (006325—$10.95)

☐ **ABRAHAM LINCOLN: The Man Behind the Myths by Stephen B. Oates.** He has been called the Great Emancipator and a white racist, a devotee of democracy and an incipient tyrant. His life has been cloaked in the mists of time and distorted by both the devotion and the enmity that he inspired. With his pioneering research Oates offers us a picture of Lincoln as he really was. (007348—$6.95)

Prices slightly higher in Canada.

Buy them at your local bookstore or use this convenient coupon for ordering.

NEW AMERICAN LIBRARY
P.O. Box 999, Bergenfield, New Jersey 07621

Please send me the books I have checked above. I am enclosing $_____ (please add $1.50 to this order to cover postage and handling). Send check or money order—no cash or C.O.D.'s. Prices and numbers are subject to change without notice.

Name _____

Address _____

City _____ State _____ Zip Code _____

Allow 4-6 weeks for delivery.
This offer subject to withdrawal without notice.

There's an epidemic with 27 million victims. And no visible symptoms.

It's an epidemic of people who can't read.

Believe it or not, 27 million Americans are functionally illiterate, about one adult in five.

The solution to this problem is you... when you join the fight against illiteracy. So call the Coalition for Literacy at toll-free 1-800-228-8813 and volunteer.

Volunteer Against Illiteracy. The only degree you need is a degree of caring.